Comprehensive National Power
A Model for India

Comprehensive National Power
A Model for India

Editors

P K Singh
Y K Gera
Sandeep Dewan

(Established 1870)

United Service Institution of India
New Delhi

Vij Books India Pvt Ltd
New Delhi (India)

Published by

Vij Books India Pvt Ltd
(Publishers, Distributors & Importers)
2/19, Ansari Road, Darya Ganj
New Delhi - 110002
Phones: 91-11-43596460, 91-11- 47340674
Fax: 91-11-47340674
e-mail : vijbooks@rediffmail.com
web: www.vijbooks.com

The views expressed in the book are of the authors/contributors and not necessarily those of the United Service Institution of India / publishers.

Contents

Introduction

The concept of 'National Power' has exercised the minds of strategists and thinkers across the globe since times immemorial. Comprehensive National Power or CNP in short is a concept which refers to the overall power of a Nation State and is a conglomeration of a wide range of national assets capabilities and potential. Some of the ingredients that are commonly measured to determine CNP are – military and economic strength, potential of the population based on health, education and intellectual capacity, natural resources, scientific and technological output, governance and a host of other equally relevant parameters.

The modern Chinese methods of measuring CNP that were first undertaken in the decade of the 1980's, and thereafter, subjected to continuous rigorous study are perhaps the most cited-among CNP assessment models. However, the Chinese were not the first to seriously study the constituents of national power. Soon after the end of the Second World War coinciding with the beginning of the 'cold war' scholars began to delve into matrices that determine a nation's relative power in the global order. Broadly the chronological sequence of some of the better known theses is as follows:-

(a) The earliest equation for calculating national power was defined by Klause Knorr in 1956 and included economic capabilities, administrative competitiveness and the ability to mobilize for war.

(b) Clifford German produced a complex non-linear multivariable index in 1960. In his hypothesis nuclear weapons capabilities was central to determining power equations.

(c) A semi non-linear multivariable index was proposed by Wilhelm Fucks in 1965.

(d) Ray Cline in 1975 produced a national power equation in which both hard power and soft power capacities were built in. This, in our view was the first CNP formula which with some variants was used by the US Army to develop long term trends in the international system.

(e) Ashley Tellis and other scholars of RAND in the year 2000 advanced their concept for determining CNP. However it is not known if they published any calculation equation or results of computing for international comparison.

The Chinese scholars also propagated many methods of CNP calculation. Some of these are:-

(a) The Chinese Academy of Social Sciences advanced a system in 1996 which covers eight aspects and 64 indicators.

(b) The Chinese Military Academy represented by Huang Suofeng in 1996 and 1999 spelt out a method in which he held that CNP should be the organic integration of capacities of survival, development and coordination.

(c) The China Institute of Contemporary International Relations gave out an analytical hierarchical approach to determining CNP.

(d) Hu Angang and Men Honghua gave out their formula for CNP which defines eight components of strategic resources and 23 major indicators to constitute a computable CNP equation. Their equation adopts different weighted averages for different indicators and is dynamic in nature.

Within the Chinese political thought, the main goal of the Chinese State is to maximize China's CNP. The inclusion of economic and cultural factors and soft power measures within most CNP indices is intended to prevent China from making the mistake of the Soviet Union in over-investing in the military i.e. hard power at the expense of the civilian economy.

In India too, quite a few attempts have been made to compute and benchmark India's CNP against major nations. On close scrutiny, these appear to have lacked depth and omitted to include all relevant parameters that impact on the totality of CNP. For instance, none of the studies undertaken so far gave a reasonably accurate measure of military power and perhaps more importantly, the contribution of military strategy and a cohesive national defence policy towards national power. Again, most studies have ignored the role of foreign policy in shaping national power which is a major shortcoming. Political factors like stability and good governance were not taken into account and natural resources and environmental issues ignored. Also, most of the studies placed an over-reliance on secondary data without tempering that data through the filter of expert opinion. All these factors add up to reinforce the case for a de-novo look at the concept of CNP in the Indian context.

Any workable CNP model will necessarily see interaction between hard power, soft power and transformation variables in some form or the other. In any new model, it is the determinants, sub-factors and indices, which perhaps will be the main drivers of change. The new model will also have to examine the merits and de-merits of absolute quantification vis-à-vis the relative ranking approach.

The impact of 21st Century issues like the ferment in the Arab world, the turmoil within Islam, terrorism, fourth/ fifth generation warfare, competition for scarce resources, environmental degradation, sustainable development, aging population in the developed world or the youth bulge in the developing /underdeveloped regions etc will also have to be factored for any study to be sufficiently authoritative.

It is in this context that the USI has attempted to give a de-novo look to the subject of India's CNP. Rear Admiral Raja Menon steered this study on "India's Comprehensive National Power – Model for India" and oversaw its conduct and provided guidance and valuable suggestions. A special mention goes out to Dr Montek Singh Ahluwalia, Deputy Chairman, Planning Commission for having given an insight on "India's Transit from 2010 to 2025 – The Biggest Hurdles" during the seminar on the project. The study team comprised Mr Mohan Guruswamy, Ambassador Kanwal Sibal, Mr

Naresh Saxena, Mr Prakash Singh, Lt Gen Vinay Shankar, Vice Adm Vijay Shankar, Mr Dipankar Gupta, Mr Amitabh Kant, Mr Manohar Thyagaraj, Mr Jayadeva Ranade, Capt PK Ghosh, Mr Zorawar Daulet Singh, Maj Gen YK Gera and Capt Sandeep Dewan; each of whom has done yeoman service towards the study.

We believe this is the first comprehensive study in India that has delved into the determinants of Comprehensive National Power and then attempted to arrive at conclusions of where India currently figures in the global order. The study has also analysed each of the identified determinants with a view to suggesting remedial measures that would – if followed upon and implemented, enhance our CNP.

The CNP Project that the USI has undertaken is a foundational work for all future studies on the subject. It is expected that more such studies will follow. And these would further refine methodologies and perhaps lead us to different sets of factors and matrices. Eventually we hope that there would be awareness of the concept of CNP and a national consensus will emerge on the steps India must take to further develop its CNP in order to realize the Nation's aspirations.

Comprehensive National Power - An Overview

When the project to write a relative matrix of CNP was accepted, the first effort ran into a huge and unseen obstacle – namely, how to balance the choice of matrices chosen to describe a developing country, with that of a developed country. Would the matrix eventually be true to the description of India, or to the comparison? It soon became clear that there could be no compromise on the matrix to describe India. The comparative matrix could wait for a solution as time went by. As a result, the matrix to describe India has been expanded hugely in areas where India's outcome is still in doubt – for instance, education and skill creation, which would gainfully employ the youth bulge – OR – have them wander unemployed and turn to violence and fundamentalism. But a matrix with vastly expanded skill creation determinants was found to be totally out of place with the matrix chosen by Rand for the United States. The reasons became rapidly clear. India is determined to get *somewhere*. The United States is already *there* and equally determined to *remain* there. Hence the RAND study was clearly right in choosing determinants that reflected their anxiety and not those of India's-like keeping girls in school after puberty, adult literacy, and coping with the mismatch between the people's purchasing power and the lowest price of a laptop.

So what about the comparison? It was decided tentatively that it might be possible to compare the omnibus determinants of two countries in disparate stages of development, even if the sub determinants are entirely different. For instance, the determinant of skill creation in India might mean the creation of brick layers, plumbers and carpenters, while the same determinant in the US might mean the creation of medical laboratory technicians, plasma welders and biotechnology laboratory assistants. A comparison was possible of the "creation of skills", although the skills were different. Hence, to create an accurate picture of India was paramount, as only this picture would lead policy makers to make wiser choices to improve India's comprehensive national power. Determinants like poor state of policing, could eventually lead to a collapse of law and order, and this must lead to a reform of the police that citizens trust. The situation is different in countries like the US, although police reform may still be a demand in that country from human rights groups. The police in the US are responsive, efficient, and courteous and exist in relatively bigger numbers to a percentage of the population.

The argument of whether the determinants should be true to India or the comparison, has led backwards, to- what should be the *Objectives of the Study*? In accepting that the determinants should hold fast to Indian reality, we accept that the primary objective would be '*to attempt to quantify and describe those attributes of India that most accurately portray its capability to exert its national will*'. The irrelevance of much of the India – specific determinants to countries like the USA, and vice versa , necessarily leads us to draw a second objective that can only be derived from the comparison. The second objective is '*to assess how the powers compared in this study could exert their national power to leverage the international environment to the greater national good*'. Clearly the communities and bureaucracies that could use the two portions of the book are different. The bureaucracies whose task is to leverage the international environment, in all countries, are not those who have to grapple with female literacy and access to primary education.

This observation also deals us to another conclusion – which is that a dialogue between the two communities could arise from this book , where those who have to accept that Indian power is ' what it is' will say that this needn't be so, if some people in the other community delivered on areas where Indian backwardness is simply unacceptable. A counter argument could be, that Indian power is inherently much larger than is deployed to leverage the international situation, and the ineffectual leveraging comes from the timidity of the second bureaucracy arising from poor mechanisms, or the failure to appoint people of merit to head their institutions. In any case, the book would hopefully generate a lively debate.

Embarking on a CNP study in India, one is made aware of the earlier studies carried out in the United States and China. The Chinese attempts are of greater importance to India, both as an Asian neighbour and for the unresolved disputes between the two countries. Chinese studies originate with Deng Xiaoping and hence carry strong political overtones of Deng's attempts to define power as something more than Mao's idea, of something originating from the barrel of a gun. At the same time, Chinese studies either give, or perhaps are forced to pay obeisance to ancient Chinese history, to show that comprehensive power was something they always understood. This is a stretched analogy, because it is precisely because China and India missed out on the 'Age of Enlightenment and Reason' that their GDPs plummeted from what was earlier, a level proportional to their share of the world's population. Students of CNP refer to the studies conducted by the Chinese Academy of Social Sciences and the Academy of Military Sciences (in the Chinese NDU). Other studies exist in China, done by universities and a classified study referred to in a Hong Kong journal in 1995. The most notable ones from the USA is the Rand study. There is also an important study that was published by the World Economic Forum and the International Institute for Management Development in Lausanne, which placed countries in order of international competitiveness. In the Lausanne study Singapore is placed second behind the United States, and Hong Kong third. So clearly Lausanne is dealing with a subject different from CNP.

A study on comprehensive National power would be incomplete without a background reference to the rise and fall of countries and empires, or an assessment of the inbuilt longevity to power. In this genre, Gibbon set off a series of rise and fall books that have not been repeated in the latter part of the twentieth century, which saw some spectacular rises and equally dramatic falls. The question for us is whether our set of determinants would have captured the early hints of the fall of Hitler's Germany and the USSR if the same tools had been used to study those countries at their zenith. In the historical context the 75 years of USSR power is but a moment. The first set of determinants was tested against the USSR's indices and it is conceded that it would *not* have indentified the USSR's fatal flaw. The list was amended again to identify fatal weaknesses in seemingly invincible powers. In that sense, this Indian methodology attempts to incorporate determinants that would hopefully, not measure, transient power, like that of Kim Jong Il, at his apogee. The determinants incorporate the best ideas of Kennedy, Spengler and Toynbee, but do not confine it exclusively to their single track opinions. The weightage for institutions is however very strong in our list, and this aspect covers the two demands of longevity and the opinions of the pundits.

There is another aspect in the choice of determinants where one could have erred in implying the inherent belief, that war is inevitable. The background to the Chinese studies is fairly explicit about international competition becoming quite severe, even if the word hostilities are not mentioned. This is ascribed by the authors to Deng's demands, which at the time was relatively non-bellicose, moving away from Mao's 'barrel of a gun' concept. Our study if it errs at all towards one side or the other, does so on the side of the longevity quotient of national power.

To make the comparison table, the countries virtually chose themselves. On the weightage of gross economic power the USA, China and a future India are automatic choices. Japan is in relative decline and so is Russia-but some people hold out hopes of their reviving. This controversy makes them possible swing states. The European states are also in relative decline, and we have the difficulty of comparing the UK to Germany. The latter is a much larger economic power, while the former punches much above its weight externally. France has always had an independent commitment to overseas power projection, and Indonesia is the second largest Asian state. Brazil and South Africa complete the list.

Conceptualising Comprehensive National Power

On the Rise and Decline of Nations: Understanding the Divergent Trajectories of Europe and Asia

Why Western Europe grew rich and consequently surpassed the rest of Eurasia by the mid-nineteenth century is a question of ongoing debate among economic and political historians. Four civilizations – Egypt, Mesopotamia, India and China enjoyed a head start in the global competition for wealth and power. The subsequent technological retreat and loss of these civilizations has once again become a subject of renewed interest as some of these regions are once again displaying signs of a revival.

Eurocentric models of world history[1] maintain that Western Europe possessed unique features that explain its success in the industrial revolution as follows:-

(a) Europe became wealthier than Asia allowing a more capital-intensive path of development. They became wealthier because they managed to lower their fertility rate from the sixteenth to eighteenth century allowing Europe to escape the trap of population growth keeping down per capita growth.

(b) Economic institutions such as property rights – a set of institutional arrangements that aligned the private rate of return with the social rate of return – explain Europe's rise and the origins of capitalism.

---

[1] Eurocentrism is a term coined during the period of decolonization in the later 20th century to refer to the practice of viewing the world from a European perspective, with an implied belief, either consciously or subconsciously, in the preeminence of European culture.

(c) Max Weber's "Protestant ethic", which spurred efforts to dominate and create wealth. Weber saw a rationalization in all forms of western interactions one that India and China lacked (contemporary material success of these two polities, however modest, has frontally challenged this Weberian thesis of an unchanging East?).[2]

Eurocentric conventional wisdom – and argued by the colonial rationalization of Hegel's *Philosophy of History* and Marx's *Asiatic mode of Production* – also asserts that in Asia "elites focused much more on grabbing the surplus from the people and from one another than on enlarging the surplus through further investment or innovation. The great eastern Eurasian agrarian empires and civilizations (such as China and India) had larger populations, more splendid courts, and richer elites, but they were a dead end for a humanity trapped under a monstrous regiment of kings and priests."[3]

More recent scholarship, however, shows that as late as 1750, Asia was similar to Western Europe across of range of metrics. As Kenneth Pomeranz puts it, the core regions of Eurasia "the Yangzi delta, the Kanto plain, Britain and the Netherlands, Gujarat—shared some crucial features with each other, which they did not share with the rest of the continent or subcontinent around them...relatively free markets, extensive handicraft industries, highly commercialized agriculture."[4] East Asia also had a high transportation capability. China, for instance, transported 30 million *shi* (1 *shi*=160 pounds) of grain over long distances to feed about 14 million people in the eighteenth century, five times Europe's long-distance grain transportation in the same period.

A recent comparative analysis has shown that Chinese grain markets were as efficient as their European counterparts as late as 1780.[5] Asia had

---

[2] Ming Wan, *The Political Economy of East Asia: Striving for Wealth and Power,* 2008, pp. 78.

[3] J. Bradford DeLong, A Review of Ken Pomeranz's *The Great Divergence,* 2000.

[4] R. Bin Wong, *China Transformed: Historical change and the limits of European experience,* 1997. Kenneth Pomeranz, T*he Great Divergence: China, Europe and the Making of Modern World Economy,* 2000.

[5] C.H. Shiue and W. Keller, *Markets in China and Europe on the eve of the Industrial Revolution, American Economic Review,* 2007, 97:1189-1216.

more large cities than Europe (22 percent urbanization in Japan compared to 10-15 in Europe) indicating an ability to transport bulk goods.[6] The Chinese and Japanese also appear to have had similar or higher life expectancy than West Europeans.[7] In areas of industrial technique, China's early lead has been documented: In textiles, China had a power-driven spinning machine in the thirteenth century, 500 years before England would leverage such production in the industrial revolution. In iron manufacture, the Chinese learned to use coal and coke in blast furnaces to smelt iron and were turning out as much as 125,000 tons of pig iron by the later eleventh century – a figure not achieved by Britain until 700 years later.[8] Moreover, the best available estimates of international comparison of wealth show Asia ahead of Europe as late as 1820.

Shares of World GDP, 1-2001

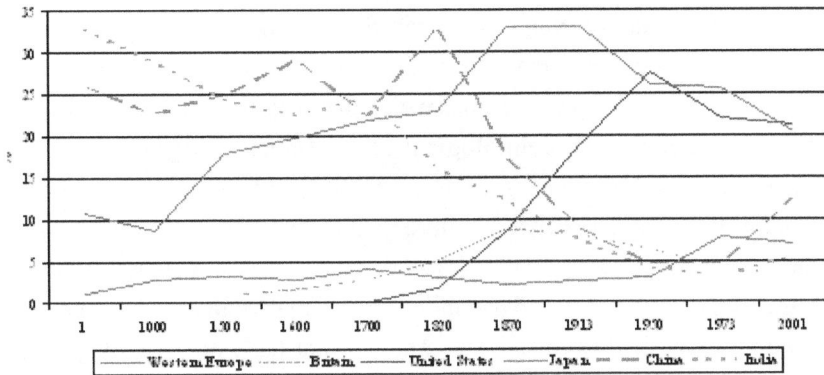

Source: Angus Maddision, The World Economy: Historical Statistics (Paris: Development Centre, OECD, 2003), 261.

Chinese civilization had a clear half-millennium as the world's leader in technological innovation from 500 to 1000. Thereafter innovation in China appears to flag. Little seems to have been done in developing further the high technologies like textiles, communication, precision metalworking

---

[6] Ibid. Gilbert Rozman, Urban Networks in Ching China and Tokugawa Japan, 1973.

[7] William Lavely and R. Bin Wong, *Revisiting the Malthusian Narrative: The Contemporary Study of Population Dynamics in late Imperial China,* Journal of Asian Studies, 57, No. 3, August 1998.

[8] Mark Elvin, The *Pattern of the Chinese Past,* 1973, pp. 85.

(clock-making) that provided the technological base on which the Industrial Revolution rested. China's technological lead: printing in the thirteenth century, shipbuilding in the fifteenth century, porcelain-making in the seventeenth century somehow could not be converted into a "useable" power. In fact, Chinese industrial history offers numerous examples of technological regression and oblivion. It was almost as if China had attained a sense of "completeness". As Patricia Crone observes, "China is a star example of a successful civilization...China reached the pinnacle of economic development possible under pre-industrial conditions and stopped: no forces pushing it in a different direction are in evidence."[9]

It is not entirely clear why this occurred. Moreover, between 1400 and 1800, it is believed that the population of China grew from 80 million to 300 million.[10] Hardly indicative of an economic decline, this is corroborated by Angus Maddison's grand empirical economic survey (See chart). India too was a major manufacturing exporter in the seventeenth, with her cotton textiles much sought after in world markets and competing on at least equal terms with the East India Companies well into the eighteenth century. Habib provides evidence that technological adaptation in Mughal India was impressive in areas such as cash crops like tobacco and maize and shipbuilding, though there was a failure to introduce basic innovations such as book-printing, mechanical clockwork, optical improvements such as spectacles and telescopes, and had fallen behind in iron and steel technology despite an early lead in this field.[11] Again, what has not been adequately addressed, however, is the absence of conversion of wealth to power.

Jared Diamond offers a very brief explanation on why the dominant powers of the last 500 years have been West European rather than Asian (especially China). The Asian areas in which big civilizations arose had geographical features conducive to the formation of large, stable, isolated empires which faced no external pressure to change and as a result stagnated. In these conditions policies of technological and social stagnation

---

[9] Patricia Crone, *Pre-Industrial Societies,* 1989, pp. 172-173.

[10] J. Bradford De Long, Book Review, 1998 of David S. Landes, *The Wealth and Poverty of Nations: Why Are Some So Rich and Others So Poor*, New York, 1998.

[11] Irfan Habib, *The technology and economy of Mughal India*, India Economic and Social History Review, 27:1-34, 1980.

could persist – until the European colonialists arrived.

China was a very notable example; in 1436, a new Ming Emperor outlawed the building of ocean-going ships, in which China was the world leader at the time (Zheng Ze, the Chinese admiral who was a trusted lieutenant of the Yung-lo Emperor, took 30,000 men and seventy ships on seven expeditions to the Indian Ocean from 1405-1433 marking the apogee of Chinese sea power that had originated in the fifth century).[12] It has been argued that China's continental obligations in the early fifteenth century diverted attention away from naval power projection. The invasion and occupation of Annam (northern Vietnam) in 1407-27) along with a Mongol threat from the northern frontiers had created instability on China's land borders. William McNeill argues that "land frontiers against steppe raiders and potential conquerors remained more important than anything happening in the ports where European ships put in."[13] And by the time the Chinese defeated the last steppe power in the mid-eighteenth century, the European powers was already in control of the sea lanes and vital ports of Asia. Similarly, Japan learned about guns from Portuguese explorers in 1543 and by 1600 had the world's best guns; but as these threatened the power of the Samurai class, it restricted and finally banned their production.

Diamond concludes that such bans could be imposed only in politically unified and isolated nations. He also says that India, on the other hand, may have been too fragmented for a monumental rise in power similar to Europe's.[14] On the other hand, the late-19th-century Japanese leap is seen to have resulted from the destruction of Japan's internal barriers by the demands of Britain and the Western powers for free trade. But while *laissez faire* worked to destroy cartelization in Japan, it did not do so in India— where the caste system, unchallenged by governmental authority, prevailed.[15]

---

[12] Jared Diamond, *Guns, Germs, and Steel: The Fates of Human Societies*, New York, 1999.

[13] William McNeill, *World History and the Rise and Fall of the West,* Journal of World History, Vol. 9, No. 2, 1998, pp. 215-36.

[14] Jared Diamond, *How to get rich*, July 1999.

[15] Mancur Olson, *The rise and decline of nations: economic growth, stagflation, and social rigidities*, 1982.

Europe's many natural barriers allowed the development of competing nation-states. Europe's geography favored balkanization into smaller, closer, nation-states, as its many natural barriers (mountains, rivers and forests) provided defensible borders (for the military technology of the time) and made the establishment of political unity on a continental scale impossible. As a result, governments that suppressed economic and technological progress soon corrected their mistakes or were out-competed relatively quickly. This was a classic example of the anarchy of Hobbes' "state of nature" at play - where the geopolitical context compelled European nation states to produce efficient fiscal-miltary structures at the domestic level (since the recurring prospect war impelled the state to find efficient ways of raising tax revenues). For instance, from 1688-1815 saw a remarkable expansion in the share of national expenditure undertaken by the British state - from a tiny percentage to 20 percent. And an overwhelming share (~80%) of British government expenditure was for military purposes. This amounted to a defence budget of 16 percent of GNP of which 60 percent was allocated to the Royal Navy.[16]

In such a context of "a primitive form of arms race among the city states and then the larger kingdoms", it is not surprising that new techniques of warfare and military technologies occurred more frequently in Europe than elsewhere.[17] For instance, firearms, which had been developed and widely used in China, enjoyed little progress once the Ming dynasty (1368-1644) stabilized the countryside. The Jesuit Matteo Ricci was perplexed by the highly developed technical skills of the Chinese, which were used not for military purposes but for pyrotechnic shows. He wrote, when I was in Nanjing (1599) I estimated that in the month-long New Year celebrations they used up more saltpeter and gunpowder than we would need for a war lasting two or three years."[18]

Similarly, in Japan, Tokugawa Ieyasu, who ended the civil war and established a stable shogunate government in 1603, forbade feudal lords to

---

[16] Ronald Findlay and Kevin H. O'Rourke, *Power and Plenty: Trade, War, and the World Economy in the Second Millennium*, 2007, pp. 351.

[17] Paul Kennedy, pp. 22.

[18] Quoted in Jonathan Spence, *The Memory Palace of Matteo Ricci*, 1984, pp. 45-46.

own firearms and banned information about guns.[19] In India too, while the Mughals were good at manufacturing muskets and heavy brass cannon, they fell behind in the manufacture of lighter iron cannon that were more efficient on the battlefield. And while the impetus for constant improvements existed in Europe, in Asia the ruling regimes facing fewer challenges to their authority were less inclined to improve their armaments. There were two important consequences of the arms spiral in Europe – one it preserved a balance of power in the continent and second was its eventual naval mastery.[20] Again geography seemed to have helped. Europe's peripheral location on the western edge of Eurasia had protected it from the Mongols, while Muslim cities such as Baghdad and Damascus were devastated by Genghis Khan's successors. At other times, Europe's location placed it at the mercy of Muslim middlemen, giving Europeans a strong incentive to engage in maritime exploration.[21]

Thus, while in Europe geographical factors created conditions for more rapid power transitions (Spain succeeded by France and then by England), in Asia several sub-systems coexisted without impacting or competing with one another. Nothing demonstrates this further than the perfunctory material and political intercourse between China and India over the past two millennia, contrary to popular contemporary claims. Further, a common European culture ensured that ideas could flow smoothly across frontiers, even when their originators could not.[22]

Thus, an intensely competitive interstate system in Western Europe was more conducive to technological, military and organizational innovation than the autonomous, hierarchical orders in China and India. Further, the size of the Asian economies was large enough to serve as big self-sufficient consuming markets in their own right. Such an option of autarky was simply not feasible for Britain and the small states of continental Europe. Thus unlike, in the East, international trade was a *necessary* condition for the growth of Europe. The political importance of trade also had important

---

[19] Mark Elvin, *Pattern of the Chinese Past*, 1973.

[20] Paul Kennedy, pp. 23.

[21] Ronald Findlay and Kevin H. O'Rourke, *Power and Plenty*, pp. 360.

[22] Ibid., pp. 359.

second order effects like giving rise to legislation that was favourable to commercial interests. That the European powers were well acquainted with the relationship between trade (wealth) and military power is reflected in the words of a Dutchman, Jan Pietersz Coen:

> "You should well know from experience that in Asia trade must be driven and maintained under the protection and favour of your own weapons, and that the weapons must be wielded from the profits gained by the trade; so that trade cannot be maintained without war, nor war without trade."[23]

The configurations of the domestic political economy also influenced the likelihood of technological progress. The nature of the relationship between the state and merchants (private enterprise) was different between China and Western Europe. China lacked a free market and institutionalized property rights. The Chinese state was always stepping in to interfere with private enterprise - to take over certain activities, to prohibit and inhibit others, to manipulate prices, to exact bribes. The Chinese central government was motivated by a desire to preserve an agrarian polity or to control important resources (i.e. iron, salt). Innovations in the Chinese court were judged by their consequences of the balance of power and influence.[24] The Ming code of laws also sought to block social mobility, with severe penalties for those jumping professional barriers (perhaps not dissimilar from the structural immobility of the caste system in India). As the noted Sinologist, Etienne Balazs observes,

> "Chinese society was highly authoritarian…no expression of public life that can escape state control. There is to begin with a whole array of state monopolies, which comprise the great consumption staples: salt, iron, tea, alcohol, foreign trade. There is a monopoly of education, jealously guarded. There are clothing regulations, a regulation of public and private construction; the colours one wears, the music one hears, the festivals – all are regulated. There are rules for birth and rules for

---

[23] Quoted in C. R. Boxer, *Portuguese Conquest and Commerce in Southern Asia, 1500-1750*, 1985, pp. 3.

[24] David S. Landes, *Why Europe and the West? Why not China?*, Journal of Economic Perspectives, Volume 20, Number 2, Spring 2006, pp. 3-22.

death; the providential State watches minutely over every step of its subjects, from cradle to grave."[25]

It has also been suggested that China's "cultural triumphalism" also created an "intellectual xenophobia" making it a bad learner, especially after its own scientific and technological achievements had slowed considerably by the seventeenth century. Even when the threat from European colonialists was making itself evident in the Indian Ocean, an insecure Chinese majority found it difficult to respond:

"...military defeat was the technical reason why Western knowledge should be acquired, but it was also the psychological reason why it should not be. Instinctively the Chinese preferred admitting military defeat, which could be reversed, to entering a psychological crisis; people could stand humiliation but not self-debasement....The mandarins sensed the threat to Chinese civilization irrespective of the economic and political issues, and they tried to resist this threat without regard to the economic and political dangers. In the past the Chinese had never had to give up their cultural pride: the foreign rulers always adopted the Chinese civilization. Hence there was nothing in their history to guide them through their modern crisis."[26]

Political fragmentation across Europe implied that the state had to compete with aristocracies, the church, and urban residents and it was difficult to suppress inconvenient ideas; the Chinese emperor ran a centralized bureaucracy and faced few institutionalized power centres outside the state. The political economy and decentralization of political power in Europe was such that even an erroneous grand strategy (as is conjectured to have occurred in China and India insofar as these empires failed to balance even when the external threat became evident) could not be implemented. As Paul Kennedy observes, "it was inconceivable in the fractured political circumstances of Reformation of Europe that everyone would acknowledge the Pope's division of the overseas world into Spanish and Portuguese spheres – and even less conceivable that an order banning overseas trade (akin to

---

[25] Etienne Balazs, *Chinese Civilization and Bureaucracy*, 1964. pp. 23-23.

[26] Carlo M. Cipolla, *Guns, Sails, and Empires: Technological Innovation and the Early Phases of European Expansion, 1400-1700,* 1966, pp. 120.

those promulgated in Ming China and Tokugawa Japan) would have any effect."[27]

Such political competition and diversity in organizations and technology allowed Europeans to experiment with new ways of doing business and politics and enabled them to leverage the opportunity of the industrial revolution and the ensuing diffusion of military-industrial technologies. [28]

Deconstructing CNP

A tentative interpretation of the past millennia suggests that Asia did *not* fail to acquire wealth. There is diverse empirical evidence to show a mercantile and agricultural economy flourishing in eastern Eurasia. Angus Maddison's estimates suggest that there was sufficient Asian capital upto the early nineteenth century to finance technological and military innovations. Yet, these nations failed to build the social capabilities to either develop or rapidly adopt the physical and organizational technologies of Western Europe's industrial revolution. And, in the instances when the capability was attained the incentive to preserve and develop it further was lacking (classic case is China's abrupt dismantling of its formidable naval capabilities in the fifteenth century). Such failures arguably emanated from a combination of the internal structure of these societies (i.e. In India - the caste system, lack of dissemination of knowledge beyond a privileged class) and the absence of compelling external geopolitical pressures (and an inability to accurately assess the seaward threats of the time) to convert wealth to military power.

Given this historical backdrop, it is reasonable to conclude that the path from acquiring wealth to power is neither linear nor inevitable. There are identifiable intervening variables that influence a state's 'conversion capability'. The principal intervening variable is the State's extractive and goal making capacity: If in the process of its creation, wealth dissipates in a decentralized fashion (untapped because of a weak state) or after successful state extraction wealth is appropriated by non-state interests (i.e. where an oligarchy penetrates the state for its own ends thereby diminishing or

---

[27] Paul Kennedy, *The Rise of and Fall of the Great Powers*, 1989, pp. 20.

[28] Ming Wan, *The Political Economy of East Asia: Striving for Wealth and Power*, 2008, pp. 83.

subverting the state's original goals) national power *will* remain unrealized.

Further, globalisation has imposed additional challenges to the ability of the state to accumulate CNP. In the words of Robert Gilpin, to "retain domestic autonomy and possess valued industries in a world characterized by the internationalization of production, global integration of financial markets, and the diminution of national control" is the contemporary challenge.[29]

The following influence a state's extractive capacity:-

(a) **Economic structure** – material and natural resources. This determinant has a dual feature in the sense that aside from providing the surpluses to transform physical and human resources into tangible capabilities it also serves as a non-coercive instrument of power by itself.

(b) **Elite Cohesiveness** - "the degree to which a central government's political leadership is fragmented by persistent internal divisions"[30]. Elite cohesion directly affects the state's ability to set national goals and abide by them.

(c) **Societal Cohesiveness** – degree to which citizens within a state treat each other as having equal claim to the state and citizenship. Social or national cohesion affects the state's ability to mobilize the masses for strategic ends.

(d) **Science & Technology**

(e) **Governance** – broadly defined as the ability of the state to penetrate and engage society and maintain its monopoly over legitimate use of violence. The state's ability to mobilize individuals and resources is greater when society cooperates with the state rather than resists it.

---

[29] Robert Gilpin, The Political Economy of International Relations (Princeton, NJ: Princeton University Press, 1987), 404.

[30] Randall Schweller, 2006. Alternatively, it has been argued that elite cohesion should be taken as part of social cohesion: social cohesion is to be understood at both the elite and the societal level.

(f) **Human Capital and Development** – Measures the institutional and knowledge capability of the system to leverage its human resource endowment (demography).

(g) **Accountability index** – impacts the legitimacy of the ruling regime. A state's legitimacy is derived from two sources:-

(i) security, economic and welfare performance.

(ii) normative authority in the sense that the prevailing political arrangement is deemed to be universally acceptable to the polity. (This determinant captures the latter.)

The above may be considered as the "building blocks" or "inputs" of CNP. These building blocks embody latent power and only the state's political performance can convert these building blocks into useable power instruments.

And since in an anarchical or "self help" international system, the ultimate currency of useable power is military force the principal objective of a security seeking state is to convert its "building blocks" into military capabilities. Thus, for CNP to be complete the chain, the extractive process *must* produce a tangible output - combat capabilities. This is captured by the determinant of Military Capability.

The final component of CNP one that provides it a strategic character is the "plan of use". In our study the 'Foreign Policy' Determinant attempts to measure the capacity of the state in terms of its autonomy, grand strategy (or the institutional and ideational ability to generate and adapt one), and the quality of the strategic bureaucracy (those assigned to implement national security goals) as they combine to maneuver the state in international life by influencing other actors in the system.

Broadly, we are conceiving power as a combination of material capabilities (that have been generated and transformed through the extraction and mobilization process of national performance) and strategy (as power is not exercised in a vacuum but "against the resistance of opposing wills".) Thus, "the state must be able to set goals, obtain the resources to achieve those goals, and encourage non-state actors in society (for example, business enterprises, social classes) to cooperate in the attainment of the state's aims."[31]

It may be noted that for potential great powers such as India and perhaps even China, anecdotal and empirical observation would suggest much of the state's performance and energies is being channeled or consumed in the first realm itself – the building blocks – rather than actually completing the dynamic interaction with the second realm to produce coercive capabilities and grand strategies. The reasons for this would perhaps lie in structural weaknesses in the first realm itself. For instance, the governance and legitimacy challenges of the Indian and the Chinese state, which in turn emanate from the relatively lower levels of societal and elite cohesion, may be diverting disproportionate resources and strategic attention away from developing military capabilities and grand strategies toward a premium on internal security and other dilemmas. It has been argued that both countries are domestically 'weak states' which largely constrains their internal and external behavior.[32] Thus, to assess whether a state is likely to be successful in extracting and mobilizing societal wealth and converting these resources to coercive instruments of power, one must be able to analyze the relative distribution of power between the state and society.[33] But since state power is generally uneven across policy areas, it is necessary to identify the functional areas where the state is strong or weak. For instance, the Indian state might be strong in areas of political empowerment of different ethnicities but weak in allocating resources toward military-technical and scientific innovations or national security. It is the state's capacity in the latter area that concerns us more.

But we are also concerned about the legitimacy of a state's political system since this directly impacts the stability and the extractive capacity of the state. For example, in a comparative perspective, India's presumed

---

[31] Ashley Tellis etc., *Measuring National Power in the Postindustrial Age*, RAND MR1110A-10, 2000, pp. 130.

[32] Namrata Panwar, *Domestic Social Cohesion and State Power: Comparative study of India and China*, Working draft for "Southern Political Science Association Annual Meeting 2010", Atlanta, Georgia, January 7-9, 2010.

[33] Ashley Tellis etc., *Measuring National Power in the Postindustrial Age*, RAND MR1110A-10, 2000.

advantage over other potential great powers is the normative appeal and domestic acceptability of its political system. This provides the state with a vital if intangible source of legitimacy. In contrast, the Chinese state's legitimacy relies almost entirely on the state's economic and welfare performance that seeks to compensate for the absence of an overarching normative unanimity in the body politic. And "if the state's legitimacy is based solely on performance, its legitimacy is hostage to performance failures."[34]

It is hoped that our CNP study would offer insights into this notion of stunted or latent power and identify the structural breakdown or weaknesses in the CNP production process.[35] To be sure, while there are other instances of stunted power in the international system (Japan, Germany etc.), these cases emanate less from a structural breakdown within the state than from external constraints that have integrated these states into a security community hence precluding the incentive or the option for developing an autonomous CNP. US grand strategy in the post-1945 phase has integrated Western Europe and Japan into durable alliance structures, which neither of these stunted power centres can easily exit from.

The Paradox of Unrealised Power

Finally, some analysts have drawn attention to "the paradox of unrealized power" that is the inability of a state to translate potential power into actual power (achieving a political outcome). This is caused by two factors:-

(a) The lack of will or skill in the effective use of power.

(b) The capabilities of an actor must be juxtaposed in the context of a "policy contingency framework" specifying who is trying to get

---

[34] Ibid., pp. 114.

[35] It is also true that India has acquired a modicum of great power military capabilities in some aspects of its force structure largely because of a fortuitous set of geopolitical circumstances. Whether this unique structural advantage - that has enabled India to leverage the external system to compensate for internal deficiencies - should be incorporated within this study is debatable. Nonetheless, in the long run these external opportunities *cannot* relieve the Indian state from constructing an autonomous military-industrial base.

whom to do what.[36] Power unlike monetary resources is not fungible and a power resource that might be useful in one context could become a liability or simply irrelevant in another. The principle theme that these studies seek to convey is that conceiving power "as an undifferentiated quantifiable mass" will offer little insights into the actual political success of the studied state units.

The quest for contextualizing power by relating it to hypothetical contingencies and specific geopolitical contexts, however analytically appealing would be methodologically next to impossible to incorporate in our study. What this implies is that the results of our CNP study would reveal little about the political outcome of a situational context where power is exercised by one of the eight members of our CNP peer group. What our study does claim to do is enable a measurement of the "capabilities that permit the power wielder to make effective threats" or inducements to compel or deter other actors.[37] Whether these capabilities (of state A) are actually transformed into actual power will depend on the strategic actor (state B) on which putative power of state A is exercised and the situational context in which such a strategic interaction occurs.

In other words, the scope of our study enables an understanding of the internal generation of CNP (that results from an intricate division of labour within a state) and not whether that the data we crunch has political relevance in predicting outcomes. In this sense, we are closer to Ray Cline's notion of "perceived power", which is distinct from actual power.[38] In a similar vein, Kenneth Waltz notes "ranking states does not require predicting their success in war or in other endeavors. We need only rank them roughly by

---

[36] David Baldwin, *Power Analysis and World Politics: New Trends versus Old Tendencies*, World Politics, Vol. 31, No. 2 (Jan., 1979), pp. 161-194. Harold and Margaret Sprout, Man-Milieu Relationship Hypotheses in the Context of International Politics, Center For International Studies, Princeton University Research Monograph (Princeton, NJ: Princeton, 1956), pp. 39–49. Jeffrey Hart, *Three Approaches to the Measurement of Power in International Relations*, International Organization, Vol. 30, No. 2 (Spring, 1976), pp. 289-305.

[37] Klaus Knorr, *The Power of Nations: The Political Economy of International Relations*, 1975.

[38] Ray S. Cline, *World Power Assessment: A Calculus of Strategic Drift*, 1975.

capability."[39]

Nonetheless, what our study could do is analytically account for macro-structural constraints that have system-wide impact. For instance, the nuclear revolution and economic interdependence distinguish the present international system from all previous eras. (Nuclear weapons have at the very least complicated and limited the exploitation of conventional use of force, and economic and financial interdependence have produced disincentives for coercive foreign policy options). These two variables determine the international context in which power is actually exercised.

One possible way to account for this would be to make a subjective judgment on the weightage provided to the determinant military capabilities (and its sub-determinants – conventional and strategic force structure) and assign weights to the sub-metrics of economic determinants by rewarding those states that have more symmetrical linkages or "mutual vulnerability" with the international economy (lower foreign debt, external imbalances are not sever, energy dependence is manageable etc.) rather than asymmetrical interdependence (single commodity vulnerability, lack of diversification in export markets energy sources, high dependency on imported capital).[40]

The Objectives of the Study

The idea of CNP is premised on the primacy of the state as the principal actor in the international system. Yet, to gauge the relative power of different state units, one needs to disaggregate state power whereby each constituent or *determinant* of national power has a relative capability to be gauged (the importance or weight that each determinant is assigned is inherently subjective). The notion of CNP, however, implies that the sub-components of power are greater than the sum of its individual parts. Thus, the

---

[39] Kenneth Waltz, *Theory of International Politics*, 1979, pp. 131. According to Waltz, for states a "rank depends on how they score on all of the following items: size of population and territory, resource endowment, economic capability, military strength, political stability and competence."

[40] One idea behind economic interdependence and power is that if a state's international transactions have a low opportunity cost (implying the existence of alternatives domestic or reliable external options) relative to others its political flexibility is greater (i.e. its ability to absorb a sanction, naval blockade, limited military conflict or natural disaster is greater).

interdependencies within the state's various internal components are implicitly recognized and these determinants dynamically interact to produce what is known as CNP.

Mathematically, one possible function would be defined as,

$$CNP = F(D1, D2....D7) * S$$

Where,

D = Determinant

S = Strategy (in our nomenclature: Foreign Policy Determinant).

Objectives

(a) To identify the international power hierarchy and India's relative position in this group. Since this exercise would inherently involve contrasting 'apples with oranges' or 'great powers' (such as the US) with 'emerging powers' a process of standardisation is required. Yet, standardizing the determinants could lead to a selection of sub-determinants that are simply not susceptible to a useful relative assessment given the asymmetrical stages of development among the peer group. Nonetheless, a rationalized choice of sub-determinants in light of the above and data collection constraints would yield a hierarchical ranking of major powers in the international system.

(b) The above methodological dilemma (inherent in any CNP study that deals with a world of 'apples and oranges') enables a parallel India-specific exercise to offer Indian policy planners a comprehensive scrutiny of the same determinants of CNP (as in part a.) but increasing the number of sub-determinants, thereby flagging areas that require priority policy attention (which might not have been captured if a parsimonious analysis had been undertaken).

The above implies that the study is not simply content with providing a snapshot of the contemporary international hierarchy but seeks to gain some insights into the complex process of how CNP is produced in the dynamic organism called the state.

An Overall Perspective of Comprehensive National Power – Methodologies and Thought Processes

From the days of Sun Tzu to the present, political scientists and strategists have postulated that power is inextricably linked to political action. The primacy of power play in international relations has been aptly described by Vernon Van Dyke as "Importance of power in politics is attested by the universal view that whatever else international politics may be, it is also a struggle for Power".[1]

However Morgenthau felt compelled to bring out the nuances of power play and hence flagged four major distinctions about the usage of power in international relations.

Firstly he clarified that Power and influence were clearly distinct from each other. While the former decided outcomes, the latter shaped decision making.

Secondly he distinguished between Power and Force. He opined that the former is more of a psychological concept. Those with power merely needed to threaten its usage for achievement of results. However he also stated that resorting to the usage of force often revealed a perception of a lack of power.

Thirdly he talked of Moral and Immoral power. In this Morgenthau asserted that the former held actions justified by ideology (Communism, Liberalism, Democracy, Fascism, etc.) An aspect in which he adopted a

---

[1] Vernon Van Dyke, *International Politics* (Meredith Publishing Company, New York)

cynical approach since he believed that the purpose of ideology was to win hearts and minds and to acknowledge the quest for power would be to abandon any moral superiority. Then the debate shifted to the morality of the issue.

Finally he talked of a distinction between usable and unusable power stating that the possession of power did not signify its usage. As a corollary to the entire debate on "power equations" arose the concept of quantifying the "power" of a state and so arose the idea of comprehensive national power (the name/ terminology came much later as we will see) or the aggregate power of a state. While most of the western thought processes identified "power" mainly with its military capacity and "hard power" (its presence or lack of it) thinkers like Morgenthau added the ideological factor and more importantly the ethical dimension or morality of usage of power. Unfortunately aspects of "soft power" and other formats of power were ignored making the debate one sided, static and overwhelmingly military oriented.

It was in this context that during the Cold War period, a nation's power was largely determined by the strength and capability of its military forces. Accordingly, the Soviets developed the concept of Co Relation of Forces (COF) as a means of carrying out such measurement,(the concept will be compared with the more wholesome Chinese approach and discussed later in the article). The accent of this concept was overwhelmingly military in accordance to the thought process then in existence. However with the dismantling of the power blocks and a current transition towards a multipolar world , sheer military might no longer remained the defining factor of strength and power. Instead, elements such as economics, technological ability etc become increasingly critical in the competition for power and influence in the world.

The evolving (and enlarging) concept of national power, thus, engaged the attention of international strategists not only with a view to rationalize the recent history but also to prognosticate future international power equations that were developing.

However the quantification of this enlarging concept of national power proved to be extremely complex, nebulous and complicated affair given its qualitative and quantitative constituents. But, notwithstanding its complexity and dynamic nature its ambit became a little clearer along with its definitional approach. Thus Comprehensive National power could well be defined as the aggregate power (comprising of hard, soft and smart power constituents) of a state and its ability to use its national capacity in the achievement of its national objectives.

The Chinese Concept

Having taken cue from Deng's dictum the Chinese developed the most well rounded approach towards measurement and the process of quantification of national power. They can also be credited with developing the phrase and the modern idea of "Comprehensive National Power" during the early 1980s when the initiative to measure and compare national strengths became persistent. The driver for this development took place as Deng Xiaoping modified Chairman Mao's party line that "world war was unavoidable," to predicting that "world war probably can be avoided."[2] The Marxist-Leninist "foundation" of Deng's new assessment of the security environment was that "the growth of the world's forces of peace exceeds the growth of the forces of war." In a Cold war period that signified that the United States and the Soviet Union were at a stalemate in their military struggle, but the strength of countries that were opposed to war was also increasing. The international environment was evolving and the importance of economic issues was growing. Hence in such a scenario military force could no longer be the sole judge and primary index to a country's strength which would be determined by numerous other factors as well. Thus there needed to be means for measuring the sum of the "forces restricting war,"

Deng wrote: *"If at the end of the new century China attains a "comparatively well off level," then there will be a major increase in the power restricting war. If China again goes through thirty to fifty*

---

[2] Zhu Liangyin and Meng Renzhong, "Deng Xiaoping zonghe guoli sixiang yanjiu" (A study on Deng Xiaoping's Comprehensive National Power thought), in *Xin shiqi junshi jingji lilun yanjiu* (Studies of new period military economic theory), eds. Li Lin and Zhao Qinxuan (Beijing: Junshi kexue chubanshe, 1995), p 42.

years of construction, and comes close to the level of developed countries, then at that time it will be even harder for a war to be fought.[3]"

Thus Deng has been attributed the foresight to establish the theoretical foundation and basis of the concept[4]. However it is unlikely that Deng himself ever used the terms "Comprehensive National Power" which would have probably come around through analysis of his statements on the priorities of China's national construction and the significance of this development to the growth of China's strategic power. The authorship of the term is claimed by   Senior Colonel Huang Shuofeng of AMS writing his book *"On Comprehensive National Power"*.

The basic concept of "Comprehensive National Power" however has ancient cultural roots even in Chinese strategic discourse and has "evolved from the concepts of 'power,' 'actual strength', and 'national power.' [5] Studies of Herbert Goldhamer provide examples of ancient Chinese strategists who emphasized the need to conduct calculations about the future[6].

According to the Chinese, *CNP* (總合國力) (*zonghe guoli)* refers to the combined overall conditions and strengths of a country in numerous areas. It is the aggregate sense of all factors such as territory, availability of natural resources, military strength, economic clout, social conditions, domestic government, foreign policy and its initiatives, and finally the degree of wielding international influence. Thus CNP is an evaluatory measure done both qualitatively, as well as quantitatively of the current and future strengths of all these above factors. While the former is resorted to for general discussions of country strengths and weaknesses, the latter is used to calculate numerical values of CNP through the use of formulae and their own extensive index systems and equations. It is noteworthy that the Chinese seem to reject the usage of GNP (Gross National Product) as a means to

---

[3] Ibid. p 44

[4] Ibid p 43

[5] Wang Songfen, ed., *Shijie zhuyao guojia zonghe guoli bijiao yanjiu* (Comparative studies of the comprehensive national power of the world's major nations)(Changsha: Hunan chubanshe, 1996), p.23

[6] See Herbert Goldhamer, *The Adviser* (New York: Elsevier, 1978); and Herbert Goldhamer, *Reality and Belief in Military Affairs: A First Draft* (Santa Monica, CA: The RAND Corporation, 1979).

evaluate national power as is prevalent in US. A closer inspection reveals that the concept of CNP and the associated analytical methods are not rooted in traditional Marxist-Leninist dogma or Western social science but in many ways unique.

Contextually the ongoing "debate" about CNP is also important for RMA (Revolution in Military Affairs) researchers, because- according to Chinese analysts - fore knowledge of a nation's CNP can determine which side will win a war by better implementation of RMA[7]. Thus future CNP scores can not only help in identification of the status hierarchy and the power potential of a state but also which state is likely to implement RMA to a higher degree and hence be the eventual winner in an overt war. Unfortunately numerous Chinese authors have made predictions about future CNP, but few provide detailed accounts about the associated methodologies for measurement and evaluation.

Some of the fairly detailed accounts of calculating CNP have appeared in two books by two different Chinese institutes. While one has been published by the Academy of Military Science (AMS) it is contrasted by the other book published later by the civilian Chinese Academy of Social Sciences (CASS). It is noteworthy that both these have approached the problem within the stated ambit outlined by Deng Xiaoping and some of the authors were apparently directly involved with Deng's estimates. While the AMS study propounds a more orthodox view the reformist view was presented by a team of researchers from CASS who had Gao Heng a noted author as their senior advisor. Seemingly Gao helped to invent the key Chinese concept of structural multipolarity, which he published in 1986. This coincided with Deng Xiaoping's national security adviser announcing the concept[8].

---

[7] According to Li Qingshan, "Through the analysis of belligerent countries' Comprehensive National Power, even before a war has begun, people frequently can know the results in advance." Li Qingshan, *Xin junshi geming yu gao jishu zhanzheng* (The new revolution in military affairs and high-technology warfare)(Beijing: Junshi kexue chubanshe, 1995), 191-192.

[8] See Gao Heng, "Shijie zhanlue geju zhengxiang duojihua fazhan" (The strategic world structure is developing toward multipolarity), *Guofang daxue xuebao* (National Defense University Journal), no. 2 (1986): 32-33.

Interestingly both the studies are based on the hypothesis that US is a declining power and those of other growing power centres (or poles or nodes) is rapidly reducing and hence the world is slowly moving towards multi polarity. The other notable and surprising aspect of both studies is that they have avoided mentioning China as a future "super power" (unlike the Chinese and world media) preferring to label China as one of the future five equal "poles".

The main point of divergence between the two studies arises from estimating the rate of growth of China in contrast to the decline of US. They also differ on how to assess military power of a state. There is also a contrast in the debate carried on in the two studies about the future strategic environment by the civilian and military mindsets in China. It is apparent that CASS and AMS have used different rates of growth and decline. AMS growth estimates have projected China's CNP increasing seven times faster than the CASS pace;

Chinese scholars, today use the concept of CNP to make assessments in their particular areas. For the military strategist CNP scores can aid "warfare more specifically in future warfare to predict "who is capable of winning a victory in a new RMA war."[9] and for others it can assist in a umber of way including providing pointers towards "all directional economic war,"[10]. However the concept comprises of various qualitative and quantitative components.

Qualitative Factors

While the overall concept of the CNP is fairly distilled it is noteworthy that the specific components of the CNP - are nuanced and at times dissimilar in their composition – depending on the interpretation of the particular analyst. Some Chinese authors prefer to adopt a qualitative approach towards CNP by dividing the entire ambit into broad areas while others prefer a quantitative analysis with detailed definitions of each component. Undoubtedly some factors remain common between the two efforts but inconsistencies exist.

---

[9] Li Qingshan, *Xin junshi geming yu gao jishu zhanzheng*, p. 191

[10] Tong Fuquan and Liu Yichang, *Shijie quanfangwei jingji zhan* (The world's all directional economic war)(Beijing: Junshi kexue chubanshe, 1991).

This dilemma has been commented upon by the Chinese who feel - that "Because different countries' national conditions are not the same and researcher's personal goals are different, interpretations of the concept of national power vary."[11]

An overview of the qualitative approaches would make it easier to understand the quantitative methodologies later.

Economic Aspects

While military strategists have a tendency to view the entire concept of CNP from the prism of war and its associated consequences, civilian thinkers relate to the concept in a more nuanced fashion. Writers Tong Fuquan and Liu Yichang have tried to analyse the concept by accentuating economic issues of nations. They have accordingly divided CNP into four major parts— with economics playing the prominent and crucial role which is followed by politics, science and technology, and military affairs. Thus they feel that "Actual economic strength is, of course, the major component part of Comprehensive National Power" [12] The other three areas are not discussed as independent factors but with regard to their relationship with the overall / specific economic scenarios. The authors firmly believe that a country with strong economic power will correspondingly wield a powerful political influence. However, they do admit that Japan is an exception to this rule in which case economic influence and clout has not translated into an equally potent strength in international political affairs.

Similarly a direct linkage exists between the extent of a country's economic power and the level of its scientific and technological prowess. The authors opine that even military power- which is seen as the primary factor for other analysts - is to be viewed within the ambit of its relation to other factors mentioned above.

Another important aspect that needs attention is the correlation between military budgets and the military power. In most cases military expenditures is both a reflection of whether a nation's military strength is strong or weak, while providing an important indicator to the power of its economy and most

---

[11] Wu Chunqiu, *Guangyi dazhanlue*,p.95

[12] Tong Fuquan and Liu Yichang, *Shijie quanfangwei jingji zhan*, p.232

importantly the ability to imbibe and disseminate military related technological aspects.[13] However a country lacking in military power is unlikely to score high on CNP.

Strategy

The Chinese have an acute sense of history and the military thinkers such as Sun Tsi laid importance to attacking the strategy of the enemy – an aspect that has found reflection in modern times by writers such as Xi Runchang of AMS. Xi explains that his particular stress on the importance of strategy does not ignore the position of the other components but is "done in order to give prominence to this important area that people often overlook."[14]. Xi, has accordingly proceeded to evaluate national strategies based on various aspects the main being as to how a country's leadership "effectively utilizes" its strategy. Xi writes, "In the current information age, for any major nation in the strategic competition, whether they take action early or take action late, is extremely important...."[15]

Taking the example of China and Russia – Xi feels that since both these countries were late entrants in the field of strategic competition and hence were overtaken by "ambitious" countries like America, Europe and Japan who moved quickly to implement their strategies.

Xi's compatriot from AMS, Wu Chunqiu, however supports a slightly different point of view in which he suggests that CNP and grand strategy have an "unbreakable internal connection" of a "dual nature."[16]. In a vicious circle of sorts, he feels that CNP is wielded to attain the goals of grand strategy (for which a strong CNP is required) – yet on the other hand its development becomes one of the aims of grand strategy. Thus in Wu's opinion strategy cannot be a component of CNP evaluation.

---

[13] It can argued that some Gulf countries especially Saudi Arabia have impressive military budgets but that is no reflection on their scientific capability or international clout.

[14] Xi Runchang, "Shijie xin geju zhanwang" (Prospects for the new world structure"), in *Shijie zhengzhi xin geju yu guoji anquan* (The new world political structure and international security), eds. Xi Runchang and Gao Heng (Beijing: Junshi kexue chubanshe, 1996), p.46

[15] Ibid., p.45

[16] Wu Chunqiu, *Guangyi dazhanlue*, p. 94

Wu feels that - "In the current age when peace and development have become the main trends in the world, numerous countries, to different degrees, recognize that economics are the foundation; science and technology, especially high technology, are the guide; education is the guide of the guide; national defence is the backup force; and national policies are the key factor playing a unifying and coordinating role." Furthermore, citing the breakup of Soviet Union as an example Wu explains that countries can learn from mistakes made by other countries by analyzing the development patterns of both the national strategy and the Comprehensive National Power of these particular countries.

RMA and its Utilisation

Since ancient times Chinese strategists such as Sun Zi and Wu Zi have both propounded that victory (or defeat) in war can be predicted in advance if a comparison of certain factors that contribute to a country's strengths is done appropriately. The Chinese strategists of today also believe in this age old dictum and the present day CNP discourse is often shaped accordingly.

Li Qingshan, a People's Liberation Army (PLA) colonel puts forth a similar argument in his book *The New Revolution in Military Affairs and High-technology Warfare. He states* "Through the analysis of belligerent countries' Comprehensive National Power, even before a war has begun, people can frequently know the results in advance."[17] He however concedes that as war develops, there will be fluctuations in the strengths and functions of the various component factors. Thus what plays a direct role in the outcome of the war are the changes that take place in this comparison of forces during the process of war, as well as the results of diplomatic struggles, ideological struggles, and economic struggles.

Commenting on the RMA factor in CNP he opines that RMA will not override previously existing premises for making strategic assessments and that high-technology weaponry "can change the appearance of warfare, but it cannot change the laws of victory in warfare". Thus he links RMA and CNP by stating "…Historically, in numerous wars the victors have

---

[17] Li Qingshan, *Xin junshi geming yu gao jishu zhanzheng* (The new revolution in military affairs and high-technology warfare)(Beijing: Junshi kexue chubanshe, 1995), p192

been both those who have technically inferior weaponry and those who have technically superior weaponry. Technology is not the only factor determining victory or defeat in war."[18] However its level of usage is still critical in determining the outcome of war and goes on to state that RMA warfare "is still a comprehensive test of the level of countries' strength."

Taking the military line of approach Li delineates CNP into five major components or areas —politics, economics, military affairs, science and technology, and foreign affairs—each of which are interlinked and are to be viewed within the ambit of their role in war. For Li "Warfare is the continuation of politics and reflects a country's strategic intentions" – and RMA (and its usage) is a critical component in attaining victory since it is determined by a country's scientific and technological development.[19]

Quantitative Factors

Two prominent Chinese books propose a quantitative approach to the problem of evaluating CNP. Both these are slightly divergent in their approaches to the common problem in that they originate from military and civilian perspectives since they are a product from AMS and from CASS respectively. The two books are *Comparative Studies of the Comprehensive National Power of the World's Major Nations,* by a team of largely civilian analysts coordinated by Wang Songfen, of CASS. The other book is *On Comprehensive National Power,* by Senior Colonel Huang Shuofeng, of AMS who claims to have worked with Deng Xiaoping.

The CASS study

Originally published in December 1996, this book puts forward a detailed dissection of the characteristics of the CNP component factors and fairly comprehensive measurement methodologies in calculating the CNP. It also provides extensive data tables from the results of examining the CNP of 18 countries.

---

[18] Ibid p.191

[19] See Wang Zhenxi, "The New Wave of the World Revolution in Military Affairs," *International Strategic Studies* 44, no. 2 (April 1997): 8-9.

Based on three guiding principles this book divides CNP into eight major areas. They comprise of natural resources, domestic and foreign economics, science and technology, military affairs, government and foreign affairs capability, and social development. The three of the basic principles on which the authors relied to determine the above eight general factors include the following

(a) Both material power (tangible factors such as economics, military affairs, etc.) as well as spirit power (the intangible factors, such as international relations, leverage politics, etc.) need to be included in an assessment of CNP

(b) CNP is composed not only of actual power; but potential power also has a contributing role.

(c) The components of CNP and their roles have changed throughout history and will continue to do so in the future; therefore, new aspects may be added or dropped when evaluating different time periods.[20]

The CASS Indexing system:

Having taken a quantitative approach to evaluating CNP one of the major tasks that the authors from CASS faced was to evolve and create measurable   and uniform standards that can evaluate all the eight factors above as applicable to various countries. This was undeniably a complex task since it not only involved the measurement indices of tangible and intangible factors but also the correlation between them. Additionally the authors wanted to include "both indexes for total amount, and indexes for amount per person; both quantity indexes and quality indexes; both efficiency indexes and consumption indexes."[21]   Finally the authors arrived at a matrix of 64 indices for the eight areas of measurement. These indices are enumerated in the table below

---

[20] Wang Songfen, ed., *Shijie zhuyao guojia zonghe guoli bijiao yanjiu* (Comparative studies of the comprehensive national power of the world's major nations)(Changsha: Hunan chubanshe, 1996),p. 36

[21] Ibid p.64

Table 1: The Comprehensive National Power Index Framework[22]

Natural Resources

Man Power Resources: total population; life expectancy; the proportion of the economically active population in the total population; the number of university students per 10,000 people

Land Resources: the area of national territory; the area of cultivatable territory; the area in forest

Mineral Resources (reserves): iron; copper; bauxite

Energy Resources (reserves): coal; crude oil; natural gases; water energy

Economic Activities Capability

Actual Economic Strength (total): gross domestic product (GDP); industry production capability (electric energy production, steel output, cement output, logs output); food supply capability (total grain output, degree of self-sufficiency in grain); energy supply capability (volume of energy production, volume of energy consumption, crude oil processing capability); total cotton output

Actual Economic Strength (per person): GDP per person; industry production capability (electric energy production, steel output, cement output, logs output); food supply capability (total grain output, average calories per person); energy supply capability (volume of energy consumption)

Production Efficiency: social labour production rate; industry labour production rate, agriculture labour production rate

Material Consumption Level: volume of energy consumption based on GDP calculations

Structure: the proportion of the tertiary industry in the GDP

Foreign Economic Activities Capability

---

[22] As cited in "Geo Political Power Calculations" **n.4**

Total import and export trade; total import trade, total export trade

Total international reserves; international reserves (not including gold); gold reserves

Science and Technology Capability

Proportion of research and development in the GDP; number of scientists and engineers; the number of scientists and engineers per 1,000 people; proportion of machinery and transportation equipment exports in total exports; proportion of high-technology intensive exports in total exports

Social Development Level

Education Level: education expenditures per person; proportion of people studying in higher education; proportion of people studying in secondary school education

Cultural Level: adult literacy rate; number of people per one thousand who get a daily newspaper

Health Care Level: health care expenditures per person; number of people doctors are responsible for; number of people nurses are responsible for

Communications: number of people who have a telephone per 100 people

Urbanization: Proportion of the urban population in the total population

Military Capability

Number of military personnel; military expenditures; weapons exports; nuclear weapons (the number of nuclear launchers; the number of nuclear warheads)

Government Regulation and Control Capability

Proportion of final government consumption expenditures in the GDP; proportion of central government expenditures in the GDP;

investigation through interviews asking nine questions

Foreign Affairs Capability uses ten factors in a "nerve network model" to carry out a broad assessment.

Source: Wang Songfen, ed., *Shijie zhuyao guojia zonghe guoli bijiao yanjiu* (Comparative studies of the comprehensive national power of the world's major nations)(Changsha: Hunan chubanshe, 1996), 69.

CASS Weighted Index Methodology

Stage I: Basic Plan

The evaluation of the CNP is basically a two stage effort in which analysts from the Office of Statistics and Analysis at Institute of World Economics and Politics (IWEP) at CASS divide their measurement into the Basic Plan and the Weighted Plan.

At the Basic Plan stage first the basic 64 indices are calculated and standardized using various formulae through index calculation methods, which "combine R. S. Cline's comprehensive calculation method of assigning values and the comprehensive index calculation method used in the book *Japan's Comprehensive National Power.*"[23]

Later, this data is separated into calculated unit values. The hard indexes are divided into two groups, direct indexes (those directly related to GDP growth per person) and indirect indexes (those inversely related to GDP growth per person)[24] The former set of data takes the biggest value as 100, the latter set takes the lowest value as 100 to "successively calculate the deserved value of the different countries for those indexes." For assessing intangible areas, the group often resorts to investigative methodologies in which a group of renowned experts are closely questioned on the subject and the results computer analyzed quantitatively.

In the case of foreign affairs which is another intangible or "soft area" the CASS group has designed a nerve network model with ten factors related to capability in foreign affairs activities—population, territory, natural

---

[23] Wang Songfen, ed., *Shijie zhuyao guojia zonghe guoli bijiao yanjiu,*p. 71

[24] As cited in "Geo Political Power Calculations" available at http://www.fas.org/nuke/guide/china/doctrine/pills2/part08.htm

resources, military affairs, economics, science and technology, politics, ideology, system of organization, and international image. The values so allotted are standardized later. Thus based on these different methodologies, the numerical value of the 64 indexes, the eight major areas, and eventually the CNP is calculated.

Stage II: The Weighted Plan

To overcome the aberrations and distortions that may arise during the basic Plan stage – the Weighted Plan is resorted to[25]. For example countries with extensive natural resources and relatively sparse population score high on CNP even though this is not a true reflection of their international standing, economic or national power. The main reason for this aberration is their strength in per-person rates of economic capacity and high standard of living (social factors). Secondly certain issues and factors follow time specific regimes for example during times of conflict or less than war situations, weapon manufacturing and enhancing military capacity would enjoy high national priority while at others would be less accentuated - hence appropriate time specific revisions have to made periodically to ensure standardisation.

Lastly, the number of indexes in each of the eight major areas not equal-(ie -natural resources has fourteen, while foreign economic capability has two) —but each index, regardless of its value or importance, is allotted the same weight eventually. [26] Hence during the second stage of CNP measurement, the quantitative results of the basic plan are revised through qualitative analysis.

However in this analysis some guidelines and dictums are kept in mind. Primarily that economic development forms the most important activity for most nations in peace time hence it's primacy in CNP calculations. Meanwhile measuring military capacity and capability is also the one of the most important aspects of CNP along with the professional efficacy of the military in carrying out its duties in peace as well as in war.

---

[25] Wang Songfen, ed., *Shijie zhuyao guojia zonghe guoli bijiao yanjiu*, p.168
[26] "Geo Political Power Calculations"n.4

It is noticeable that the Chinese analysts themselves face this problem as to which factor to accentuate – a form of this debate is also visible between the military studies of CNP and the civilian one. In any case, availability of natural resources forms the "material base" of CNP measurement by CASS.[27]

The different weighted values of factors are shown in the table below:

Table 2. Weighted coefficients of major component factors

National Power Factor	Weighted Coefficient
Total CNP	1.00
Natural resources	0.08
Economic activities capability	0.28
Foreign economic activities capability	0.13
Scientific and technological capability	0.15
Social development level	0.10
Military capability	0.10
Government regulation and control Capability	0.08
Foreign affairs capability	0.08

Source: Wang Songfen, ed., Shijie zhuyao guojia zonghe guoli bijiao yanjiu (Comparative studies of the comprehensive national power of the world's major nations)(Changsha: Hunan chubanshe, 1996), 169.

In addition to the above, the different indices of each the constituents of major factors are also assigned weights. For example, there are four indices constituting the military factor. They include —the number of military personnel, military expenditures, weapons exports, and nuclear weapons (in case the country possesses them) and they are equally assigned weights of 0.25 each. Similarly the science and technology capability factor has been

---

[27] Wang Songfen, ed., *Shijie zhuyao guojia zonghe guoli bijiao yanjiup.169*

divided into research and developments in the GDP and the index for technology personnel. Both have weighted coefficients of 0.30;

Based on these weighted revisions and by using the data generated for the 64 indexes as evaluated under the basic plan - the numerical value of the eight major areas and finally the calculated CNP for each nation is reached.

It is interesting to note that forecast of CNP of 18 nations were made for the years 2000 and 2010. Known as Forecasted Weighted Plan these were based on the principles of the weighted plan. The calculated predictions were done by evaluating the potential future role of that particular nation and its futuristic influence/ capability with respect to the different component factors – the weighted coefficients of which were adjusted accordingly. To give an example – the growing significance of education, communications research and development in particular, within the ambit of science and technology,, the weighted coefficients for science and technology and social development level was raised from 0.15 to 0.17 and from 0.10 to 0.12, respectively for futuristic projections. On the other hand the weights allotted to the two economic factors and military affairs capability remained the same though foreign affairs capability, were reduced to 0.07. In all these predictions using the new weighted coefficients, the data gathered from the basic plan were taken as the base.

The AMS Index System

In comparison to the methodology used by CASS system for calculating CNP the AMS system is slightly different though the overall aim remains essentially the same. The essence of the calculation methods are propounded by Huang Shuofeng in his book "On Comprehensive National Power". The *book* provides a fairly detailed analysis of the major component factors of CNP and their numerous indexes as seen from the AMS's (or rather Huang's) perspective.

Huang feels that relying only on theoretical research for analyzing CNP is grossly inadequate and advocates the usage of systems theory and mathematical methods for developing a qualitative and quantitative approach to the problem. Consequently, Huang describes CNP as a large and complex system composed of many levels or subsystems, within which there are interlinked component factors. Overall he divides the CNP index system into four major index subsystems. These comprise of:-

(a) Material power or hard power factors : is made up of the hard factors, natural resources, economics, science and technology, and national defense

(b) The Spirit power or soft power factors: Also known as intellect power – it determines the effectiveness of the material form (hard) national power. It includes politics, foreign affairs, and culture and education. Both Material and Spirit power reflect a country's needed strength for existence and development.

(c) The coordinated power: reflects the leadership mechanism's organization, command, management, and decision making levels;

(d) The environmental factor: reflects the restricting conditions of Comprehensive National Power.[28] This subsystem comprises of three partsnamely:-

   (i) The international environment (that analyses the world architecture with in the ambit of different balances of power),

   (ii) The natural environment (a country's natural resources, ecological conditions etc),

   (iii) The social environment (the political set up, hierarchy , economic and social systems)[29]

Commenting on the above four major index factors Huang writes that there being no absolutes - even the hard factors contain some aspects that are soft in nature, but for the purpose of analysis they are designated to a subsystem based on their dominant characteristic for eg , it is universally understood that national defence is a hard factor, but a few of its components like its associated ideology and military theory, fall within the ambit of being soft factors.

---

[28] Huang Shuofeng, *Zonghe guoli lun p.162*

[29] Ibid p.164

Each of the components of the major sub indexes is itself a sub-sub index, and together they all form a CNP appraisal index system. For each of these sub-sub-indexes, Huang provides detailed lists of their contents in his book. However only a few have been elaborated below as examples and for the sake of comparison.

(a) "Foreign Affairs Power Subsystem: Foreign political relations; foreign economic relations; foreign military relations; diplomatic activities capability; international contribution capability."

(b) "National Defence Power Subsystem: Standing army (nuclear, conventional) and reserve forces; national defence investment; national defence science and technology and national defence industry; national defence bases and installations; strategic material reserves and logistics safeguards; national defence education and training; national defence system establishment; the national defence ideology of the people and troop morale; military theory."

(c) "Political Power Subsystem: National strategy goals; political stability; policy level; the nation's leadership, organization, and decision making capability; national embodiment power."

(d) Science and Technology Power Subsystem: Science and technology troops (scientists and engineers, technological personnel); investment in science and technology (total, proportion of the GNP); science and technology level (high science and technology, general science and technology); science and technology system; scientific and technological progress speed; scientific and technological progress contribution; scientific and technological results and applications."[30]

While working out "The Structural Networks of Comprehensive National Power System," Huang has adopted a slightly nuanced position towards defence/ military power in that he has attempted to delineate "direct" military power from "indirect" military power. Accordingly while direct military power includes measures of nuclear forces and conventional forces, indirect military power on the other hand comprises of associated aspects such as total armed manpower; the professionalism of the soldier,

---

[30] Ibid pp. 169, 170, 172

his weapons , their efficacy , weapons acquisitions , reserve and strategic reserve capability, logistic etc.

The AMS Dynamic Equation

According to the AMS perspective, the foundation of calculating Comprehensive National Power of any nation rests on the Dynamic equation as conceived by Col Huang. Importantly, in establishing his equation, Huang also emphasizes the dynamic aspects of CNP by reiterating that one of the primary characteristic of CNP is that it is continuously evolving with the passage of time. This evolution is dependent not only on changes in global geo political structures and the international environment but also on aspects like changing regimes of science and technology, micro and macro economics, energy and foreign policy etc[31] hence in an effort to deal with such a dynamic aspect dealing with variations and with changing developments of CNP - Huang assessed that, *a type of "motion equation"* was needed. That was based on the principles of systems theory, coordinated studies, and dynamics studies. Consequently, the results generated by Colonel Huang were quite different from those arrived at by civilians working at CASS.

The growth factor and development process of CNP has been described as "the process of taking a group of factors and turning them into output, under fixed domestic and foreign environments, and natural conditions." This process Huang has depicted numerically by the equation that is also called Comprehensive National Power function

$$Y_t = F (x_1, x_2, ..., x_n; t)$$

In this equation:

the CNP n component factors are $x_1, x_2, ..., x_n$

the amount of their inputs is combined, and the output volume—the

CNP—is represented by Y_t

t is the variable for time

$x_1, x_2, ..., x_n$ are functions of t.

---

[31] Ibid p.175

This equation shows the relationship between the input amount of the individual component factors and the total volume of output.

Huang's efforts to deal with numerous interconnections and the deluge of associated data have led him to use "macro variables . . . with the biggest roles in the allocation, control, and guidance of comprehensive national output Y_t." Contextually he has selected three of the four major index subsystems from his CNP index system to be the following variables:

(a) Hard variables - represented by H_t;

(b) Soft variables - mentioned as S_t;

(c) Coordinated variables, represented by K_t.

Hence the new national power function can then be written as :

$Y_t = F (H_t, S_t, K_t)$

So that calculations can be made using this new form of the national power function, it is rewritten using Newton's third law, where F = kma:

$Y_t = K_t \times (H_t)a \times (St)b$

In the above function:

H_t stands for the "mass" of CNP

S_t represents the "acceleration" of CNP

K_t is the coordinated coefficient

a is the "hard elasticity index"

b is the "soft elasticity index."

The two elasticity indexes also help in establishing if the particular country conditions is developed or developing and whether it is at war / facing unrest, or whether it is at peace and is stable.

In the AMS system of calculating the CNP it is obvious that the system has numerous subsystems and sub-subsystems, contextually the methodology for measurement like the CNP dynamic equation also have several layers of equations many of which are not explained or mentioned by the author

Huang. However the author does provide examples of sub-equations for population growth, gross national product, national income growth, scientific and technological power, and national defense power

Methods of Assessment and Measurement

In addition to the above equations and sub equations Huang has mentioned four different methods of measuring and evaluating CNP: the methods of assessment are

(a) The index number method: This method is used to compute the hard factors in the dynamic equation

(b) A specialist evaluation method: This method is used for assessing the soft factors in the dynamic equation

(c) The weighted coefficients method: This method is assigned to the coordinated factors;

(d) The vague judgment method: This method is used for assessing some of the undetermined factors.

Under the index number method, after the data have been generated through the different sub equations of the CNP dynamic equation, index numbers are established for it. These index numbers are set based upon a unified ratio, in which the value of the U.S. data from each equation is given the index number of 100. The indexes of the other countries being evaluated are then set accordingly. Later, using the new indexes, the CNP of the different countries is calculated using the national power function[32]

One of the most potent aspects of measuring CNP of nations has been that of predicting the values for the future- this has been carried out by Huang, however, the only explanation he provides of his methods to arrive at the projected values is: "In order to forecast the future world strategic structure, we used the Comprehensive National Power developments equation model, using the 'leading trend analysis method' to make calculations."[33]

---

[32] "Geo Political Power Calculations" n.4

[33] Huang Shuofeng, *Zonghe guoli lun*   p.220

Re- appreciation of the Dynamic equation

In an effort to overcome some of the lacunae Huang Shuofeng wrote his second book titled, *On the Rise and Fall of Nations. In this book Huang* further develops his qualitative and quantitative analysis of the CNP in order to project its role in the prosperity and decline of nations.

The original dynamic equation as propounded by Huang also finds identical mention in his second book however he gives further details regarding the science and technology power sub-equation in his second effort.

Since the main thrust of his second book is mainly to evaluate the rise and fall of nations using the concept of CNP – Huang first calculates the 1996 scores of overall CNP and its various factors for six countries. In the re- evaluation it is discovered that his new quantitative analysis of the United States, Japan, Germany, Russia, China, and India differ from those he derived in his earlier book 7 years before.[34]

It is noteworthy that the original "Comprehensive National Power dynamic equation" measures only a country's strength at a given time; it does not indicate how this power and its component factors influence the nation in its development. Unfortunately the older version of the equation allows for the comparison of CNP for different countries, but they do not illustrate the outcome of the interaction and competition between these countries.[35]

To overcome these above constraints in the dynamic equation, the goal of the new one is to quantitatively analyze this "competitive and developing evolutionary process," in order to determine the rise and decline of nations. Accordingly the author divides this aspect of rise and decline of nations into two parts

(a) Evaluating the individual country by itself,

(b) Assessing two nations that are in competition with each other.

---

[34] "Geo Political Power Calculations" n.4

[35] Huang Shuofeng, *Guojia shengshuai lun* (On the rise and fall of nations)(Changsha: Hunan chubanshe, 1996),p. 379

The first situation can be used to analyze how a country's power is influenced by domestic conditions and the international environment which the author refers to as "an environment where the initiative is in one's own hands," [36]

The second part deals with a more intricate issue and as to how national strength is affected by the competition or interaction between two forces The equation can also be adapted to examine an internal struggle for power between a country's old state system and a new one with a new national strategy[37]

Talking about the competing aspects between two countries the potential results of such an eventuality could be categorized into four general categories:

(a) Both countries could get into a nuclear conflicts and be destroyed

(b) One country could dominate the other.

(c) One country could force another into a "fatal position."

(d) Both countries could co exist peacefully by promoting prosperity

Hubei Science Commission Calculations

The CASS team and Colonel Huang from AMS are not the only Chinese analysts to do research on CNP and attempt at calculating it. Numerous articles/books on international relations written by Chinese analysts attempt at predicting the CNP and the future evolution patterns of relevant nations and the futuristic security architecture of the international environment.

However what sets the CASS and AMS study apart from the rest is that unlike others who just mention the concept in generic terms and make predictions without proper explanations, these two studies provide extensive details and explanations about their assessment and calculation processes, as well as numerous data tables of their results.

Notwithstanding the above it is important to briefly analyse the research

---

[36] Ibid p.382

[37] Ibid p.385

done by some other authors. Contextually research on the subject conducted in the early stages by Yu Hongyi and Wang Youdi of the Hubei Science Commission finds mention in the CASS study.

The formula used by them for calculating CNP was given as "function (F), dimension (D), structure (S), level (L), and four- dimensional vector comprehensive national strength (CNS) measurement formula, in which CNS = F (FDSL).[38] The FDSL measurement formula based on the calculation results of the 12 countries is shown in the table.

Table 4 . Hubei Science Commission CNP Calculations (1985)

Country	Function Dimension (FD)	Structure Level LS	CNP
United States	0.5049	0.9262	0.6838 (1)
Soviet Union	0.2048	0.8252	0.4111 (2)
Japan	0.1434	0.8815	0.3555 (3)
Germany	0.0854	0.8839	0.2748 (4)
England	0.0621	0.9178	0.2386 (5)
France	0.0609	0.8907	0.2329 (6)
China	0.0757	0.6409	0.2202 (7)
Canada	0.0489	0.9225	0.2123 (8)
Italy	0.0454	0.8757	0.1993 (9)
Australia	0.0207	0.9133	0.1374 (10)
India	0.0298	0.6256	0.1365 (11)
Egypt	0.0057	0.7509	0.0656 (12)

Source: Yu Hongyi and Wang Youdi, "Zonghe guoli cedu pingjie (Measuring the value of comprehensive national power)," Keji jinbu yu duice (Scientific and Technological Progress and Ways of Dealing with it) 1989: 5, in Shijie zhuyao guojia zonghe guoli bijiao yanjiu, Wang Songfen, ed., 50-51

---

[38] Yu Hongyi and Wang Youdi, "Zonghe guoli cedu pingjie (Measuring the value of comprehensive national power)," *Keji jinbu yu duice* (Scientific and technological progress and ways of dealing with it) 1989, 5, in Wang Songfen, ed., *Shijie zhuyao guojia zonghe guoli bijiao yanjiu*, 50-51

Western Thought Processes

As had been mentioned earlier the Western focus on measurement of the power of a state was distinctly different from what the Chinese had envisaged as CNP. Contextually, over the ages many western strategists had approached this issue with differing perspectives. Some strategists approached the problem of Measuring National Power as a Single variable.

Single Variable Approaches

Military Power Inis Claude and Karl Deustesche[39] used Gross Military Capability as an indicator of national power of a state. There were other strategists who followed the traditional singular military approach like Alcock and Alan Newcombe who used Military Expenditure[40] while George Modelski and William Thompson with their maritime mindset used the size of naval forces, as a measure of projectable national power.

Economic Power Analysts with an economic bent of mind and economists convinced about the primacy of economic issues in the measurement of power index of a state have chosen to use it as a singular variable. Hence Kingsley Davis, a demographer and Organski,[41] a political scientist, have advocated use of national income for representing national power. While on the other hand Charles Hitch and Roland McKean have used the variant of Gross National Product (GNP) to measure national power[42].

While single variable approaches were appealing due to their sheer simplicity in reality they were grossly insufficient to assess the national power of a state given the sheer complexity. Hence such methodology was criticized by scholars for their lack of realism. Thus evolved multivariable approaches in measuring national power which attempted to represent the true power of a state.

---

[39] See Inis Claude, *Power and International Relations*, (New York – Random House), Karl W Deustesche, *The Analysis of International Relations*, (Englewood Cliffs:Prentice Hall)

[40] Norman Z Alcock and Alan G Newcombe, *The Perception of National Power, Journal of Conflict Resolution,* Volume 14 (1970)

[41] See Kingsley Davis, *Demographic Foundations of National Power*, Morrow Burger , AFK Organski, *World Politics*, (New York – Knopf)

[42] See Charles Hitch and Roland McKean, *Economics of Defence in Nuclear Age*, (Cambridge – Harvard Press)

Clifford Model

One of the better known models for measuring national power that appeared in the early 60s was known as the Clifford model. It was conceived by F Clifford, a German scholar of international relations. The model was a complex non linear multivariable index that attempts to identify the discrete variables as well as specify their interrelationships. The same is enumerated below,

G = N * (L+P+I+M),

where, G = National Power

N = Nuclear Capability

L = Size of land mass

P = Size and quality of population

I = Industrial Base

M = Size of the military[43]

Wilhelm Fuchs model

A similar nonlinear multivariable index that became famous was subsequently proposed by Wilhelm Fuchs in 1965. The equation was simpler than the one used by Clifford and it sought to derive national power from three summational variables :

population size (p),

energy production (z),

and steel production ($z1$) - arranged in one of nine formulas for measuring national power (M), all of which were variants of one another and took the form of $M = p2z$, $M = p3/2z$, etc[44]

---

[43] For a more detailed treatment see F Clifford German, *A Tentative Evaluation of World Power*, Journal of Conflict Resolution, Volume 4 (1960)

[44] For a more detailed treatment see Wilhelm Fuchs, *Formeln zur Macht: Prognosen uber Volker, Wirtschaft Potentiale*

Ray Cline Model

One of the most famous contemporary methods that evolved from the West and found acceptance amongst the academia and the Western strategic community (mainly the US) was conceived and proposed by Ray Cline who was the former Director of US Intelligence and later a Deputy Director of the CIA. Cline's model evolved a nonlinear multivariable index that attempted to integrate both capabilities and commitments to create a formula that would rank the perceived power of states.

This model formed the basis of some improvements and variants that were later used by the United States Government to predict and forecast the long range trends in the international hierarchy. It proposed simple formulae that could be used to quantify national power, even though two of its factors are intangible. The methodology did not necessarily allow the actual and precise measurement of total national power, but enabled its partial quantification. This was due to the fact that the first three factors in the suggested formula were tangible elements and can be quantified objectively. However the last two factors are subjective and defy suitable quantification. Unlike the Chinese – Cline does not suggest an appropriate methodology to quantify qualitative factors by an elaborate system of weighted indexes etc. The formula given in the model is as follows:-

$$PP = (C+E+M) * (S+W),$$

Where,

PP = Perceived Power

C = Critical mass (population and territory)

E = Economic capability

M = Military capability

S = Quality of strategy

W = Will to pursue strategy

Measuring National Power in the Post industrial Age

A group of scholars like Jacek Kugler, William Domke, and Lewis Snider begun to revisit the vexing question of power.[45] Their work tended to focus not so much on creating quantitative assessment factors (indices) for measurement of constituents of national power *per-se*, as the Western scholars of the 1960s and 1970s had done earlier - but rather they laid primacy on deepening the notion of national power to include measures of capacity building related to the societal realm.

As per their formulation, National Power is ultimately a product of the interaction between two components comprising of the country's ability to dominate the cycles of economic innovation and thereafter, to utilize the resultant of this domination to produce effective military capabilities. These capabilities/ capacities in turn reinforce existing economic leverages while producing a stable political order. As a consequence such an effort in turn also provides benefits for the international system as a whole.

Thus the ability to dominate the cycles of innovation in the international economy is the critical impetus beneath the production of power: thus its significance is that national power has fundamentally *material* components, without which all other manifestations would be devoid of substance. Taking each realm separately as follows

National Resources: The first realms, "national resources," are simply the "building blocks" a country needs if it is to develop

National Performance The second realm, "national performance," seeks to capture the mechanisms that enable countries to convert the natural resources identified in the first realm, which represent latent power, into tangible forms of usable power.

Military Capability The third important realm, "military capability," seeks to capture the indicators of national power that are ultimately personified by the combat proficiency of a country's military force. These capabilities could be classified into:-

---

[45] For a detailed treatment see Ashley Tellis, Janice Bially, Christopher Laine & Melissa McPherson, *Measuring National Power in Post Industrial Age,* (Rand Arroyo Centre)

(i) The strategic resources of a military which include budgetary allocations, manpower resources, military infrastructure, the defence industrial base, and the inventorial assets and the logistical support.

(ii) The means by which these strategic resources are converted into effective capabilities - for eg – threat perceptions and response strategies, ability to imbibe technology the efficacy and nature of civil-military relations, foreign military-to-military relations, doctrinal and training approaches, organizational architecture and the capacity for carrying innovational modifications.

(iii) The professional capabilities of the combatants including war fighting competencies.

International Futures (IF) Model

Developed by Barry Hughes, International Futures (IF) is a large-scale integrated global modeling system that serves as a thinking tool for the analysis of country-specific, futuristic estimations with a time line extending upto 100 yrs and by taking into account multi dimensional issues. It explores non linear human leveraging factors.

IF is data-based and also rooted in theory. It represents major agent-classes (households, governments, firms) interacting in a variety of global issues like demography, economics, social, and environmental factors. The menu driven interface of the International Futures software system allows display of alternative scenarios over time horizons from the year 2000 up to 2100. The system is also capable of developing scenarios for the future.

Soviet Concept COF

It is interesting to note that the concept of evaluating national power has undergone considerable changes even from the time of Cold war. The Soviet methodology to measure power was termed as *sootnosheniye sil* in Russian. These two words can be correctly translated as "correlation of forces," (COF) "relation of forces," or "relationship of forces"—all conveyed the idea of a relationship or distribution of power.[46] It referred to a Soviet method

---

[46] See Raymond L. Garthoff, "The Concept of the Balance of Power in Soviet Policy Making," *World Politics,* October 1951, p. 87.

of assessing world power and reflected Moscow's view of a bipolar world. During the Cold war and in consonance with the Soviet tradition, policy priorities and strategy were derived from Moscow's evaluation of nations' relative power in the correlation. In this manner, the correlation evaluation of forces was multidimensional. It was a broader concept than the traditional Western concept of "balance of power,"

It was a qualitative and quantitative method which comprised of all things that determined relative power: public opinion, political allegiance, economic prosperity, class struggle, and military might. This holistic concept the analysts contrasted unfavourably with what they saw as a Western view too focused on counting inventory.

The Soviets were very sensitive about miscalculating COF. They felt that an underestimation of the enemy's true military capabilities could lead to "adventurism" or actions incurring unwarranted risks (an action they could ill afford); while on the other hand an overestimation of strength could lead to "opportunism" or a failure to seize a gain, which a correct calculation of the COF would have permitted.[47]

The COF concept was supposedly dynamic because history is dynamic, but given the lack of information with regards to the methodologies used – it is not possible to compare the CNS dynamism with that of COF.

COF was in many ways similar to the CNP concept propounded by the Chinese though admittedly the latter is much more holistic. COF was well suited the Cold war scenario where as CNP with its military-economic foundation is much better suited for the dynamic variations of the multi polar world of today.

Comparison of some Western Methods with Chinese CNP

Having had a brief overview of the various thought processes and "model systems" for assessing power being followed in the West it relevant to compare the Chinese CNP with these thought processes a little more closely.

It must be understood that before formulating their own concept of CNP Chinese had closely studied many western models in an effort to

---

[47] Ibid p.92

'better' the existing systems.

In general, Chinese authors have proved to be explicitly critical of foreign quantitative analysis methodologies to assess national power. Contextually some foreign formulae for assessing national power have been frequently mentioned, both negatively and positively. The formulae are those created by Ray Cline and William Fuchs, and the Japan Economic Planning Department, Comprehensive Planning Office, (in a study entitled *Japan's Comprehensive National Power*).

In 1984 when Premier Deng Xiaoping, set up a team of Chinese scholars tasked to analyse the future security environment in the world, as part of a study on China's national defence strategy for the year 2000 the scholars studied western literature on the subject. One of the initial western authors studied was Ray Cline and his "National Power Equation" but his formulae were discarded.

It was considered too "static" and was indifferent to the dynamic nature of CNP and its variations over time. One of the major reasons for such rejection was that Cline did not include science and technology as a factor and that his means for judging the soft, intangible factors were neither objective nor unified.

William Fuch's formulae was also studied in detail but that too was rejected because it was restricted in its approach in that it measured only hard factors while ignoring the soft ones. Military aspects and those of science and technology were glossed over.

Lastly the Chinese scholars found the 1987 Japanese study "done in order to serve the Japanese Government's established guiding principles and policy."[48]. They (Chinese scholars) felt that the index system propounded by this study was too narrow and unscientific- leading it to be discarded. (*The World's All Directional Economic War*, Tong Fuquan and Liu Yichang)

However it would be incorrect to presume that all Chinese scholars have discarded Western methodologies for measuring CNP. Despite the claim of absolute "originality in approach" a lot of the Chinese methodology

---

[48] Tong Fuquan and Liu Yichang, *Shijie quanfangwei jingji zhan*, p. 234

was partly "borrowed" from Western thinking.

CASS, for one of their measurement techniques (as mentioned earlier) was unique in that it not only adapts aspects of Cline's methodology but amalgamated it with features of the Japanese study.

Again in sharp contrast to Huang's observations of Cline, Xi Rnchang believed Cline's standards to be "relatively objective," including the standards for the soft factors,(mainly on aspects such as strategy). Xi went on to use for his own calculation Ray Cline's national power equation.[49]

Again the Chinese equations themselves suffered from many shortfalls. For eg the original Huang "Comprehensive National Power dynamic equation" measured only a country's strength at a given time; it did not indicate how this power and its component factors influenced the nation in its development. Unfortunately the older version of the equation allows for the comparison of CNP for different countries, but did not illustrate the outcome of the interaction and competition between these countries.

Overall while there is little doubt that the Chinese methodology to assess aggregate national power by numerous studies is markedly different from traditional Western processes. However before criticising such process for their "restricted approach" lack of "holistic over view " it must be remembered that in the prevailing geo strategic circumstances of a Cold war – the accent was on military strength and on singular "hard approaches" hence the models too reflected this thought process. The issue of predicting a hierarchical world order and the strategic futures through CNP is a much later development.

Later Western models however have changed that approach considerably. The Rand study is much more wholesome and "in keeping with times". It studies the interaction between two components comprising of the country's ability to dominate the cycles of economic innovation and thereafter, to utilize the resultant of this domination to produce effective military capabilities. Thus in a well rounded fashion it lays primacy on deepening the notion of national power to include measures of capacity building related to the societal realm.

---

[49] Xi Runchang, "Shijie zhengzhi xin geju,"p. 44

Hence it can be summarised that the "unique" Chinese approach is only a cog in the process of evolution of measuring national powers.

Indian Calculations

Given the growing popularity of the Chinese CNP concept as a important tool to measure the national power of a nation and hence to tailor strategies (and even tactics) on the basis of futuristic projections of CNP - , the National Security Council Secretariat (NSCS) attempted to evolve a "National Security Index (NSI)" on (more or less) similar lines except that it has gone so far as to give primacy to Human security index above national security while computing NSI.[50] For a "poor democracy" this addition of a social dimension is a path breaking step.

The NSI constitutes an average of five indices. These include, Human Development Index (HDI), Research and Development Index (RDI), GDP Performance Index (GDPPI), Defence Expenditure Index (DEI) and Population Index (PI).

Each of these major indices is further sub divided into sub-indices for example: Human Development Index HDI - which reflects the socio-economic conditions of a country – is based on a number of sub indices such as life expectancy index, education index, per capita income index, etc

Research and Development Index (RDI): this is a reflection of the technological prowess of a country constitutes the weighted average of three separate unequal indices, namely Patents Index, Index of R&D Expenditure as a percentage of GNP and Index of R&D Scientists and Engineers per million.

GDP Performance Index (GDPPI): The GDPPI is important for calculating a country's overall economic strength and the rate at which this capability is evolving. The main index comprises of the weighted average of two separate indices — the "GDP Index" and the "GDP Growth Index".[51]

---

[50] Karl Hwang "New Thinking in Measuring National Power" Study by University of Ljubljana, Slovenia, 23"26 July 2008, p.2

[51] "Evolving A Comprehensive National Security Index" available at http://www.financialexpress.com/news/evolving-a-comprehensive-national-security-index/73228/0 (Contributed by National Security Council Secretariat). India's National Security, Annual Review 2002

Shortcomings

The NSI suffers from numerous short-comings. It is also not known if the NSI is used to predict a nation's power in the years to come. The efficacy of NSI as a tool in strategic decision making is also open to debate. Apart from that, the ambit of the calculations is all too restricted and "static" in a generic comparison to the Chinese CNP calculations. The NSI in addition, does not take into account resource abundance, environmental health and good governance aspects of a country.

It also places Human security index above national security while computing NSI – which is unique and can be greatly advantageous for power computation of a poor Third world country – yet prove to be of not so much value for First world nations.

Conclusion

Calculation of aggregate national power has seen its slow evolution from times immemorial. At different times in its evolution – models have managed to lay stress on aspects that have been considered important at that particular time. Starting from singular variables (mainly with respect to the military or hard power constituents) in the West, the models have started including multi variable aspects.

With increasing complexity later models have realised the importance of quantifying the qualitative aspects including soft power constituents. Later Western models have incorporated such ideas in their calculation.

Given the Chinese idea of creating the wholesome concept of CNP and the importance of the scores to the aspiring Chinese because it can identify: their status in the hierarchy in world politics. It also identifies the power potential of China's allies, adversaries and rivals apart from indicating which country would be best suited to exploit the RMA in times of war and less than war situations. Thus providing a clear indication as to which side had a clear advantage and a possible victory in war.

In addition the importance of the CNP calculations lies in their deciphering the future course of action for "competing" in the hierarchy of world politics and its usage for adjusting national strategies accordingly.

The Chinese seem to have used CNP scores well for "fine tuning" their national strategic approaches. Unfortunately in the case of countries like India (with NSI which has been path breaking in some aspects due to the stress on social factors like human security and hence an apt tool for assessing power of third world countries) it is debatable if such assessments have ever been templated on conceptual policy directives. Hence probably in the Indian case it has been reduced to an academic exercise in futility – with access of the results to a few.

The "usage" of western origin models by western governments in adjusting national strategic approaches due to changing "aggregate power assessments" by various models is debatable. (Note: Except COF results that were used extensively by the erstwhile Soviet Union during Cold war era).

In the end it can only be summarized that CNP or any other power assessment tool which is only useful if the scores are used by the concerned government in shaping policy directives- otherwise it will remain an aspect of academic curiosity.

Methodology of the Study

Choosing Determinants

The task of assessing comprehensive National Power (CNP) has taken some strides in the last two decades largely owing to Chinese interest in the subject. The rise of China gives the study much traction in strategic circles. As can be seen in the Chinese studies, the choice of determinants will decide the outcome. Whether the study is done with purely quantitative factors, or qualitative ones or a mixture of both, the process must gather respectability when tested against proven historical examples of the rise and fall of nations. The Chinese studies, done mainly by the Chinese Academy of Social Sciences (CASS) and the Academy of Military Sciences (AMS), produces rankings of CNP that co-relate to GDP rankings in seven out of ten cases[1]. This does not assure the skeptic that such studies have advanced the knowledge of determining power very much. There are a number of other reasons why the choice of determinants needs a much closer look. The US study also mentions that relative rankings may not change very much whether a large number of determinants are chosen or whether hugely important single indices are used. For that reason this Indian study has wider objectives than creating snapshots.

The Anamoly of Military Power. All Chinese studies place Japan second to the United States, and yet argue that military power is one of the chief constituents of CNP. This is impossible to reconcile when Japan's transnational military power is a legal impossibility. The AMS study in fact alludes to CNP being reflected in a nation's ability to leverage the Revolution in Military Affairs, but yet relapses into statements that CNP is more than

---

[1] Michael Pillsbury, Geopolitical Power Calculations, January 2000, NDU Press, quoting Wang Songfen ed. Comparitive Studies of the Comprehensive National Power of the World's Major Nations: Human Chubanshe, 1996

military power. The CASS study posits an entirely new theory that the RMA doesn't pertain exclusively to the military, but is a combination of national will, military power and science and technology. There are huge ambivalences when it comes to deciding whether CNP reflects the Nation's ability to win wars at some instant in time, or whether it reflects the eventual outcome in the on- going competition to be considered the world's most powerful nation – without going to war. A great deal of the Chinese ambivalence in choosing determinants comes from Marxist –Leninist texts as 'sacred' and the as yet incomplete shift from Maoist dogma that world war is inevitable, to Deng's belief that achieving supreme status in CNP by China will make war unnecessary[2].

The ambivalence is reflected in the difference in results obtained by the AMS and CASS. The former clearly gives greater weightage to military power and sees the order among nations departing from those of the CASS study where CNP varies but little from GDP rankings. The military power anomaly becomes more pronounced in the AMS study when the GDP rankings are clearly seen to outweigh the poor transnational military capabilities of countries like Brazil and Canada while placing their power index above the UK and the latter above Australia. Once the determinants are set, there is little escape to change the outcomes, despite the results appearing to be bizarre.

Many analysts suggest that national power can exist without any military power. This belief comes, as stated earlier from the number of studies that rank Japan high in order of power, based entirely on the size of its GDP. The inference is that such countries can influence world events by the force of economic pressures, entirely devoid of military force. This belief leads the analyst into further suggesting that non military power exists in other forms too, and such options together constitute soft power. This subject was hotly debated and it was difficult to identify a single case of a 'country' that was able to exert power by means entirely devoid of the military. Ideas and religions have done so, and there are no bigger examples of the force of ideas than the conversion of South East Asia to Theravada Buddhism and

---

[2] Pillsbury, quoting Zhu Liangyin and Meng Rengzhong, A Study on Deng Xiaoping's Comprehensive National Power thought in Li Lin and Zhao Qianxuan Eds.

the conversion of China to Mahayana Buddhism by a single individual—Kumarajiva[3]. This study has confined itself to a 'country' as the unit for the assessment of national power and does not deal with the flow of culture and values across national boundaries. Reverse examples were found to be plentiful, where great cultures and traditions were systematically denigrated and devalued, as belonging to a 'conquered' people and hence belonging to an inferior culture. The everyday visible examples of the renaissance of Indian culture and food, in the world of the 21st century is seen as a restoration of 'old' culture by the country's surge to wealth and power. The culture didn't change, but perceptions did.

The Anamoly of the US. The definitive US study on CNP (Tellis)[4] shows that in the post-industrial age, the measure of CNP has to be dramatically different. The US view is that it has acquired a kind of hegemony- a result of winning the cold war- and that hegemony should be preserved. In other words, the US position is unique. It is concerned with 'preserving' its hegemony and not so much as transiting to a better position in the world. This hegemony is seen to be a Grand Mix of economic innovation and its conversion to military capability. The US view is that CNP can be broken down into three broad sub heads of national resources, national performance and military capability. However the Determinants under each of these sub heads are unique and in rather wide variance with Indian or Chinese studies. The chart of the US listing of determinants is shown below.

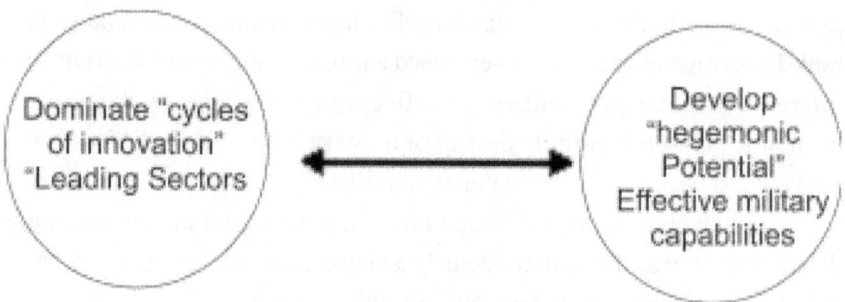

Dominate "cycles of innovation" "Leading Sectors

Develop "hegemonic Potential" Effective military capabilities

Fig. 1 : Explaining the Generation of National Power
(Source: Tellis, CNP)

[3] Sun Shuyun , Ten Thousand Miles Without a Cloud, (Harper Collins: New York , 2003)

[4] Ashley Tellis, Janice Bially, Christopher Laine, Measuring National Power in the Post-industrial Age, MR 1110 RAND Monograph Reports

A Revised View of National Power

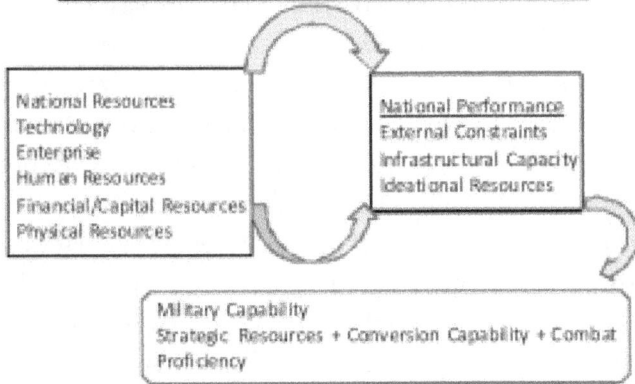

| National Resources
Technology
Enterprise
Human Resources
Financial/Capital Resources
Physical Resources | National Performance
External Constraints
Infrastructural Capacity
Ideational Resources |

Military Capability
Strategic Resources + Conversion Capability + Combat Proficiency

A study of the US determinants immediately shows what the strengths of the US are in the early 21st century, or are seen to be. It is perfectly understandable that preserving hegemony would require that the US regenerate itself constantly. The determinants are so chosen as to give an idea of where that regenerative capacity is. These determinants are quite inapplicable for India in its current state of development. If this study is to lead to benefits for the Indian policy maker, a far more detailed analysis of India's weaknesses are necessary. Only their articulation and measures to overcome them would result in getting to a stage where it has any regenerative capacity at all. Without that regenerative capacity, there can be no reliance on Technology, for instance, the chief national resource of the US. But countries like India without cutting edge technologies are not at a disadvantage during their growth period, as they can often slipstream behind the leaders to close the gap. The US study also identifies the close link between the knowledge revolution and its effects on both economic resurgence and military power and hence for the US, it is the capability of the state to effect that conversion that is the true indication of latent national power.

The Anomaly of the USSR. Samples of CNP studies done for 1988 show the USSR as the second most powerful nation in the world. Such a result brings deep discredit to the CNP process as it failed to see the entire collapse of a giant nation two years later. On the other hand, the opaqueness of the Soviet state which defied attempts to accurately define state capacity may be taken as an excuse for making an inaccurate assessment of power in 1988. Could such errors happen again? It certainly did in the case of Saddam Husain's Iraq which allegedly had the most powerful military machine in the Middle East in both 1991 and 2001. Whatever the internal weaknesses of the Iraq state may have been, the armed forces of Iraq were well supplied and equipped by Middle East standards, but failed to withstand an attack on the country for more than 100 hours. There could be an argument that with 13000 nuclear weapons and the capacity to mobilize 13000 tanks and 250 divisions, the USSR was the second most powerful nation in the world. But what does such estimation tell us? If CNP is useful as an estimate only at the instant that it is made, it contributes little to our knowledge of power. At the same time, the study cannot guarantee the longevity of the estimates. The USSR anomaly was the factor that led the study group to include the determinant of 'Accountability to the People'. Without a genuine and free process where the government seeks its mandate from the people at regular intervals, the writ and power of the government (which represents the power of the state) is in serious doubt, as occurred in the USSR. The weightage given to this factor is still controversial and will be dealt with later. However, when one considers that the entire political process that governed the USSR rose and collapsed in 72 years, it will be seen that the power of the state, was, in terms of history – momentary. It is a challenge to capture that brittleness of power that cannot be ignored by analysts who might seek only to create a momentary snapshot.

The Special Determinants for India. The study group recognizes that a CNP study that is only a 2010 snapshot of India's pure power, would not lead to any exciting inferences. What India has, is the potential to be a great power. The word great is only used as a rough quantitative adjective to imply a capacity to influence many other powers in the region, by say, 2025. But India is yet to fulfill the promise that well wishers expect of it. Much of this hope rests on two factors. The first is that some actors in the country have preformed so well that despite the huge list of pending reforms, the country has posted startling GDP growth figures. The second is that the country has a noticeable youth Cohort who, it is hoped will drive the growth rates further up, if they are gainfully employed. If they are not gainfully employed, the youth dividend could turn into a millstone, the weight of which would drag India to disaster. We are then looking at a per capita income of about $ 5000, when growth stagnates and India bumbles along in decrepitude. The alternatives are startling. How can the study group capture the starkness of these choices? The answer has been to choose determinants that resemble no other study of national power, but have the unique validity of describing India.

For this reason this study is divided into two distinct phases. One describes India in terms that admittedly are not valid for other countries. The second brings a comparison of the most valid determinants to arrive at a comparative table of CNP. In describing India, many sub-determinants have been chosen, which could be said to be contained in others. Educating women and girls is gone into in great detail for the transformation that it causes in population, family, literacy, nutrition and health. So although one causes the other, both are defined in this study, so that the bureaucracies responsible for each are identified. So the large number of determinants in Education and Human resources is meant to only identify the details of where India could go horribly wrong. The study is to that extent prescriptive for policy makers in Delhi, apart from giving omnibus descriptions of relative CNPs of selected countries.

The Structure of the Study. Today, India is not a significant power in the world. Its GDP is lower than that of four European countries. Although Afghanistan is its strategic frontier, three European countries have more troops fighting the Taliban, and have lost more soldiers in that fight than has India. In the fight against piracy in the Indian Ocean, other have shouldered a disproportionate share of the anti-piracy patrolling than has India, which still patrols outside the coordinated activity of TF 151[5]. Although its GDP is big, its poverty, its illiterates and the difficulties of opening a new business in

---

[5] Combined Task Force 151, A multinational force established in Jan 2009 to conduct counter piracy operations off Somalia. The Indian ships coordinate with TF 151 but are outside it.

India are all reflected in the economic picture drawn in this study. So why is looking at India so important in analyzing the CNP of important countries of the world? The answer lies in India's future the promise that India holds out, of rising to prosperity and power through the democratic process. So India is important in the future. If that conclusion is a given, there is little point in taking a snapshot of India as of today.

What is of interest for a student of strategic affairs, is how Indian power might rise in the next ten years. To understand this transformation, it is necessary to establish a datum, as of today. This attempt forms the first part of the book. In this portion, a number of countries who figure in the power competition are compared, but on the basis of determinants that really describe India. This may be a bit unfair to the other countries, which shouldn't have to be judged on how strenuously they are trying to educate women or feed children, as they have done all that. However the broad groupings of determinants iron out these inequities and provides a level playing field in section II as will be explained.

Determinants. There are seven major heads under which determinants have been grouped. These are indicated below:

(a) Economic Strengths

(b) Human Capital and Development

(c) Governance

(d) Accountability Index

(e) Sciences and Technology

(f) Military Capability

(g) Foreign Policy

Economic Strength. It is agreed without reservation within the group that wealth leads to power. This relationship is not a permanent state of affairs, as the link between wealth, prosperity and the decline of nations is also understood. In the case of very large countries like India and China, huge GDPs can be generated without a concurrent rise in equity and welfare. These anomalies are addressed in the Human Capital area of determinants.

Moreover at the same time, enormous power can be (temporarily) generated without a proportionate rise in wealth. An example is the Soviet Union which, at the height of its power in the cold war generated only 30% of the GDP of the US. This anomaly has been addressed in other parts of the book. The choice of sub-determinants attempts to smoothen out the lumps where large GDPs may generate little money to spend for government, by looking at Tax Revenue/GDP ratios.

Human Capital and Development. Most countrywide analysis on the development of human capital in India begin by laying blame for the appalling state of public education on Macaulay's Great Minute on education[6]. An actual reading of the Minute doesn't support this diatribe. On the other hand, a reading of the unpublished minutes throws up another picture altogether. The Great Minute actually confines itself to the medium of instruction. The emphasis is on the kind of education that makes a 'native' employable. Some sentences are relevant. 'We have to educate people, who cannot at present be educated by means of their mother tongue, and this is proved by the fact that we are forced to pay our Arabic and Sanskrit students, while those who learn English are willing to pay us.' Macaulay was probably ahead of his time in knowing the effects of market forces, as he says, 'On all such subjects, the state of the market is the decisive test... A petition was presented last year to the committee by several students of Sanskrit college. The petitioner stated that they had studied in the college for ten or twelve years, that they had made themselves acquainted with Hindu literature and science; that they had received certificates of proficiency , and what is the result of all this? Notwithstanding such testimonials, they say, we have but little prospect of bettering our condition, without the kind assistance your honourable committee, the indifference with which we are looked upon by our countrymen, leaving no hope of encouragement or assistance from them'.

In the year 2008, the situation doesn't seem to have greatly improved after central and state governments have fiddled with educating the Indian people for 61 years after the British left. An MIT assessment on the state

---

[6] Mr. (Lord) Macaulay's Great Minute (English Versus Sanskrit and Arabic) 2 Feb 1835, in WFB Laurie , sketches of some Anglo Indians, p. 169

of Human capital development says 'A recent study shows that the public education sector may be beyond saving[7].' The MIT study concedes that India's Human Capital resources is huge, but in the MIT International Review, it presents a possible solution as coming from sustainable investment in private schools delivering standardized , high quality education.

Public expenditure on education in India is still below the levels of other emerging economies, but if private investment is included, it is the same as in developed OECD countries, but only in primary and secondary schools. In tertiary education, it is still much lower than in emerging economies, even if one includes private participation. Today, 51% of India's population is under 25 and 67% under 35. So does this bulge portend economic success or disaster? A Swedish social scientist says that when 15 to 29 year olds constitute more than 31% of the population, violence in society will be endemic. This is not difficult to understand. The total number of males in the volatile age group who have grievances against the state will be larger. This is exacerbated when the Youth bulge is predominantly male and can't find partners. Other comments about India's Youth bulge are that India has a huge labour force, or the largest reservoir of military manpower. There are others that say that with 51% of the people below 25 , and 80% of them disaffected with the state, is it any surprise that there is so much terrorism?[8]

Governance. In this section, the constituent parts of 'governance' are expanded to include the two great societal ills of India – communal division and caste inequalities. These are first explored. The remaining six sub-determinants describe the catastrophically unsatisfactory state of the civil bureaucracy, the police, the Judiciary and the mechanisms that deliver justice. In China, a country which is far better 'governed', the institutional weakness of the political system not being accountable to the people, is described in the next determinant of our study. Governance may be unsatisfactory in the minds of most people in most countries. This study however believes that better governance would lead to higher growth.

---

[7] Harnessing India's Human Capital Through Educational Opportunities, MIT International Review, Spring 2008

[8] Alya Mishra, India: Vocational Education Upgraded OECD Education Today, on http// community.OECD,org/docs/Doc-1357

A broad overview of public governance is available from the World Governance Assessment Project Working Paper[9]. The India portion entitled 'Assessing and Analysing Governance in India' brings out much revealing data. The study is based upon public opinion polls conducted in four states: Andhra Pradesh, Bihar, Delhi and Kerala. Summarising the data for the four states, average readings for India, as pertaining to civil society, political society, government, bureaucracy, economic Society, and judiciary come out as indicated in the table and graph shown below.

Average Score for India: Comparing Ratings for Arenas

Arena	Civil Society	Political Society	Gove-rnment	Burea-ucracy	Economic Society	Judiciary	Average
5 Years ago	3.24	2.98	3.07	3.29	2.86	2.95	3.06
Now	3.28	3.07	3.01	3.20	2.98	3.00	3.09

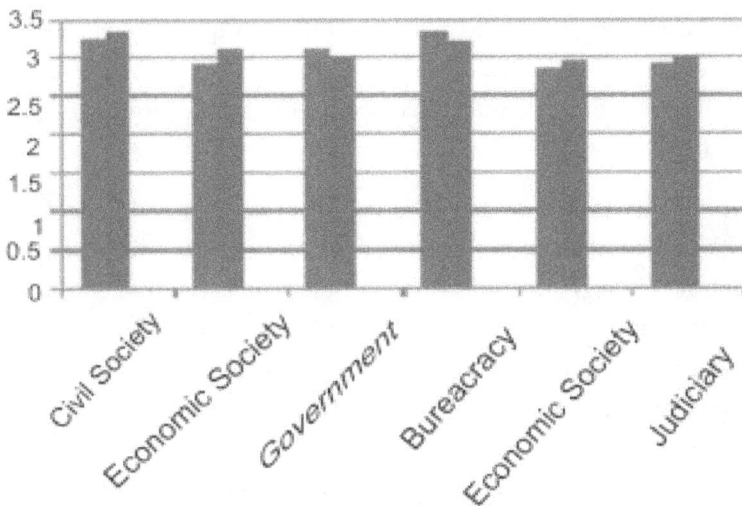

Combaring Current Ratings of Governance Arenas in India

[9] Julius Court, Assessing and Analysing Governance in India: Evidence from a Survey, United Nations University, World Governance Assessment Project Working Paper No. 1, Feb 2001

Mechanisms. Astute critics of governance will agree that most people know what needs to be done to improve governance, but it will not be done because the mechanism to govern is broken. In India, criticisms are leveled against the bureaucracy, the police and lately, the Judiciary. The Maoist problem is indicative, where the tribals accuse the administration of having not provided well for them all these years. Their aversion to seeking a political solution comes from a disillusionment that all governments will eventually use the same oppressive mechanism to govern. Some big questions need to be asked.

In assessing bureaucratic effectiveness, there was an accusation that a course attended in, say, 1960 should not entitle a bureaucrat to go untrained until 2000. Therefore the Indian Institute of Public Administration (IIPA) was set up in New Delhi. IAS officers were to attend a mid- career course at this institution in their forties. Today officers attending are between the ages of 36 and 52 and of the 110 or so secretaries to the government of India , less than 10% have attended this course.

Police reform is so overdue that the Indian Police Service still functions according to the Indian Police Act 1861[10]. This act has gems in it like police duties to prevent 'furious riding' down a road, or arresting a person 'easing himself' or driving cattle too fast. According to the act, a police officer can actually be anybody, appointed as such, without any qualification. It required a brave police officer's PIL to force the Supreme Court to ask states why they shouldn't reform the police. The body entrusted to write a new act has been at it since 2005.

Accountability Index. As stated earlier, this factor unused in the Chinese and US studies of CNP has been deliberately included to introduce the element of the longevity of the power of the state being studied. There are too many examples of totalitarian states whose power, at their apogee was great, but who crumbled a few years later. The USSR (70years) Hitler's Germany (13 years) Mussolini (16 years) are examples that come to mind. Two states where elections are not free and the choices are limited – China and Cuba are currently surviving in their 62nd and 58th years. There are statements from Chinese leaders that as long as Governance is good, the

---

[10] The Indian Police Act 1861.

power of the party will not wither. We doubt that this is true, and notice that in both the CAMs and CASS study, the political system has not been introduced at all. To introduce a factor that might represent the longevity of the political system, this determinant is included.

Science and Technology. The US model has its innovative capacity at the heart of its CNP, generating simultaneously, both wealth and power. In the modern world, the value of goods has scientific inputs as its chief constituent, with neither material, labour, capital nor brand value matching the technology quotient. There are other developments. The corporate model of the western world of R &D within one's own country is being replaced by partial research contributed from all parts of the globe, through internet and telecommunications. As a result, Asia has also begun to contribute to the final product, with China being (3rd), Japan (5th), India (6th) and Singapore (9th)[11]. So the fourth wave, where internationalisation of R & D becomes globalized is currently in progress. Could India with a better education strategy raise itself from a sixth position to being in the first three?

Foreign Policy. The simplest definition of foreign policy could be- to leverage the international situation to further one's national interests. If this definition is acceptable, there is no doubt that some countries punch well above their weight and some below. Nations with a past history of power and who have retained large foreign policy establishments like the UK and France, diplomatically leverage the international situation better. India's diplomatic establishment is woefully undermanned, underfunded and badly organized internally. There are some unpleasant reasons why this is so, apart from institutional incompetence. National power cannot be hidden from public view forever, and the arena where it will be judged is the external environment. Where does the power of India's diplomatic establishment to leverage the international situation lie today, and how might it grow by 2020? The government has recognized the inadequacy of the establishment and sanctioned a doubling of the cadre and a spanking new building. Will the Foreign Service rise to the levels expected?

---

[11] Internationalisation of R&D , Discussion paper BIAC, Business and Industry Advisory Committee to the OECD

Assessing CNP of Nations. Comprehensive national power between India and the US, Germany, France, Japan, Russia, Indonesia, Brazil and South Africa will be compared. The choice of these nations may be arguable. The US, China, Japan and Russia choose themselves. India has been chosen as the next most populous nations in Asia. Brazil and South Africa are the choices from South America and Africa. Germany and France choose themselves from Europe. It is true that some interesting 'Other countries' might emerge. They include Turkey and Vietnam. However, looking at the year 2020, the number of players seems to reduce in the first divisions' league.

The list of such determinants for India is huge. The CNP of other countries are based only on determinants and not any sub-determinant. The study group is not particularly interested in how the other countries might change their micro-strategies, other than to mark major trends. For India, which is a country to reckon with ONLY in the future, and not today, the intricacies of each determinant's composition is of interest.

Weighted Indices. Many alternate studies exist, other than CNP, such as the Lausanne study and the Legatum Prosperity Index. These emphasize productivity, prosperity and the economy. CNP studies from China have weighted indices which, on the average give twice or more weightage to the economy as they do to the remaining factors. All cases of the rise of Great Powers have been powered by their economic rise, as is occurring in China today, and is thought will happen in India in another ten years. So clearly, the economy needs to be maneuvered into a position of carrying greater weightage relative to social, military and diplomatic factors. This has been done.

The economy is studied under five sub-determinants and these five have below them, about 36 sib-determinants. Presumably these have weightages too. For instance Mineral Resources is a sub-determinant, which can play an odd role. Japan without any worthwhile resource is the world's second richest nation. The Chinese study places Canada and Australia among the powerful nations of the world, mostly owing to their abundant resources. At the same time, Saudi Arabia, the most long lasting source of hydrocarbons is never considered to be a player in any study. These conclusions must be explained. In our study, sub-determinants are also weighted, and weightages are what enables us to arrive at base points for sub-determinants. However, even with weighted indices, it may be impossible for any determinant to compete against the overwhelming weight of the economy. If economic factors balance out between two nations, their performance in the social, military and institutional capabilities will prove decisive.

Non-Quantifiable determinants. It was always clear that there would be determinants that are non-quantifiable. The US study for instance, includes no quantitative analysis. But there are some determinants, like the state of the economy and Human Capital Development that are so well researched, and provide such rich statistics, that it would be impractical to ignore all that data. This still leaves us with the problem of non-quantifiable determinants. These have been addressed through polls. These polls are not really 'public' opinion polls but emanating from a quasi-expert audience, consisting of many nationalities and many specializations. Such an audience is the student bodies of the National Defence College, Delhi and the Armed forces College of Defence Management, Secunderabad. These two student bodies together total around 150 officers, between the ages of 38-42 (CDM) and 48-51 (NDC). The two big determinants addressed by this body are Military Capability and Foreign Policy.

Part II of the Study

Studying the non-traditional threats to security, or in other words, the social and non-military aspects of a nation's power, brings home with great clarity that India's rise to a great power status is not a given. Many might say that this is self-evident and refer to poverty, illiteracy and the questionable accuracy of the poverty line. In this study, which attempts to quantify as many variables as possible, we have made an attempt to list the great reasons which may prevent India from greatness, or those difficulties, the overcoming of which will ensure an untrammeled rise. There have been listed as

(a) Poor and unreformed governance mechanisms

(b) An unreformed Police force

(c) Failure to move 300 million to cities

(d) Non-Delivery of Justice

(e) Inadequate Skill Creation

(f) Archaic Higher Defence Management

The choice of these factors as being overwhelming may be contestable. But the reason why some others such as Land Reforms in the Northern States or rooting out corruption, have not found their way into the list, is because, at the highest levels, any number of things 'to do' can be listed. In most cases, that exercise would be pointless, as the reasons why they have not been 'done' in 60 years is that the mechanisms are increasingly breaking down. The list has therefore been chosen on the basis of 'who' is to be reformed, so that the mechanism begin to function autonomously as it is meant to, instead of appointing commissions or committees that will tell the same broken mechanisms to deliver. The possible outcomes of India's efforts to create reform, will lead to alternate scenarios. The scenarios will be evolved in a structured manner, bring out two or three Macro scenarios – where reforms take place and the huge population and employment transition occurs, and a scenario where the success of the reforms are partial or minimal, and Indian growth slows down or peters out by 2020. The country will then be brought down by government mechanisms unable to move 300 million people to cities preserve law and order and deliver justice.

Projecting CNP to 2020. There are CNP studies that project their findings into the future, most notably, the Chinese studies. The clearest CNP projections are from CASS which has 1990 as the base and CNP is projected to 2020. In 2010, the USSR is shown as barely 10% behind the USA, and Japan is projected to overtake the US by 2020 with China well behind the USA, Japan, Germany, France and South Korea. India is placed in a lowly position in 2020[12], just above Mexico well behind Canada, and a little behind Australia. The determinants that led to these extraordinary results are not clear. Some of them are understandable. India had not liberalized so there is no surprise there, but Japan, Germany and France are big surprises indeed. The AMS study makes much more sense, placing China, just a quarter percent behind the USA in 2020, with Germany in fourth position followed by India. The projection beyond the base rates, appear to be based upon the GDP.

---

[12] Pillsbury, Table 11 and 13, Geopolitical Power Calculations.

This study will attempt to use both GDP and opinion polls to project the major determinants from 2010 to 2020. Some of the critical factors mentioned earlier, whose outcomes are still uncertain, and where reforms have only recently been initiated, will be bracketed into scenarios. So as far as India is concerned there will definitely be two outcomes, at least – where reforms occur and where they do not. The outcomes for China, where political reform is considered a must at some stage, to maintain the economic momentum, will also be diverted into scenarios, as will the outcomes for the USA. In case of the USA, where the government is fully aware of the role of innovation in creating power, scenarios can be drawn up where the US reinvests itself, and another where it does not.

Economic Determinants

Given our analytical and strategic interest in the relationship between the economy and power or leverage in international affairs, we are interested in assessing the advantages and vulnerabilities that have been associated with how India has responded to and acquired material wealth from economic globalisation. Discerning the quality and composition of India's growth as opposed to simply recording the rise of an aggregate statistic (GDP) is vital. This approach is essential if we are seeking to evaluate whether India is on a trajectory to emerge as a robust great power in the coming decades.

The first part deconstructs India's growth model and explores why India's growth has not produced a robust manufacturing sector. The second part undertakes a comparative analysis using select sub-determinants from the CNP dataset and evaluates India's relative position vis-à-vis her peer group.

Sectoral Share of GDP – Time Series

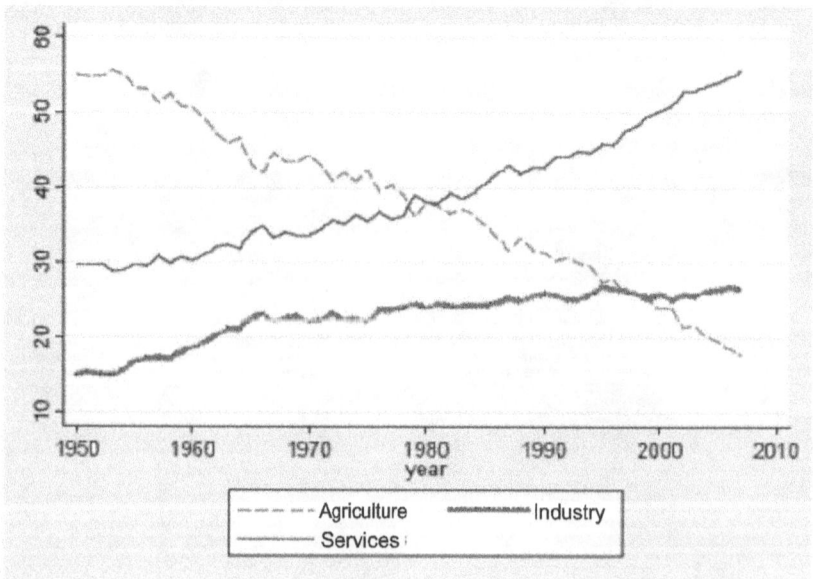

Note: Data used is from the Central Statistical Organisation (CSO) from 1950-2007.

While India's share of services has increased from 37 to 55 per cent, the share of manufacturing (included in industry) has remained nearly constant at 16 per cent of GDP. The change in the share of manufacturing during this period in India has been about 2.5 percentage points lower than the average country at the same stage of development, while the change in the services share was about 10 percentage points higher than average (even though its employment performance was below average). In contrast, according to a recent Assocham study, China's share of its manufacturing sector to GDP is 35 per cent; South Korea, Malaysia and Indonesia's is 30 per cent; Argentina and Brazil's manufacturing sectors contribute 24 per cent to their national economies.

What explains this Indian puzzle – niche skill-intensive services within a structural bias for a generally services-oriented economy coexisting with a large agrarian base while the manufacturing component (especially labour-intensive manufacturing) lags far behind?

Structural constraints in India have created this pattern – a small pool of skilled workers (<"25 million undergraduates or higher degree holders) and a simultaneous national illiteracy rate of almost 40 per cent. For instance, in 2000, India spent 86 per cent of per capita GDP per student in tertiary education, while it spent 14 per cent of per capita GDP per student in primary education.[1] This is a legacy of the 1950s where India's planners invested resources in institutions of higher learning but failed to address the mass illiteracy in the countryside. As education is a dual subject (under the purview of Delhi and the provinces), despite central investment in primary education, the actual deployment and management of funds occurs at the state level and inefficiencies at that level usually stifle investment or its quality on the ground.[2] The share of elementary education in total education expenditure

---

[1] K. Kochhar, Kumar U., Rajan R., Subramanian A., and Tokatlidis I., 'India's Pattern of Development: What Happened, What Follows', IMF Working Papers, 2005.

[2] India's education budget more than doubled in the last five years increasing from Rs. 152,847 crores in FY 2004-05 to Rs. 372,813 crores in FY 2009-10. An estimated 45 per cent (figures for FY 2008-09) of education expenditures are now dedicated to elementary education. The Government of India's (GOI) primary vehicle for the delivering elementary education is the Sarva Shiksha Abhiyaan (a centrally sponsored scheme that has been in operation since 2001). Reflecting the overall trend of increased investment, the Sarva Shiksha Abhiyaan (SSA) budget too has increased significantly in the last few years from Rs.7,156 crores in 2005-06 to Rs.15,000 crores in 2010-11. It is, however, still unclear whether this increased budgetary support from Delhi is affecting outcomes on the ground.

rarely exceeded 50 per cent in India compared to South Korea in the 1950s, which allocated two-thirds of its education spending on primary education.

The two charts below show massive illiteracy coexisting with a relatively higher post-secondary or tertiary attainment (absorbed by the services sector) in India.

India's Education Distribution by Sectors, 2004

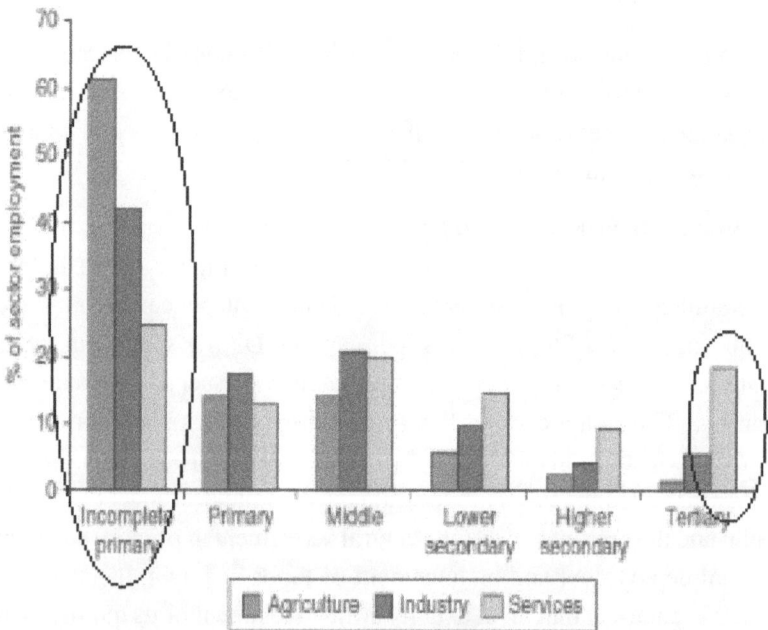

Source: India National Sample Survey Organization, Socio-economic Survey, Round 60, January-June 2004, Asian Development Outlook 2007.

Educational Attainment of the Total Population Aged 15–64, 2000

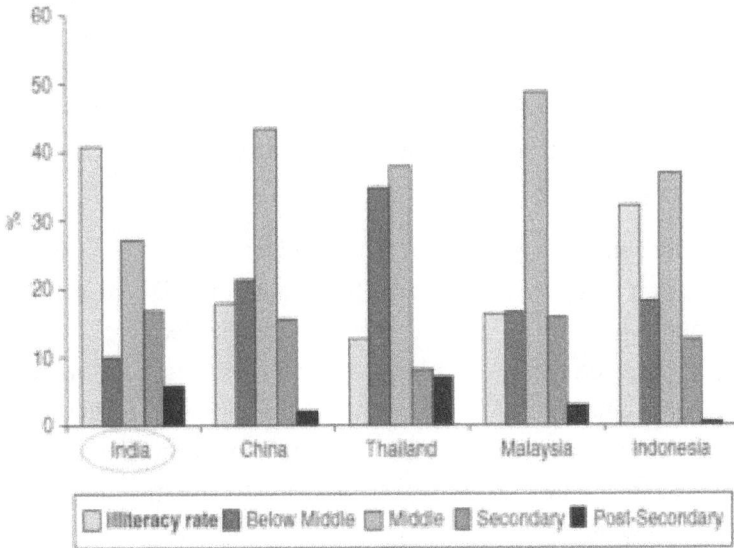

Source: Barry Bosworth, Susan M. Collins, Arvind Virmani, 'Sources of Growth in the Indian Economy', NBER Working Paper 12901, Cambridge, MA, February 2007.

A second structural factor that created an anti-manufacturing bias was the inability of the state to expand "core infrastructure" goods, and, rigid labour laws. This unique policy context created a situation of "constrained adaptation" where an inherently entrepreneurial class filled a vacuum created by structural constraints, and channeled resources toward those services industries that relied relatively less on physical infrastructure and where the *relatively* superior tertiary education sector had produced an available base of skilled workers.[3]

---

[3] K. Kochhar, Kumar U., Rajan R., Subramanian A., and Tokatlidis I., 'India's Pattern of Development: What Happened, What Follows', IMF Working Papers, 2005.

Thus, India's services sector was responsible for over 60 per cent of its GDP growth in the 1990s. And the growth acceleration was the strongest in business services, communication, and banking services, followed by hotels and restaurants, and community services. These five sub-sectors together accounted for the entire acceleration in services growth in the 1990s. This trend continued in the 2000s. Services contributed 69 per cent of the overall average growth in GDP between 2002 and 2007, this time with the addition of the fast-growing ITES sector.

A recent study of input-output structure identified 10 vital sectors in the Indian economy based on growth impacts on GDP of efficiency improvements in these sectors. These sectors include electricity, water and gas supply, transport services, railway transport services, coal and lignite, etc. The study found that India's growth rate is at least as sensitive to these sectors as it was prior to the 1991 reforms.[4] It is inefficiencies and underinvestment in these infrastructure sectors that has prevented both a take-off in manufacturing industries and deprived the latter from receiving export-oriented foreign direct investment (FDI).

In contrast, the services sector in general and the information technology and software sectors in particular, which are relatively less capital-intensive in their operations and less reliant on core 'public goods', have unsurprisingly flourished, as have certain niche manufacturing sectors that have created their own captive sources of private infrastructure. For instance, 30 percent of industrial electricity consumption is accounted for by captive generation, predominantly diesel generator sets.

More generally, supply-side bottlenecks continue to constrain Indian industry. In the 1980's, India had higher infrastructure stocks in power, roads and telecommunication, and, was only surpassed by China in 1990. After the mid-1980s, the pressure on public expenditure from rising deficits constrained public investment. From 1986, public investment in GDP began a steady decline from 11.2 per cent to 5.6 per cent of GDP in 2003–04.[5]

---

[4] Nirvikar Singh, 'The Ten Sectors that Need a Boost', *Financial Express*, 12 December 2006.

[5] T. N. Srinivasan, 'Comments on From "Hindu Growth" to Productivity Surge: The Mystery of the Indian Growth Transition', IMF Staff Papers, Vol. 52, No. 2, September 2005.

Even today, for every $1 that India spends on infrastructure, China spends $7. Over the past 20 years, India's self-reliance in the production of machine tools has fallen from 80 per cent to the current 20 per cent.

Infrastructure Investment (per cent of GDP), India and China

The gap in infrastructure stocks is now so large that for India to catch up with China's present level of stocks per capita by 2015, it would have to invest 12.5 percent of GDP per year on infrastructure. For India to maintain growth rates of 8-10 percent, it is estimated that it would have to invest $1 trillion over the next decade.

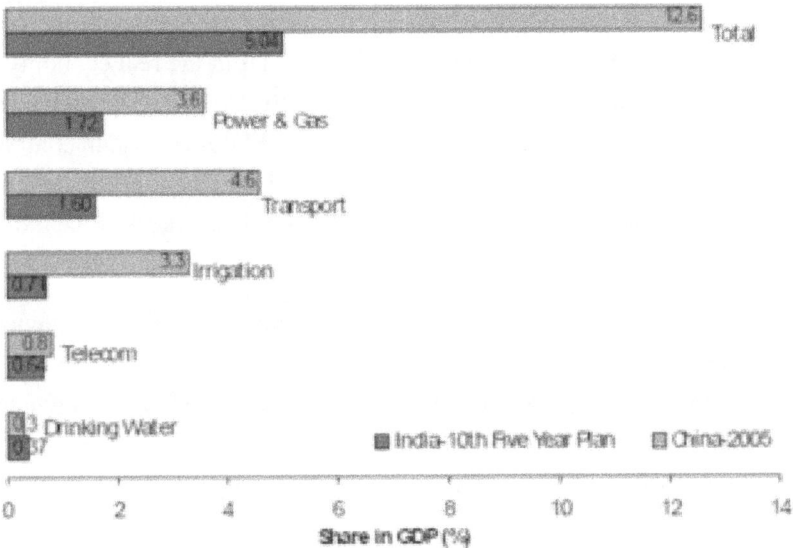

Source: Poonam Gupta, Rana Hasan, Utsav Kumar, 'What Constrains Indian Manufacturing?', ICRIER Working Paper No. 211, March 2008.

The first adverse consequence of the Indian state's inability to provide core infrastructure goods has been the internationalisation of India Inc.'s operations. It is remarkable how globalised India Inc. has become. The empirical evidence is instructive: 50 per cent of the total profits of the top 30 Indian companies come from their overseas operations. Outward investment has totalled nearly $80 billion over the past decade with most of this FDI flowing to the OECD economies led by the UK and US.[6] Reserve Bank of India data shows that outward-FDI by domestic companies in overseas joint ventures and wholly owned subsidiaries was $18 billion in 2009-10 and $44 billion in the 2010-2011.[7]

While some would laud this data as evidence of Indian success on the global stage, it is hardly a sign of strength that a capital scarce country is exporting its resources away from the home economy. Further, there is also no evidence to suggest that India's outward-FDI into core OECD economies has produced a flow of knowledge or technology transfers to the Indian economy. A prima facie survey of India Inc.'s acquisitions suggests a pattern of investments linked to servicing consumers and businesses in the core western economies.[8] By comparison, inbound FDI in the real economy is declining. According to a FICCI study, from 2000 to 2008 India received an average of $3.4 billion of manufacturing-oriented FDI each year. In contrast, China pulled in $40 billion of manufacturing FDI annually during the same period. Again, this paradox stems from the structural bottleneck in the Indian political economy that dis-incentivises investment in manufacturing sectors.

The globalisation of India Inc. has important adverse consequences for India's ability to develop a domestic industrial base that can ultimately feed into both military-technical sectors and science and technology, and research and development to produce innovation that enables economies to maintain growth over extended periods.

---

[6] In the United States alone, during 2004-2009, 90 Indian companies made 127 greenfield investments worth $5.5 billion, and created 16,576 jobs. During the same period, 239 Indian companies made 372 acquisitions in the United States, and, the total value of 267 (of the 372) acquisitions was $21 billion. The bulk of M&A investments by India Inc. in the United States were ironically in manufacturing and other industrial sectors (manufacturing, biotech, chemicals & pharmaceuticals, automotive, and telecom) rather than in services for which India is well known.

[7] James Lamont, 'Indian groups double overseas investments', *Financial Times,* June 23, 2011.

[8] To be sure, to the extent that a portion of this FDI is also focused on securing long-term access to natural resources (such as iron and coal mines in Australia and Africa or oil reserves in West Asia) that would ultimately fuel India's industrial development is certainly an advantage.

According to Demos, a UK based think tank, India produces about 6,000 Science and Engineering Ph.D.s each year as compared to China's 15,000. But more importantly, China has stepped up the internationalization of its research system, with extensive collaborative networks across Europe, Japan and the US. By the end of 2007, according to China's Ministry of Commerce, multinational corporations had established 1,160 R&D centres in China. The Indian system, in contrast, remains relatively insulated mired in structural problems. The Asian Development Bank recently noted that industrial training in India was lagging behind rapid economic growth, with only 12,000 training and vocational institutes, compared to half a million in China. Again, as India's model has created a structural bias against manufacturing, this is reflected in the atrophy of its innovation eco-system.

Number of Science and Engineering (S&E) Doctoral Degrees

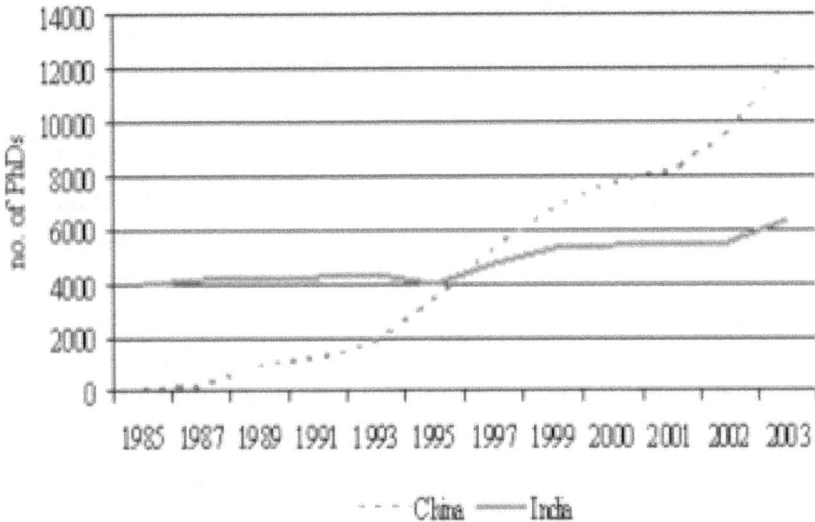

Source: 2008 Science and Engineering Indicators, National Science Board, National Science Foundation, Arlington, VA, USA; http://www.nsf.gov/statistics/seind08/

Number of Science doctoral degrees

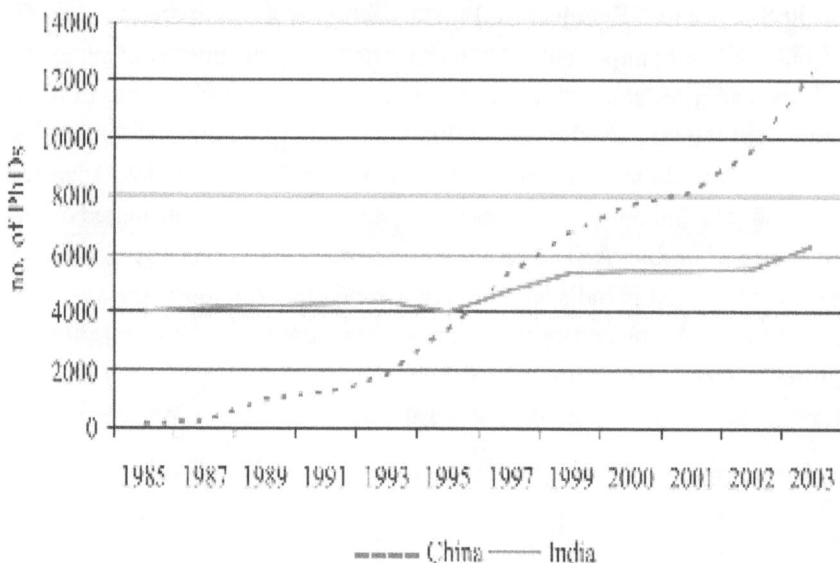

Source: 2008 Science and Engineering Indicators, National Science Board, National Science Foundation, Arlington, VA, USA; http://www.nsf.gov/statistics/seind08/

The second adverse effect of India's growth model has been its 'jobless' feature. India's jobless service-sector growth stems from the fact that the sector's growth has been driven largely by a handful of service sub-sectors—that is, ITES, telecommunications and banking. Additional employment generated by these sectors was not able to offset the rapidly falling labour-demand elasticity faced by other service sub-sectors. Further, given the skill-based model of these service sub-sectors, it is unlikely that labour-supply reallocation could occur from the unskilled countryside. In fact, recent shortages of manpower in ITES and banking have drawn its labour supply from tertiary workers intended for the manufacturing sector (such as engineers) creating a crowding-out effect. Importantly, in comparison to China, India is yet to achieve high levels of organised labour-force participation. Ninety per cent of India's 500 million workforce is in the unorganised sector!

A services-oriented focus that relies on skilled workers is therefore an unsustainable model because India's demographic trends are adding more untrained workers to the workforce than the present model can absorb. For example, despite a decade of phenomenal growth, where the ITES sector revenues have touched $70 billion (2010) – accounting for 6 per cent of GDP and 26 per cent of total exports – direct employment generated in this sector was a mere 2.3 million people. The burden of job creation, thus, will always fall upon the manufacturing sector. This impending transformation of India's economic structure has become even more imperative given ongoing demographic shifts in Southern Asia.

India, a demographic latecomer relative to the mature industrial economies and East Asia, is in the midst of a major transition in age structure. The country's working-age population as a share of the total population has risen substantially over the last three decades. And this process is set to continue over the next three decades, during which India will gain about 300 million workers.[9] When an economy's working-age population rises, so can its growth rate – a result known as the "demographic dividend". By 2020, India's working age population is projected to rise to 600 million – an increase of 100 million workers. This amounts to 10 million workers, including 65-70 per cent from the country side, entering the workforce each year.

Projected new labor force by 2030

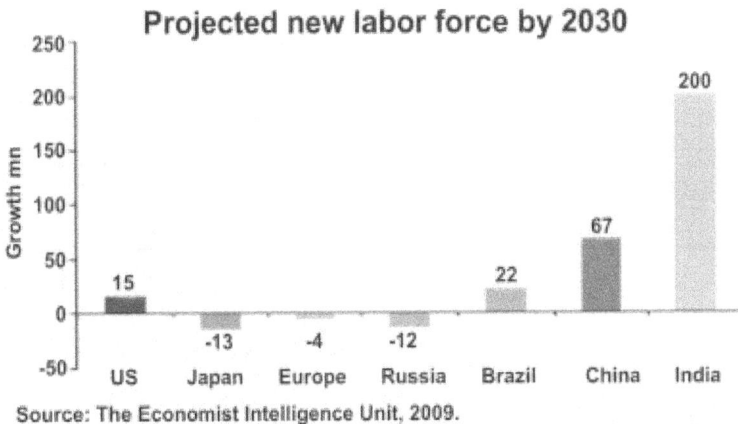

Source: The Economist Intelligence Unit, 2009.

---

[9] Shekhar Aiyar and Ashoka Mody, 'How big is India's demographic dividend? Evidence from the states', IMF, April 5, 2011.

India is poised to display the highest working age ratio in the world, catching up with China in 2020 and with Brazil in 2025.

Working age population as % of total population

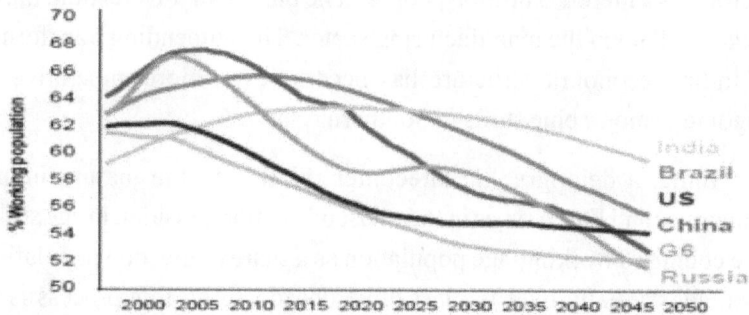

Source: Goldman, Sachs & Co., as at 30-Jun-07. The G6 member countries include France, Germany, Japan, Italy, UK and US. Working age population = share of population aged 15-60.

Source: India Revisited, Goldman Sachs, June 2010

India's labour force catching up with China

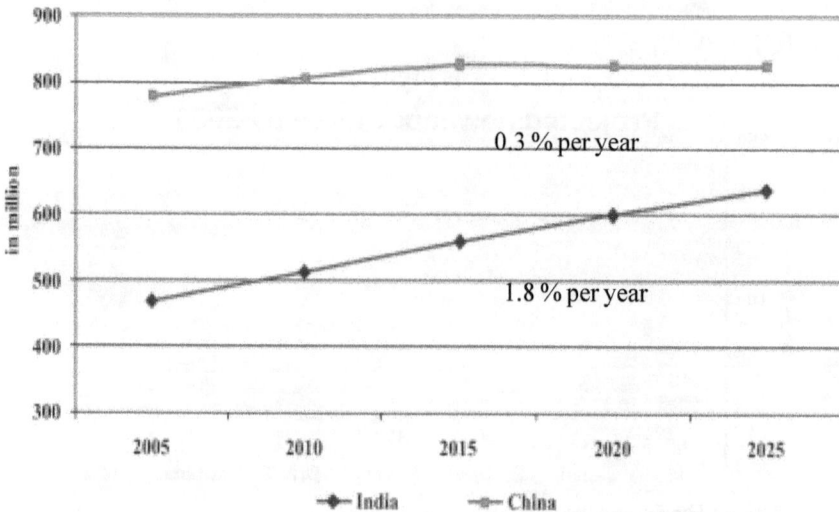

Source: McKinsey, 2010.

Leveraging this dividend, however, requires imparting a level of nutrition, healthcare and education to convert a raw human resource into human capital.[10] According to an Assocham 2008 study on the overall education ecosystem, India ranks at sixth place among the seven largest emerging economies led by Russia, China and Brazil. India performed poorly on all sectors of education – primary, secondary and tertiary. The gender parity in educational attainment in India was also the lowest among emerging economies with a rank of 116 globally.[11] A 2010 study undertaken jointly by INSEAD and the Confederation of Indian Industry also paints a picture of low innovation. In the lower-middle income group of countries, India ranks eighth below Thailand, Vietnam and Ukraine.[12]

India's Relative Performance in Healthcare

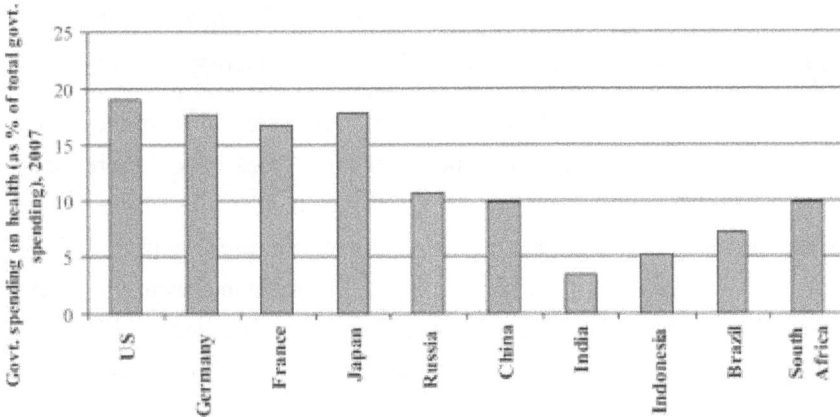

Source: Human Development Report 2009

---

[10] This is only underscored by the fact that a large portion of the demographic surge is projected to occur in what have traditionally been relatively laggard states - The share of four BIMARU states—Bihar, Madhya Pradesh, Rajasthan and Uttar Pradesh—of India's population is projected to rise from 41 per cent in 2001 to 48 per cent in 2051. 60 per cent of India's population increment will be concentrated in these four states, which have among the lowest human development indicators in the global periphery.

[11] 'India Lags behind the Emerging Economies in Quality Education: ASSOCHAM', Press Release (www. http://www.assocham.org/), December 15, 2008. The study was carried out on the basis of 20 parameters relating to primary, secondary, tertiary education and higher education and demography.

[12] 'India stands out among BRIC nations, slips on innovation second year in a row', *Economic Times,* July 4, 2011.

Perhaps the most important driver that will enable a reallocation of workers from the country side to suburban manufacturing sectors will be the agriculture sector itself. In the post-reform years, India's changing composition of GDP has squeezed out the share of agriculture from 38 per cent of GDP in 1980 to 15 per cent in 2010. Yet, agriculture's share of employment continues to account for 58 per cent (2001 census).

Such a structural decline of the countryside – growth decelerated from an annual average of 4.7 per cent per year during the 1980s to 3.1 per cent during the 1990s and further to 2.2 per cent in the 2000s. In contrast, China's agricultural sector continues to grow at over 4 per cent, despite three decades into the post-reform phase. According to the International Rice Research Institute, in 2004, India produced 124 million tonnes of rice compared to China's 186 million tonnes, despite having almost twice the area under paddy cultivation (42 million hectares versus 28 million hectares).

An unproductive and overburdened countryside have made India's urbanisation and industrialisation quest even more precarious, since releasing rural workers for labour-intensive manufacturing activities (assuming the other structural constraints that impede manufacturing are seriously resolved) can only be sustainable if land reforms and investment in agriculture itself is undertaken. Only a productive countryside can produce the additional food for a larger urban workforce and stave off bottom-up resistance to this restructuring effort in the first place.

Leveraging GDP

While mainstream empirical attention is usually drawn toward statistics that capture aggregate affluence like GDP, it is inadequate to assess the potential of a state to convert latent wealth into national resources. Per capita income is the most basic reflection of a nation's economic strength. Higher per capita income enables states to extract resources from its citizens.

The chart below shows on a per capita PPP basis, India lags behind developing countries.

World's most rapidly developing economies

Country	GDP per capita based on PPP* in 2009 (USD)	GDP growth in the past ten years (%)	GDP growth needed to catch up with the largest economies by 2050 (%)	Time needed to catch up with the largest economies (years)
Russia	15,039	10 / 5.4	4.6	17
Brazil	10,455	4.3 / 1.1	5.3	119
China	6,549	10.1 / 8.3	5.7	23
India	2,930	7.7 / 4.9	7.4	50
Poland	17,536	7 / 4.3	4.0	22
Mexico	14,534	5.2 / 2.4	4.7	55
Argentina	14,125	8.1 / 1.7	4.0	17
Turkey	13,138	8.3 / 2.7	5.3	28
South Africa	10,136	3.9 / 1.7	4.6	135
Indonesia	3,980	4.3 / 1.3	7.2	181

Maximum rate ■   Average rate ■

* Purchasing power parity (PPP) is a theory of long-term equilibrium exchange rates based on relative price levels of two countries

In terms of real per capita in current dollars, India's is a low-income economy with catch-up process that would last several decades. What is important to note is that the Indian state's ability to extract resources for multiple strategic agendas is constrained by the income level of its polity. Like all economies, India must judiciously choose where to deploy the limited societal wealth that the state is able to extract through the tax system.

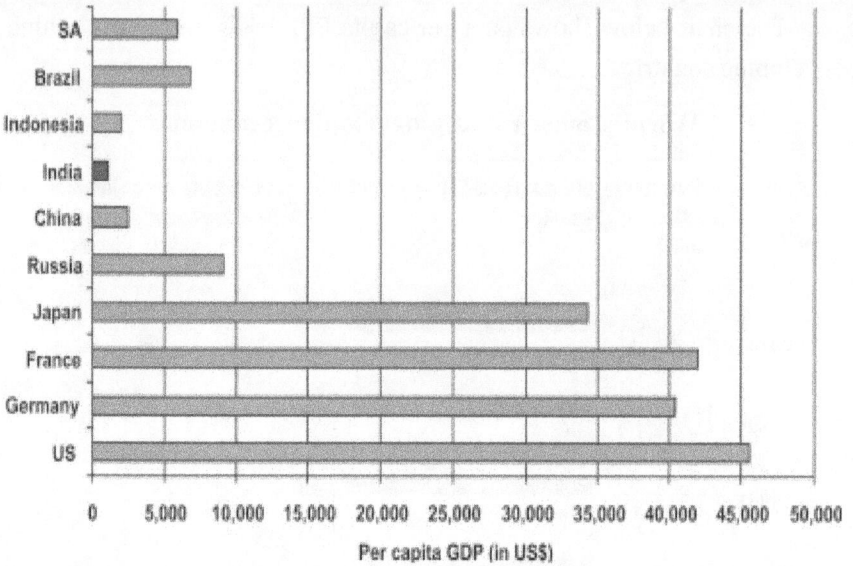

Source: Human Development Report 2009

A state's extractive capacity is considered as the most basic evidence of a state ability to mobilize societal wealth for national aims. The ratio of tax revenues as a percentage of GDP is usually viewed as the most reliable proxy to assess a state's extractive capacity.

Below is an empirical snapshot that captures the Indian state's relative fiscal power among its peer group:

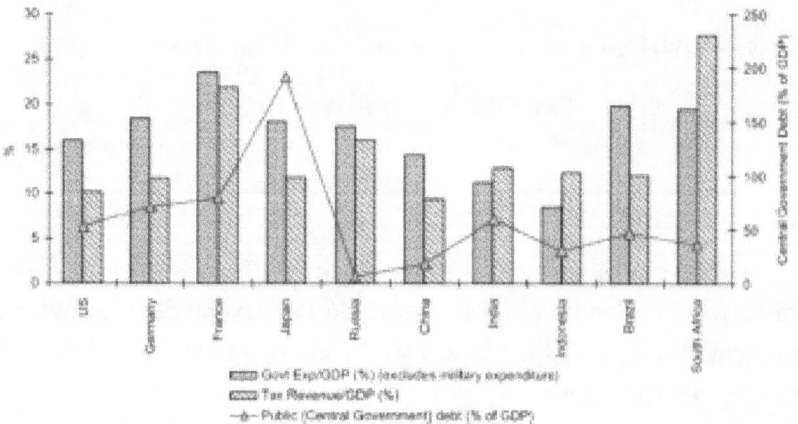

Source: Economist Intelligence Unit 2009, World Bank's World Development Indicators 2008. NOTE all metrics relate to only Central Government figures.

Since states differ in the degree of centralisation in their economic systems, let us evaluate India's relative position in terms of *total* tax revenues to GDP.

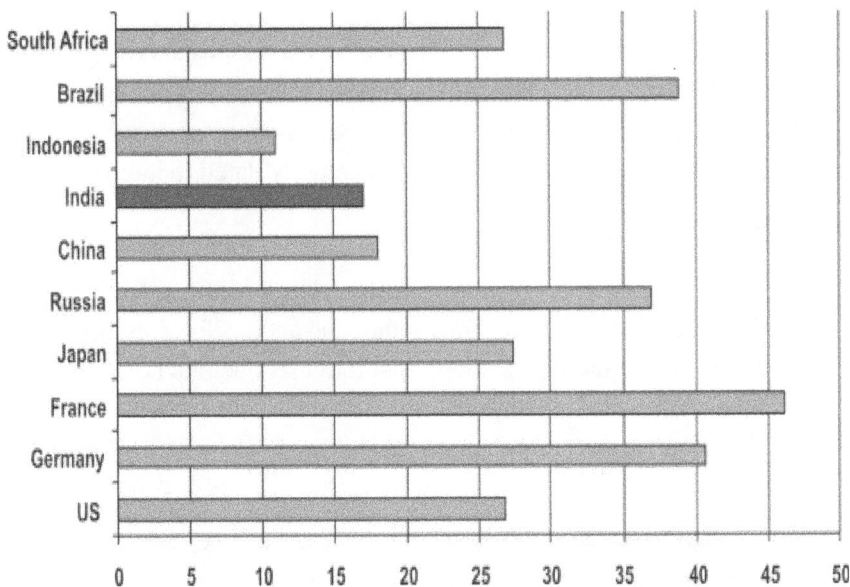

Source: Index of Economic Freedom, Heritage Foundation.

Across the OECD as a whole, total tax revenues averaged an estimated 33.7 percent of GDP in 2009.

India's total tax revenue (including provincial governments) as a percentage of GDP has barely increased from 15.4 per cent in 1991 to 18.5 per cent in 2008. It has also been argued that direct taxes are a useful measure to gauge the penetration of the state in society.[13]

---

[13] Lewis Snider argues that, 'direct taxes are relatively more difficult to collect than indirect taxes because they require more effective infrastructural power. Taxes on international trade and transactions are the easiest to levy because relatively little infrastructural power is needed to collect them … direct taxes require a more developed capacity to make the state's presence felt in the event of noncompliance than other forms.' Lewis W. Snider, 'Identifying the Elements of State Power: Where Do We Begin?', *Comparative Political Studies*, 20(3), 1987, pp. 325-326, 328. Historically, the major share of tax revenues came from indirect taxes in India, though recently the share of direct taxes has increased from 40 per cent in 2004 to 56 per cent in 2008.

India has one of the lowest tax-GDP ratios among most emerging economies in the world. While China's total tax collection is about the same, Brazil and Russia's ratios are markedly higher at 39 and 37 percent respectively.

It is perhaps surprising to note that even as services account for more than half of India's GDP, service tax contributes barely 8 percent of the gross tax revenues of the Centre. With a larger number of services being brought under the tax net every budget, this ratio is slated to improve.

Modernity of Economic System

The quality of an economic system is determined by the infrastructure stocks that enable investment to yield higher return and act as a force multiplier in the economy. The figure below shows that India lags behind her CNP peer group in the quality of its infrastructure.

Infrastructure quality by country

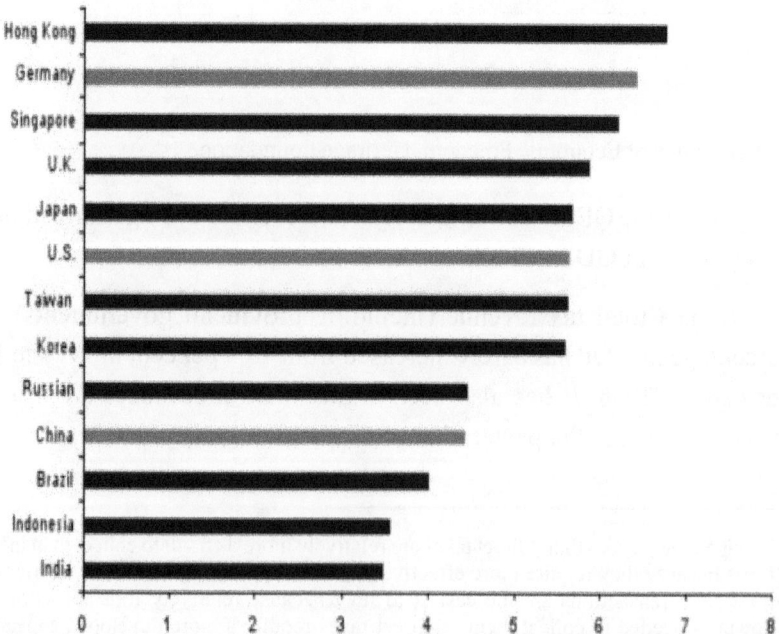

Note: In the scales (1)=poorly developed and inefficient and (7)=among the best in the world

Source: World Economic Forum Global Competitiveness Report, 2010-2011

This structural bottleneck in turn has stifled the industrial value-addition that India's economy can undertake.

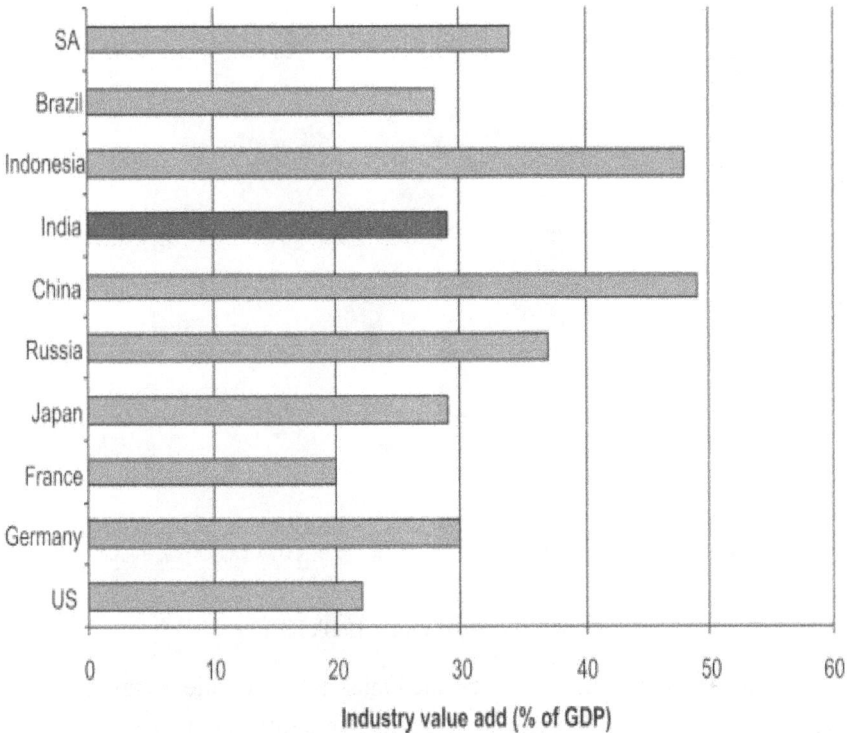

Industry value add (% of GDP)

Source: World Development Indicators, 2009.

Caveat: The above chart is a ratio and does not reveal the quality of the numerator (industrial value-addition). Germany and France's industrial sectors are far more technologically advanced than China and India's even though the latter share of GDP might be similar or greater.

For instance, an evaluation of the R&D (knowledge) capabilities of the CNP peer group reveals the technological gap between the emerging economies and the OECD economies.

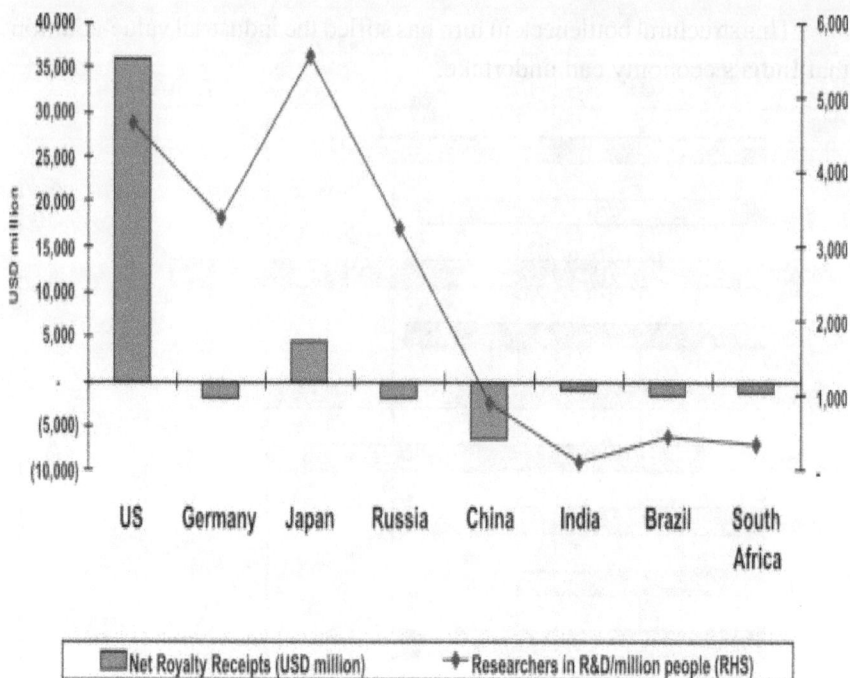

Source: World Development Indicators; World Bank KEI

Another statistic that can reveal the industrial capabilities of an economy are the share of high-tech exports in the overall manufactured goods exported.

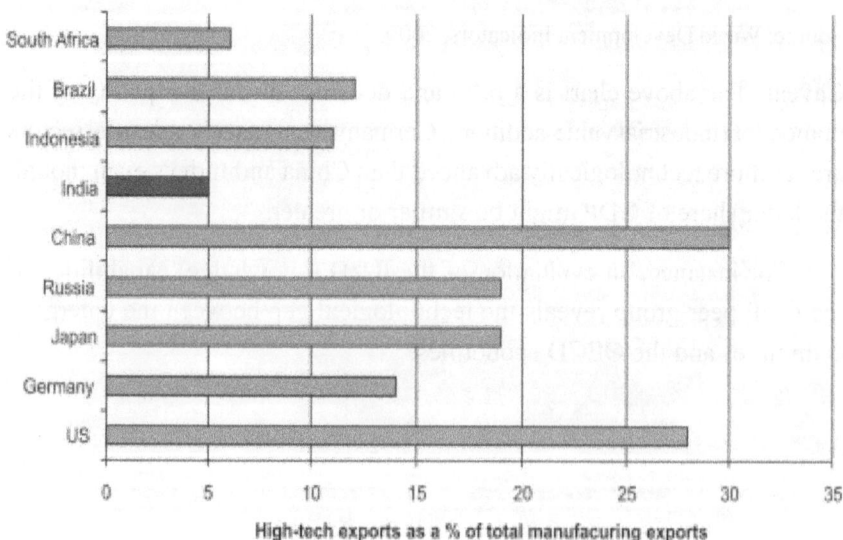

Source: World Bank WDI, 2007.

An important caveat for China's case must be noted. The figure above suggests China's industrial capabilities are extremely high. The reality, however, is more complex. 83 percent of China's high-tech exports are driven by multinational corporations, which have either off-shored some of their production operations[14] or are rerouting their exports via China that does the final assembly of high tech products that are designed and developed in the advanced economies like Japan, Germany and South Korea.

Natural Resource Endowment and Energy Security. Ultimately, despite all the innovations and productivity of an economic system, state cannot avoid the constraints of population density, water availability and energy resources.

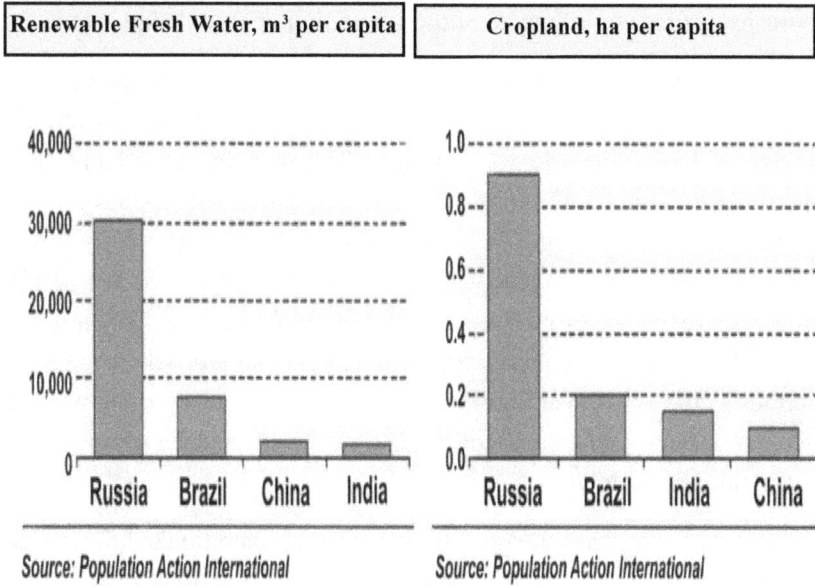

Source: Population Action International

Source: Population Action International

---

[14] Taiwan-IT companies have relocated 95 percent of their production/assembly capacity into and transferred mainland China to a top assembler of information and communication technology, such as laptop PCs, digital cameras and all i-products.

India: Measuring up on Science and Technology Innovation

Introduction

In defining the concept of 'structural power' of a hegemonic state, the political economist Susan Strange used the following aspects of such power: control of the use of force; control of the means of production; control of the means of finance; influence of the generation of knowledge.[1]

If we assume 'structural power' to be the same as national power, and thus use the same metrics for national power, then while the US is still the dominant military power in the world, its control of the second and third pegs of the definitions of national power have fluctuated. It does remain however the world's leading generator of 'knowledge' particularly in the amount of money spent on research and development (R&D) and the commercial relevance of products as a result of the money spent on R&D (this would include non-commodity sectors such as defense where the state functions as the sole buyer and sole funder). Here we refer to knowledge generation as being particular to science and technology and the advancement of technological frontiers.

If one believes that a measurable stake in the generation of knowledge is essential for a state in obtaining 'structural power' or national power, then in a study of India's comparative Comprehensive National Power (CNP), an assessment of the state of its 'innovation', especially in Science and Technology (S&T) is essential.

---

[1] "The Persistent Myth of Lost Hegemony." Susan Strange, International Organization, Vol. 41, No. 4, (Autumn, 1987), p. 565

What is Innovation? An Indian Perspective

The Indian economic story over the last decade has clearly drawn the attention of the world, evidenced by the flood of heads of state who visited in 2010. Much of this traffic drew attention to India as a customer of foreign goods, a fact which was reflected in the big-ticket deals that India struck during the visits of the leaders of the US, Britain, France, Russia and China. The largest component of India's GDP is services, a statistic which lends itself to the question: how much does or can India innovate or generate intellectual property in Science and Technology (S&T)?

According to Hussein Kanji, a venture capitalist who has extensive experience investing in India, formerly with the noted firm Accel Partners, and who is currently building his own fund: "In technology, India's innovation has yet to be released. There are a handful of domestic clones of US services (MakeMyTrip - India's Expedia; Naukri - India's Monster.com; Flipkart - India's Amazon eg.), but that's about it.

Some of these companies are innovative in the sense they help localize the service to India, but these are not good working examples of innovation. The truly innovative technology companies in India are still struggling. The reasons boil down to two factors: lack of engineering talent and lack of commercial talent to scale businesses globally. The first is counterintuitive given the success of IIT graduates in California. India has good engineering schools. But it doesn't churn out enough of a class of engineers that think outside of the box. The second is a global issue - most of this talent is clustered in Silicon Valley. But that will change over time.

The kinds of activity being invested in and succeeding right now in India are businesses that either leverage inexpensive manpower (BPOs, agencies) or localize US successes."[2] A frequent word used to describe domestic innovation in India is *Jugaad.*In December 2009, *BusinessWeek* magazine featured an article titled 'India's Next Global Export: Innovation', lauding the virtues of India's *jugaad.*[3] *The Economist,* in an article dated April 15, 2010, also lauded the virtues of India's 'frugal innovation',

---

[2] Email interview with Hussein Kanji, December 2010

[3] http://www.businessweek.com/innovate/content/dec2009/id2009121_864965.htm

highlighting innovations by General Electric (GE) and Tata Consultancy Services (TCS): "...GE and TCS are doing something more exciting than fiddling with existing products: they   are taking the needs of poor consumers as a starting point and working backwards. Instead of adding ever more bells and whistles, they strip the products down to their bare essentials. Jeff Immelt, GE's boss, and Vijay Govindarajan, of the Tuck Business School, have dubbed this "reverse innovation". Others call it "frugal" or "constraint-based" innovation."[4]

Writing about the practice of frugal innovation in the *New York Times,* David Bornstein chronicles the example of a Bihar company named Husk Power Systems, which has developed a system to turn rice husks into electricity. According to Bornstein: " What the company illustrates is a different way to think about innovation — one that is suitable for global problems that stem from poor people's lack of access to energy, water, housing and education. In many cases, success in these challenges hinges less on big new ideas than on collections of small old ideas well integrated and executed."[5]

Descriptions of innovation in India which originate in the frugal innovation paradigm speak primarily to innovation for India's domestic market, and not for global markets. By the same token, global companies like GE have R&D centers in India which produce intellectual property that is used globally. Despite successes by export-dependent industries in India, world perception clearly tilts toward that frugal innovation paradigm for India.

As the world's innovative leader, the US itself has had several recent studies that aim to chart not just US innovation, but comparative innovation globally — an indication of how seriously its policymakers take holding onto this lead position as a component of its national power. For instance, in 2006, then Secretary of Commerce Carlos Gutierrez chartered an Advisory Committee on Measuring Innovation in the 21st Century Economy. This committee issued its report in 2008 and defined 'innovation' as: "the design, invention, development and/or implementation of new or altered products,

---

[4] http://www.economist.com/node/15879359

[5] http://opinionator.blogs.nytimes.com/2011/01/10/a-light-in-india/

services, processes, systems, organizational structures, or business models for the purposes of creating new value for customers and financial returns for the firm."[6]

This study did not offer any new models for measuring innovation, but focused more on improving the fidelity of data collected from sources like the R&D Satellite Account from the Bureau of Economic Analysis (BEA) and the US Census Bureau. The definition of innovation put forth by this committee would prejudice the study of innovation toward that in the private sector only. There is good reason for that bias in that 65% of R&D funds in the US come from industry, while the federal government contributes 28%. Federally-performed research, i.e. research that is federally-funded and performed at federal institutions accounted for just 7% of total US R&D and 25% of total federal R&D investment.[7]

In January 2010, the US National Science Foundation released its biennial report titled Science and Engineering Indicators which showed that through 2007 the United States remained by far the single largest R&D-performing country. Its R&D expenditure of $369 billion in 2007 exceeded the Asian region's total of $338 billion and the EU's (EU-27) $263 billion. The U.S. 2007 total broadly matched the combined R&D expenditures of the next four largest countries: Japan, China, Germany, and France.[8]

In India, R&D investment is dominated by the state, with the spending split being 74% to 20% for industry.[9] The industry component of R&D spending cited in R&D magazine looks only at domestic industry spending on R&D, and not foreign contributions to R&D sited in India, which is typically done through in-house research centers owned by companies such as General Electric, IBM and Honeywell. Foreign companies spend around

---

[6] Advisory Committee on measuring innovation in the 21st century economy, Report to the Secretary of Commerce, January 2008, http://www.innovationmetrics.gov/Innovation%20Measurement%2001-08.pdf, p. i

[7] "Re-emerging US R&D," http://www.rdmag.com/Featured-Articles/2009/12/Policy-and-Industry-Re-Emerging-U-S-R-D/

[8] Science and Engineering Indicators, National Science Board publication, January 2010, http://www.nsf.gov/statistics/seind10/pdf/seind10.pdf, p. O-4

[9] See: http://www.rdmag.com/uploadedFiles/RD/Featured_Articles/2009/12/India_GFF_2010.pdf

$13b annually on R&D in India, which is about 40% of the government's total funding of R&D in India.[10]

The validity of such R&D in evaluating the status of domestic innovation can be challenged as the intellectual property for the product of such research would be held by foreign companies, with India's sole contribution being labor arbitrage. Rather, the fact that such a high percentage of R&D funding and performance is from 'in-sourced' research is an indicator of the native innovation environment.

According to R&D magazine: " Within India's industrial sector, five industries (pharmaceutical, automotive, electrical and electronics, chemicals, and defense) account for about two-thirds of the total industrial R&D...India's national system of innovation is dominated by the sectoral system of innovation of the pharmaceutical industry. A second leading sector is the automotive industry, which is comprised of both the vehicle manufacturers and the auto parts sub sectors. Both of these industries are also characterized by competitive structures, with a number of foreign and domestic manufacturers coexisting and competing with each other."[11]

A unifying characteristic of both of these (automotive and pharmaceutical) sectors in India is that they are export-heavy and thus native R&D expenditures by export-dependent industry are not just for local markets but for global ones. But, for the Indian economy and its industry as a whole, exports are a fraction of the domestic market, and thus innovation that occurs for local consumption has to be seen as a separate and distinct commodity.

So, whither innovation in India? The key question is: what is India's 'innovative capacity', especially in S&T? Porter and Stern define *national innovative capacity* as: "a country's potential—as both a political and economic entity—to produce a stream of commercially relevant innovations."[12]

---

[10] See: http://www.rdmag.com/uploadedFiles/RD/Featured_Articles/2009/12/India_GFF_2010.pdf

[11] See: http://www.rdmag.com/Featured-Articles/2009/12/Policy-and-Industry-Global-Perspective-Emerging-Nations-Gain-R-D-Ground/

[12] http://www.isc.hbs.edu/Innov_9211.pdf

In India's case, innovation for the domestic market and that for global markets can be seen as separate quantities. But, for the sake of analysis, can the factors that affect the quality of innovation in India be quantified and correlated across India's peer group countries for comparison purposes?

For that, we would have to select and analyze factors — that adequately measure Indian innovation against a global background. For the purposes of this study, the countries selected for comparison are the US — for obvious reasons — the other members of BRICSA, Germany, Japan and Indonesia.

Table 1

S&T Sub-Determinants	Data Source	Period	US	Germany	Japan	Russia	China	India	Indonesia	Brazil	South Africa	Weights
Numbers of patent applications (USPIO) worldwide	NSF SEI 2010, table 6-54		231,588	25,202	82,396	547	4,455	2,879	13	442	265	0.075
Researchers in R&D/million People	World Bank KEI	2006	4651	3386	5546	3255	926	111	199	461	361	0.150
Scientific Papers Published	World Bank KEI (Science and Engineering articles (million people)	2005	694	536	434	101	32	13	1	53	51	0.075
Personal Computers	World Bank KEI (Computers per 1000 people	2007	810	660	410	130	60	30	20	160	80	0.050
Internet users (per 100 people)	World Bank's WDI	2008	76	75	75	32	22	5	8	38	9	0.050
Research and development (% of GDP)	World Bank's WDI	2009	22.7	2.6	3.4	1.1	1.5	0.8	0.1	1.0	1.0	0.200
Internet Bandwidth	World Bank KEI (International internet Band width, bits per person)	2007	11277	25654	3734	573	280	32	53	1041	71	0.050

Table 1 (contd.)

S&T Sub-Determinants	Data Source	Period	US	Germany	Japan	Russia	China	India	Indonesia	Brazil	South Africa	Weights
Royalty Receipts	World Bank KEI (royalty and license fee receipts, $m)	2007	71,346	5,888	23,229	396	205	112	31	319	53	0.100
Value Added in Service Industry	WDI (Services etc. value added, percentages of GDP)	2005	76	69	68	57	40	53	37	65	66	0.050
ICT goods exports (% of total goods exports)	World Bank's WDI	2008	12.8	6.9	14.3	0.4	27.5	1.3	4.6	1.8	1.6	0.050
High-tech Exports (as a percentage of manufactured exports)	World Bank WDI	2007	28	14	19	19	30	5	11	12	6	0.050
Business Start-up Costs	World Bank KEI (cost to register a business, % of GNI per Capita)	2009	0.7	5.6	7.5	2.6	8.4	70.1	77.9	8.2	6	0.100

Descriptions of the Study Variables:

Number of Patent Applications (USPTO) Worldwide — Weight: 7.5%

This factor measures the 'output' side of innovation — other variables focus primarily on the 'input' side, but scholars agree that it remains one of the better measures of innovation 'output' by a state.

The data used for this section was culled from the US National Science Foundation's *Science and Engineering Indicators 2010* study. For this study, only the number of patent applications was used, not the number of patents granted. The NSF data refers primarily to patents filed with the US Patent and Trademark Office (USPTO).[13]

The reason for selection of patent applications is that the use of USPTO data only as a gold standard for world patenting trends could be later scrutinized for prejudice in their judgment. Obviously, *patents applied for* is not a perfect measure either, but for this study it will be considered the better measure of research output. Clearly, the US is still far, far ahead of any of its competitors in the number of patents applied for. By this measure, Indian output too in patent applications has increased. The number of USPTO patent applications jumped from 1,463 in 2005 to 2,879 in 2008, a 49% increase.[14]

While India ranks far behind the US, other technology intensive countries such as Germany and Japan and even China, it does rank ahead of Brazil and Russia, the other members of the BRIC grouping of countries. The most dramatic jump in Indian patenting trends has been in patent filings in India itself — from 17,466 in 2004/5 to 35,000 in 2007/8, a 100% increase in three years.[15] This is an indicator of the preference of Indian innovation to gear itself for local markets.

---

[13] *Science and Engineering Indicators*, National Science Board publication, January 2010, http://www.nsf.gov/statistics/seind10/pdf/seind10.pdf, p. 6-46

[14] *Science and Engineering Indicators*, National Science Board publication, January 2010, http://www.nsf.gov/statistics/seind10/pdf/seind10.pdf, tables 6-54 and 6-57

[15] http://www.rdmag.com/uploadedFiles/RD/Featured_Articles/2009/12/India_GFF_2010.pdf

This factor has been given a weight of 7.5%, higher that variables such as the number of personal computers, internet bandwidth etc., but judged to be lower than other output variables like ICT and high technology exports, as they are also a function of the native business climate.

Researchers in R&D/million People — Weight 15%

This variable is an indicator of research 'potential' and subsumes the effectiveness of a state's education system as well as how the products of that system are employed by the state and native industry, as well as academic research. It includes only Ph.D -qualified researchers. The data included in this study is taken from the World Bank Knowledge Economy Index (KEI).

According to the KEI data, India ranks dead last in this category, behind not just the major research powers, but also the BRIC countries and South Africa. This variable has been given a weight of 15%, as it is judged for the purposes of this study to be the most important indicator of S&T *potential,* and the only variable that includes a measure of the quality of academic research.

The number of researchers/million people is a reflection of the general Indian education system at large. According to David Karl, who co-chaired the Bi-national Task Force on Enhancing India-U.S. Cooperation in the Global Innovation Economy, jointly sponsored by the Pacific Council on International Policy and the Federation of Indian Chambers of Commerce and Industry: "Total outlays on the higher education system are much lower than in many other comparable countries, affecting the capacity for teaching and research. Singh's scientific advisor has warned that research from Indian universities is "hitting an all-time low." Even the research output from the world-renown Indian Institutes of Technology is slim. As a result, the country has few institutions with strong international standing, making it difficult to attract and retain top scholars and researchers."[16]

Critics may suggest that India's population renders this statistic meaningless. However, the same critical yardstick should also apply to China, which has more than eight times the number of researchers per million

---

[16] "India needs a Sputnik moment," David Karl, *YaleGlobal Online,* March 4, 2011, http://yaleglobal.yale.edu/content/india-needs-sputnik-moment

people than India. Even Indonesia has more researchers-per-million than India. Dismissing this statistic on the basis of India's population alone is not a valid critique. Clearly, India's performance in generating adequate 'weight' of S&T researchers is wanting.

Scientific Articles Published/per Million People — Weight 7.5%

This statistic is another measure of research 'output', and speaks to how well a state's research constituencies handle the transition from lab to the global knowledge ether. The data used here is taken from the World Bank KEI, which refers via NSF Science and Engineering Indicators to the Science Citation Index and Social Science Citation Index among its sources. In this measure, India is second to last, ahead of only Indonesia. It is almost three times as much behind China, with a comparable population size. And certainly dead last among the BRIC grouping. In this study, this variable has been given a weight of 7.5%, judged to be the equal of the number of patent applications filed in importance.

Personal Computers-per-1000 People — Weight 5%

For the average person, not just an S&T researcher, the personal computer has become a symbol of access to the global knowledge ether. More basic than that, a personal computer symbolizes access to the 'tools' of modern life. As such, 'computer density' is an important marker of how ready a nation is to participate in the global knowledge economy, and by inference is a marker of its innovative capacity. The data for this variable has been taken from the World Bank KEI.

Again, India is second-to-last in this category, ahead of only Indonesia among the sampled countries, and clearly last among BRIC countries. Population counter-arguments again don't hold water as China has more than four times the number of personal computers-per-1000 people than India. On the other hand, usage of personal computers can be tied to the literacy rate of a state, which could account for India's low ranking in this area. As a consequence of this 'filter', this variable has been given a weight of 5%, the lowest number given to any category included in this study.

Internet Users-per-100 People — Weight 5%

Obviously, this variable — addressing the density of internet users in a state — has to be taken in conjunction with that of personal computer density. The internet is the ultimate tool for cross-border knowledge sharing and collaboration, in addition to being a source for everyday knowledge s well as basic information about government and governance. In a state with a low personal computer density, more people that are able to use one, but who do not own their own, will have to cluster around collective-use computers.

The data used for this study comes from the World Bank's World Development Indicators (WDI). In this category, India is dead last, behind even Indonesia and clearly behind the BRIC grouping. For the purposes of this study, this variable has been given the same weight of 5% as personal computer density.

Internet Bandwidth — Weight 5%

Taken together with computer density and internet-user density, this variable describes how connected a state is to the global information highway, and thus the globalized knowledge economy. Here, India ranks dead last, behind even Indonesia on a bits-per-person basis. For this study, internet bandwidth has been given the same weight as computer and internet user density, at 5%.

R&D Funding as a % of GDP — Weight 20%

This variable describes the total money spent on R&D by a state, and as such subsumes many of the 'input' sub-variables that speak to a state's commitment to R&D. It is thus judged for this study to be the most important variable among the selected grouping, and is given a weight of 20%.

Once again, in this category, India ranks second-to-last, ahead of only Indonesia. As a percentage of GDP, China spends almost twice as much as India on R&D. Even South Africa spends 1% of GDP on R&D. The global leader in this area is Japan, with R&D spending at 3.4% of GDP. Total R&D spending is a predictor of a state's R&D performance. India's ranking in this variable is a reflection of its poor rankings in the other areas as well.

Royalty Receipts — Weight 10%

This variable is an important descriptor of the wide acceptability of a state's native-based research programs to local and global markets. The data used here in this study was culled from the World Bank KEI.

Further, the quantum of royalty payments can be related to how effectively a country's intellectual property 'system' is at protecting intellectual property — i.e. how effective is its patenting system, its courts and where necessary, its international diplomacy to protect the rights of its inventors? Here again, India ranks second-to-last, ahead of only Indonesia among the states sampled. The US is the clear leader, with royalty receipts of over $71 billion. As an important indicator of research output, this variable has been given a weight of 10% for this study, as it is judged to be more important and broad-based a descriptor than patent applications or papers published.

Value Added in Service Industry (% of GDP) — Weight 5%

This variable describes the contribution of the services sector of a state's economy to GDP, subtracting for inputs. Highly developed economies such as the US, Germany and Japan have a high percentage of their GDP from services. The data used for this study was taken from the World Bank WDI.

Among the set of countries studied, India ranks third-to-last, behind China and Indonesia. It is the lowest ranked among the BRIC countries in this regard. This variable is a good comparator between industrialized and emerging economies as services-based economies also score highly on the other indicators of innovation. But, for a country like India, where services has a far less percentage of GDP, other economic factors mitigate against according it a higher weight.

It is also not a complete descriptor of the state of innovation in a country. For instance, in India's instance, the economic growth of the last decade has been driven primarily by growth in the services industry. However, that development is not coincident with significant improvements in the other indicators of innovation. As such, in this study, services-value-added is thus judged to have a weight of 5%.

ICT Goods Exports (Percentage of Total Goods Exports) — Weight 5%

This variable describes a state's industrial exports of Information and Communications Technology (ICT) goods, as a percentage of its total goods exports. The data used for this study was taken from the World Bank WDI.

Since a state's effective integration of ICT is a recognized component of its integration with the global knowledge economy, its industrial performance in exports in this area is an important indicator of whether it imports important tools of innovation, or designs them locally and exports them. However, there is one criterion that mitigates against giving this factor a higher weight — local manufacture of foreign-designed products would count in these export figures, which means they do not speak directly to the quality of native innovation. As such, this variable is given a weight of 5% in this study. India ranks dead last in this category, behind even Indonesia.

High-technology Exports (as a Percentage of Manufactured Exports) — Weight 5%

Similar to ICT exports, High Technology Exports (HTE) , here measured against total manufactured exports, is an important indicator of a nation's globally integrated high-technology industrial base, and thus of the tools for innovation to occur. The data used for this study comes from the World Bank WDI. As with ICT exports, the key question in deciding how much importance to accord this variable is whether value-added by local industry is more than just labor arbitrage.

For instance, China scores the highest in this category, with 30% of manufactured exports falling into the high-technology category, more than even the US. But, the value-added in China itself in these exports is marginal in general. In this category as well, India ranks dead-last, behind Indonesia. While HTE as an indicator of a nation's innovative capacity is clearly important, it has been judged to have a weight of 5% in this study.

Business Start-up Costs — Weight 10%

A very important metric for a nation's innovative capacity is how innovation is conducted in the private sector. The states that spend the highest percentage of GDP on S&T R&D also have high percentages of research conducted in the private sector. For instance, about 70% of US R&D is conducted in the private sector and about 30% in the public sector. The figures in India are virtually reversed.

As a consequence, evaluating the ease with which a business can be started can be an important predictor of a state's innovative environment. Here, business start-up costs are evaluated as a % of Gross National Income (GNI) per capita. The data for this study was taken from the World Bank KEI.

India ranks second to last on this scale, behind only Indonesia. The lowest business start-up costs are in the US, which also ranks highest on other innovation indicators. Among BRIC states, India is last — Russia, Brazil and even China make it much easier to start a business. If business start-up costs are low, *competitive* innovation is also easier. For being an important predictor of innovative climate, this variable has been given a weight of 10%.

Summary

In the measurement of innovative capacity in a global context, India ranks poorly on all of the selected indicators in comparison with the selected countries. India's ranking in these areas predicts some important choices for Indian policymakers, if incentivizing innovation is a major goal.

While practical innovation or *jugaad* in India may be lauded, and even important for domestic markets, India's competitiveness as a global innovator lies in generating export-competitive innovation. As Hussein Kanji describes, Indian companies that are ready to innovate struggle with locating engineering talent. Further, the studied data clearly shows India lacking in the production of resident researchers.

Finally, the innovative 'infrastructure' of India needs to be addressed — improving internet access and computer usage, spending on education and R&D and making it easier for a business to be started. Failing all of these, despite isolated instances, India will continue to lag its peer competitors in the indicators of innovative capacity that have been selected for this study.

Foreign Policy: Comprehensive National Power

Comprehensive National Power is a concept, not much discussed in contemporary western political theory; neither in the Marxist Leninist understanding, nor in 20th century Chinese thinking. It is a completely newly born concept. Its origin lies in the People's Republic of China, a country which is quite obsessed with the general power of the nation-states. This theory has actually evolved on the basis of calculations done by combining and considering factors of national importance such as military, economic, cultural and other factors such as Human development index etc. The calculations show that they have ranked the USA at number one position with UK, Russia, France and Germany following the United States.

The Chinese have also started thinking in terms of hard and soft power. Their concept of CNP reflects both these elements. They have inferred their reference from the ex-Soviet Union that had extensive military power but lacked in other aspects. The growth of military power was achieved at the expense of civil economic power. So in terms of CNP, Russians were not given high ranking.

According to Chinese strategists, number of factors are to be taken into account in formation of a strong CNP. These are: economy, education, science, technology, resources and the general influence that the country exerts over the rest of the world. Economic innovation and effective military capability helps in creating a stable political environment which in turn helps to intensify existing economic advantages. Therefore, the physical and economic resources, infrastructure, knowledge and capital, all play a significant role in arriving at any assessment of CNP.

Where and how does foreign policy fit in this assessment? Can it be really integrated into CNP? The answer is probably no. Foreign policy is a deflection of CNP. It is more a consequence rather than a source. It is a product of CNP.

A country that is militarily strong, economically powerful, is rich in natural and human resources will definitely have effective foreign policy. However, conversely if a country is militarily weak, economically stagnant, devoid of natural resources, has poorly educated manpower cannot have effective foreign policy. Another question that now arises is how important Leadership is? Can a charismatic leadership act on the international stage in terms of CNP if his country is relatively weak?

Some critics cite examples of personalities like Nehru, Chaves, Mandela etc. In rare cases, does one find a leader with a charismatic personality, who is able to project external image of a country quite successfully, even when the inherent strength of the country isn't that strong!! There has to be an explanation for such an act, and there can be many. This particular leader embodies powerful ideas or principles; is willing to take risks; his faith rests on some critical resource of supreme importance or value; or has alliance with likeminded leaders that reinforce his strength.

Whatever be the indices of CNP, one might say that the sheer size of a country cannot be the sole determining factor for it to reign supreme in the world. However less influential on an international scenario a large nation (in terms of size) might be, the potential of the country cannot be undermined. Such a country will still attract attention and will still have a significant role on international stage. The other players, willingly or unwillingly cannot ignore the latent potential which if exploited well, can get its act together and gain authority and power and have its say. Therefore, such country has to be paid appropriate attention and engaged in all the decisions taken.

Next follows the civilisation factor. A country with poor statistics but with a rich background of old illustrious civilization & rich cultural attributes, that has contributed to global civilisation over a century, holds a very important footing on the world map. It cannot be ignored either.

The country's geographical and geopolitical location is another extremely important factor that ensures its importance. A country located in an area where great powers have interest in, or for that matter geopolitically placed in a situation where turbulence instability can have spillover effects on other countries, or in terms of its geopolitical situations because it could be a transit country for access to other important areas or for evacuation of energy resources are few very potent factors in determining its status.

If one takes India's membership to non-alignment movement during the time when Nehru seem to cast a large shadow on international affairs, the country might not have CNP statistic, but it is part of a movement or grouping and can therefore with the force of collective strength, its foreign policy initiatives and thinking, acquires a greater force and much more if it were a member of Security Council. In fact, when China became a member of Security Council, its CNP was inferior to that of India's. But the fact that, it is a member of Security Council, has correct implication on the role that China plays in influencing the foreign policy terms.

To further refine the concept of CNP, a distinction between global power and a regional power must be made or understood purely on the basis of a country being a great power. Taking an example of China, which has scaled the topmost scales in almost all possible development graphs, has intrinsic capacity to actually morph into a 'great power'. The statistics show its improved indices on all fronts and eventually might supplant the USA. But, at this moment, that would be a self-serving narrow view of CNP even if it is read as a legitimate concept because a country can have an effective foreign policy. It can be effective in terms of its regional interests. It need not think in global terms. In that case, it does not have to have many things which the Chinese concept has. Another option can be that one may have all these things but at reduced scale on regional scale. A country which aspires to global influence ingredients would be different from smaller country.

Finally foreign policy has to be related to goals. If your goals are driven by power politics as is in the case of China or settling historical grievances or extending Chinese territories or protecting its access to natural resources which are spread far and now wide, it can think in terms of CNP related to what China's foreign policy goals are. Therefore you need to have goals.

India may not have the same view of how it should conduct foreign policy. Take India's foreign policy, so far in terms of power projection, we have limited ourselves to extended neighbourhood like China, Nepal, Myanmar, Sri Lanka, Maldives, Pakistan and Bangladesh but as our economies grow, India integrates more and more into the globalised world, foreign policy horizon of India will get to expand not necessarily in aggressive sense, obviously foreign policy will acquire greater range. We also have problems to access natural resources especially energy. Therefore we have to develop a foreign policy that gives us the kind of reach where we can secure energy security. As the private sector grows, looking for opportunities abroad, our Indian multinationals which are largely investing abroad, has got a direct influence on Indian foreign policy objectives and the means that they must acquire in order to protect those interests. Technological innovation is very important and one should study the correlation between the development of the IT sector and foreign policy especially the relationship with the United States. One of the powerful elements which have gone into to build this relationship that led to nuclear deals and other things is our military growth especially naval forces because the navy has wider reach geographically in comparison to other forces. This gives more strength and a dynamic foreign policy.

Instability weakens the foreign policy posture and India suffers a great deal from that. It is one thing that world leaders say how we are growing, this flatters our ego but when we hear intelligence assessments make about India's real strength and power, there the picture is much more nuanced. India is far too much engrossed with domestic problems for India to be able to develop a coherent structured outgoing foreign policy. We are held back with the problems we have, the composition of population has big impact on our foreign policy. The fact we have a sizeable Muslim minority, we have problems dealing with the Middle East and Pakistan. We have spillover ethnic population on our borders. Our vulnerability to terrorism weakens our foreign policy posture. If there is going to be another terrorist attack, foreign would run away investments. So when we are fashioning our foreign policy and goals we have to be constantly worried. We have two powerful neighbours China and Pakistan which are collaborating with each other on missile matters, defence and nuclear matters per se.

As far as democracy is concerned, it is a strength. India and the United States are coming together and adhere to shared values. If we really start working on CNP, this will give additional and more foreign policy options and we will come back to where we started: that foreign policy is an offshoot of CNP but variety of factors which have been mentioned earlier come into play. Therefore in simple language, a strong country with a strong leadership will have a strong foreign policy.

Given the objective factors in India's favour, India is bound to be one of the leading powers of the world. There is no escaping this. We are the second largest demographically and by 2050, we will be largest economy doing very well. Militarily we are doing well, we have manpower empowered well to propel the country move fast. The reasons for not exercising effective power are internal instability, structural weaknesses, and multi religious and multi-ethnic historically. Our democracy has enabled us to deal with these factors in our society. But we should not believe that diversity is our strength. This is the line we have to take if we have to face that we are diverse country. There should be minimum consensus among the elite that this is the way we are going to deal with internal issues. That is why we are seen as dysfunctional democracy. Democracy should be our strength, which is and one can give many examples where democracy has not helped us achieve potentially what we could have achieved. Our priority has to be that of development. Our external challenges are adding to our internal challenges at home. But our challenges remain internal. That is the problem of ethnic spill over, and about our vulnerability to terrorism. We have unsettled borders. We have continuity with powerful neighbours which are our adversaries. These are the reasons which make us appear we are not bold and robust in foreign policy choices because we constantly going wrong in the house, as we have not been able to deal with street issues.

While we have exercised power, the very fact that we did not join any alliances and have still remained independent is the biggest example. We did not join any umbrella in spite of all difficulties. We have not signed NPT in the end and yet we have succeeded to get out of the bind of NPT. We have developed our own missile programme. Our navy is expanding and visible in the Indian Ocean. We have joint military exercises. We are clear on deterrence in spite of all objections. After 1962, we have not yielded an inch of territory. Our armed forces are hanging to Siachin and this shows our determination.

Once we can control our internal problems, we cannot build our national morale just by scoring with China and Pakistan. Even if we win some diplomatic victories, how it is going to help the common people. It might satisfy our ego but until the common people's aspirations are not met and their morale does not get built, it is of no use.

Role of the Military in Determining Comprehensive National Power of States

Preamble

In our search for a point of entry for understanding the special nature of contribution of the military to CNP, we tread into a minefield that encompasses civilizational factors, societal nuances, institutional characteristics that make for political systems and the continuous friction that emerges when state intervenes into the various functions that govern the growth of nations. Equally fundamental is the search for reasons that impel the urge to power.

Within these factors if we consider encounters between civilizations as a possible impulse to power, we note a peculiar paradox in the Indian experience. Invasions have occurred and the land subject to migratory forces; in turn the land sent out exploratory missions both for expeditionary purposes and for spiritual expansion. This duality of purpose gave seed to a unique brand of imperialism; a socio-spiritual (as opposed to religious) mould to empire. The Bamiyan Buddhas', Angkor Wat and the Ramayanic and Mahabharatan folklore that permeates every aspect of life in South East Asia stand in testimony to this mould. In each of these outward dynamics whether it was the Mauryan empire, the Srivijaya kingdoms or the quest for commerce, there was a common fibre and that was the Indic stamp which was first seen through the prism of Ashoka's Four Principles of Empire, that is to build and guard the empire through Dharma, to protect through Dharma, to administer according to Dharma and to secure the well being of the citizenry with Dharma[1].

[1] King Ashoka and Buddhism: Historical and Literary Studies. Ed. Anuradha Seneviratna. Buddhist Publication Society, Sri Lanka, 1994. ISBN 955-24-0065-2

Indeed, while the Indic civilization flourished, a restraining geographic boundary, in the modern sense to these exertions never quite emerged. Communities moved, spreading as they assimilated the periphery, as much influenced by the core and its centripetal tug as by the novelty of the fringes; in the process the mainstream adapting, transmitting and flourishing. Modern historians particularly those in the late 19th and early 20th century were not quite able to understand this phenomenon particularly when viewed through the Westphalian[2] lens.

In his treatise Arthashastra, on war, politics, economics, diplomacy and statecraft Kautilya, in the fourth century BC underscored the importance of dynamism in the growth of a state. To him passivity was outlandish[3] and the objective of a state was power not just to control outward behavior but also the thoughts of one's subjects and one's adversaries.[4] He outlined eight precepts that governed the general power of a state[5]:-

(a) Every nation acts to maximize power and self interests.

(b) Moral principles have little or no force in the actions amongst nations.

(c) Alliances are a function of mutuality.

(d) War and peace are considered solely from the perspective of what advantages they provide to the instigator.

(e) The 'Mandala' premise of foreign policy provides the basis of strategic planning of alliances and a general theory of international relations.

(f) Diplomacy of any nature is a subtle act of war in contrast to the Clausewitzian view of war being a continuation of policy.

---

[2] 1648 circa Treaty of Westphalia between Spain and the Dutch acknowledged to be the beginning of modern international relations based on mutual recognition of State sovereignty.

[3] Kautalya: The Arthashastra. LN Rangarajan (Ed., Rearranger and Translator). Penguin Classics, India, 1992.

[4] ibid

[5] ibid

(g) Three types of warfare are upheld, the first is open hostilities, the second is war through concealment and lastly a war that is waged through silence and subterfuge.

(h) Seeking justice is the last desperate resort of the weak. This sentiment would appear to be a common theme amongst the ancients for in Thucydides History of the Peloponnesian War, when the Melians talk of justice and fair play confronted with the prospect of conquest by Athens, the latter contend that such tactics were the last desperate move of a nation facing defeat[6].

The story of Horatius Cocles' last stand on the northern bridge across the river Tiber in defense of Rome against its enemies, encapsulates the spirit of the Roman citizen. It won for them their commonwealth and empire that spanned from West Asia to the British Isles. In a short period of 53 years (219 – 167BC) this entire area was brought under the dominion of the single city of Rome. The story goes that Horatius standing at the head of the bridge, fearing that a large body of Rome's enemies would force their way into the city, turned around and shouted to those behind him to hasten back to the other side and break down the bridge. They obeyed him and whilst the bridge came down he remained at his post obstructing the progress of the foe. The assault was reigned in. Cocles himself followed the bridge into the river. It was this enthusiasm for noble deeds and a lofty spirit engendered by Roman traditions in addition to their customs, institutional faith in the design of their political systems and their moral incorruptibility that made for Empire.[7]

One hears a similar message in the voice of Kautilya when he summarizes the wellspring of a King's power. He states in the Arthashastra "A King's power is in the end tied to the popular energy of the people; for not being entrenched in the spirit of his subjects, a king will soon find himself easily uprooted".[8] In this context the spirit of the people refers to their adherence to dharma, faith in the king and his leadership, their wealth

---

[6] Thucydides.History of the Peloponnesian War Penguin Books Ltd.1954 Pgs 400-408 'The Melian Dialogue'

[7] Polibius on Roman imperialism Regnery Gateway Inc.1980 Pgs 216-217

[8] Kautalya: The Arthashastra. LN Rangarajan (Ed., Rearranger and Translator). Penguin Classics, India, 1992.

generating capabilities and their belief in the general superiority that their way of life represented.

In as much as the decline in power of both the Mauryan and Roman empires are concerned, the words of Gibbon are equally applicable, "The decline was the natural and inevitable effect of immoderate greatness. Prosperity ripened the principle of decay; the causes of destruction multiplied with the extent of conquest; and as soon as time or accidents removed the artificial supports, the stupendous fabric yielded to the pressure of its own weight"[9]. There is also another school of thought that believes that it was the new religion that weakened the will to look for rewards in another world and not in this, that contributed disproportionately to the decline of empire; Buddhism in the instance of the Mauryan realm and Christianity in the case of Rome.

The Roman Moment[10]

The diamond jubilee of Queen Victoria's ascension to the British Empire's throne was celebrated on 22nd June 1897. The jubilee stretched over five days on land and sea. A military procession of over 50,000 soldiers included troops from India, Nepal, Canada, its African possessions, Australia, New Zealand and Naples. At sea, 165 ships manned by 40,000 sailors and 3,000 heavy guns saluting Her Majesty gave teeth and 'hard power' to the fact that the realm was always, not just protected, but also had the capacity to vanquish any foreseeable opposition. Eleven viceroys and premiers of Britain's self governing colonies stood in prominent attendance alongside kings, princes, maharajahs, ambassadors and emissaries from the rest of the world. The event was celebrated in every corner of the Empire from Hong Kong to Singapore to Hyderabad, Bangalore, Zanzibar to the Table Bay and in Ottawa. In Fareed Zakaria's words and as one historian covering the events wrote this was a 'Roman Moment'. In sheer military strength, organizational and administrative excellence, in the virtues of its political systems, the self ordained legitimacy of their imperial systems and the

[9] Gibbon, Edward. The History of the Decline and Fall of the Roman Empire. Ed. JB Bury. Methuen & Co. London, 1896.

[10] Zakaria, Fareed.The Post-American World, WW Norton and company, New York 2008 Pgs 167-168

superiority of their cultural and structural strengths there was no peer to this Empire.

In the present day environment it is difficult to even contemplate the extent, grandeur and the dominance of Queen Victoria's bequest. From the time she wore the mantle of the Empress of India (1876) the Empire had been linked by a web of 170,000 nautical miles of trans oceanic cables and 662,000 miles of terrestrial cables creating a vast network of information highways that enveloped the globe, even a fledgling radio network; invention of which made its appearance in 1896 was included in this complex. Railways and canals were enlarged, deepened and pushed through volumes of commerce inconceivable hither to. The appeal of the Empire, its literature, its norms and sense of fair play, its emphasis on the outdoors and sporting activities, dressing habits, schooling and health programs provided the necessary soft power for dominance of British ideas and the universality of the English way of life; all of which long outlived the impact of their hard power.

The indices of British power and therefore the applicability of this model do not readily conform to the scale of their Empire. After all neither geography nor demography (2% of the world's population) could conceivably drive and support 30% of global GDP of the day, energy consumption five times that of the United States and 155 times that of Russia, accounting for $1/5^{th}$ of the world's trade and $2/5^{th}$ of its manufacturing trade[11]; without the abiding support, incorruptible control and skewed systems that fed it with the life blood of its colonies

In our examination of national power it would be interesting to also see, what were the causes of the fall of this lofty empire. For many scholars the watershed year was 1899 when Britain entered the Boer War. Queen Victoria's exposition of 'hard power' was far more brittle than its 3,000 naval guns would seem to portray. After all there was one gun for every ten of the 30,000 Boer farmers that were lined up against the Empire. The events of that war are well known. By 1902 over 450,000 Imperial troops were deployed in and around the Transvaal in this 'righteous' war for control over the diamond mines of Kimberly and gold mines at Witwatersrand; they

---

[11] ibid pg.174

were confronted by a rag tag militia largely made up of 45,000 farmers. The Empire won but in a historical sense this was a strategic loss for to have waged a bloody repressive war for 3 years and to have sustained casualties in excess of 45,000 dead and wounded against a guerrilla adversary was a toll that underscored the fragility of the realm's hard power. Britain had stretched its military to breaking point and had discovered enormous incompetence in its war effort and at home the will to empire itself was on balance. She was never to recover from this calamitous reversal as the empire blundered into the First World War and bankruptcy by 1919.

It is a moot point whether the British empire unraveled because of bad politics, failure of its military to appreciate the changing nature of warfare brought about by technology and the aspirations of men, ill advised economics or even a blindness to the transformation that its own soft power had wrought in terms of the spread of education and the ready availability of a wide range of knowledge. In the end analysis it must be said that it was a combination of the four mired in the wilting of the will that brought about the demise of British power.

The Fukuyama Matrix

Francis Fukuyama in his book, 'State Building – Governance and World Order in the 21century', has argued that the modern state is anything but universal. The reasons for this, is that there is continuous friction between the determinants that make for power. The two augments that must in interplay enhance the power of a nation are the strength of a state in terms of its institutions that impartially plan, regulate and implement policies transparently and efficiently; and the scope of its intervention in the activities of state. This friction tends, in less developed nations, to either stunt growth or in the extreme to encourage corruption and evolve into a bizarre predatory system, particularly so when there are prejudices in either its institutions or in the scope of intervention.

In his analysis he has stated that there is no commonly accepted measure for either the strength of institutions or the degree to which they must intervene in the functioning of the state. Fig.1 below shows a bar graph in which a hypothetical relationship is drawn. On the X-axis is a sampling of various state functions while the Y- axis indicates the strength of institutional capabilities. It would be apparent that in areas of defence, law and order, macroeconomic management, welfare activities and safety nets, financial regulation; institutional strength must be high while in state functions like fostering innovation, supporting markets, wealth generation and willingness to venture outwards, institutional intervention must be low.

Fig.1Strength of Institutions — Scope of Intervention in State Functions.

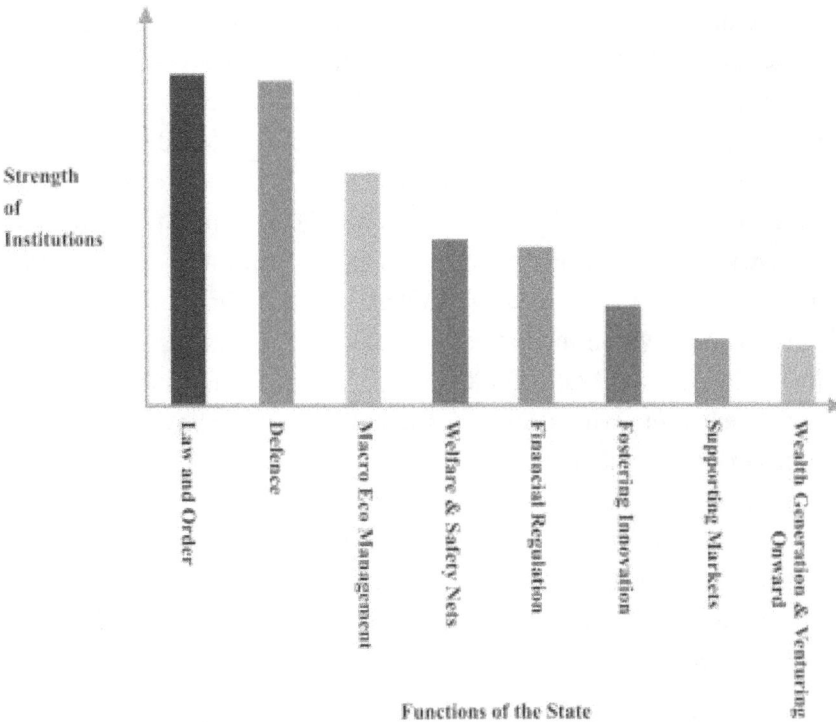

Source: Fukuyama Francis (State Building. Profile books 2004.Pgs 10-15)

Politics in the 20th century have been dominated by this interplay between the strength of institutions and the extent of intrusion of the government in the activities of the state. The century began with world order being led by the British Empire where the scope of state intervention was minimal while key institutions were strong. This prescription worked to the larger benefit of colonial powers where state activity did not go very much beyond the military, law and order and the sponsoring of business ventures. Thus one stream of development led to extremely liberal and powerful states while on the other, totalitarian states emerged which in their quest for power strived to subordinate the individual to the state's own political ends by the creation of repressive institutions. This, as is today historically well known, led to the right wing power structure in the form of Nazi Germany and the left wing version in the form of Soviet Union; both of which rose and failed very rapidly under the weight of their own contradictions.

The dilemma associated with building the power of a nation through the interplay of the two augments is that there is no fixed prescription for a favourable outcome. This is apparent from the experience of the 20th century when liberal nations with minimal state intervention developed into powerful nations while the same prescription when applied to some of the African nations such as Kenya, Zimbabwe, Nigeria and Congo resulted in systems that were predatory and debilitated potentially prosperous nations. Similarly, countries such as Pakistan, where strength of the military became such a dominant force within the nation, that it recreated the Prussian situation without the necessary larger cultural and societal strengths resulting in a Voltairesque army with a country. The break up of the Soviet Union and the mushrooming of authoritarian regimes, with their known record of being able to undertake reforms without having to face societal demands, came up against a different set of problems because of the release of pent-up urge for benefits that were in contradiction to the very goals of reform. Yet, there is the success story of the authoritarian Lee Kwan Yu's Singapore which defies conventional wisdom.

In the end analysis the empirical relationship between authoritarianism, development and power remains complex and as ambiguous as the relationship between democracy, development and power. China's case emphasizes a host of complex societal, technological factors that underscores the apparent success in striving for national power through political centralization.

The Pivots of Power

In concept, the comprehensive capability of a country to pursue its strategic objectives through freedom of action internally and externally defines its comprehensive national power. In achieving this freedom of action, three core factors play a disproportionate part. The first and primary of these is the strategic capability in all dimensions. Second, is the resolve of that nation as underscored by the will of its people and leadership to power. And lastly, is the state's ability to face up to and manipulate strategic outcomes. Klaus Knorr defined national power as the aggregate of a state's economic capability, its administrative competitiveness in terms of the influence it was willing to bring to bear globally and its readiness to use its military in order to bring about a favourable conclusion[12]. Theoretically this correlation was Clausewitzian in nature when war in fact was seen as a legitimate tool for the pursuit of strategic objectives, the other tools having been tried and found ineffective. In Knorr's construct economic factors within the larger international system was seen as a necessary base for power but not a very effective instrument of coercion for which military capability and aggressive intent were the determinants that could deliver desired outcomes. It is true that his writings were against the backdrop of the cold war; at a time when the possibility of a direct catastrophic clash between the two super powers was ruled out and the flavour of the period was proxy wars between clients. Yet, even then as now, economic sanctions whether by individual states or the international system remains a less than efficacious mechanism.

Another political economist, David Singer in the 1960s introduced the concept of a Composite Index of National Capability in order to assess the power of a state[13]. He saw power as those attributes of a state that could influence other nations in three time dimensions the short, medium and long term. The short term capability was represented by military strength and military personnel both in terms of quality and quantity. The medium term capability was characterized by industrial activity particularly in terms of iron and steel production and energy consumption. While the long term

[12] Knorr, Klaus. The Power of Nations: The Political Economics of International Relations. Basic Boooks 1975.

[13] Singer, David. 'The Correlates of War. Testing some Real Politik Models'.NY The Free Press 1980.

capability was a function of demographic factors which included the vigour of people, their will and creativity. This formulation again reflected the mores of the time. It was during the most turbulent period of the cold war and the industrial age hadn't quite given way to the information era. Therefore the structure of this formulation was to use the military in order to bring about a conclusion that could eventually permit the medium and long term capabilities to reconstitute the situation into one favourable to the patron. In fact this model would appear to be one lifted off from the World War II experience. Military victory of the allies infused industrial activity in the vanquished nation in the medium term and was capped by a tide of the American way of life. The success of this ideal is there for us to see. Yet in its relevance for contemporary times it does not factor the larger effects of globalization, civilisational factors and the dawn of the age of knowledge; all of which can inhibit the achievement of the short term objectives. Iraq, Iran, Afghanistan and North Korea in recent times are cases in point.

The Ray Cline recipe, though one that emerged during the height of the cold war, moves away from the Second World War mould and introduces soft power attributes at the very outset when change in the international environment is sought. It places before the statesman the natural subjectivity which arises, when dealing with strategic factors and the will and vigour of people, at the same time it does not lose sight of the hard objective factors that contribute to power. This blend of the abstract with the realist's point of view is its most abiding virtue.

The other significant feature of the Ray Cline paradigm is that it sees power through the eyes of the international system or a potential adversary[14]. This is a fresh and sophisticated approach to dealing in matters related to the power of a state which in part is an abstraction. In mathematical terms this concept is expressed as follows:

$$Pp = (C+E+M) * (S+W)$$

where,

Pp - Perceived power

---

[14] Cline, S. Ray. 'World Power Assessment: A Calculus for Strategic Drift' Washington: Center for Strategic and International studies, Georgetown University,1975, pg11.

C -   Population and geographic factors

E -   Total economic capacity

M-   Military capability including nuclear facility

S -   The strategic purpose expressed as a coefficient of the synergic value provided by the cohesiveness of plans and the objectivity with which these plans are executed.

W -   The national will to power of the people and resolve of leadership.

The Chinese believe that the purpose of Comprehensive National Power is to render the adversary (or the international system) powerless to stop its will. In this definition there are shades of an expanded Clausewitz when the latter defines 'war as an act of force to compel our enemy to do our will'.[15] Clausewitz, in his understanding of the application of national power, perceived two inseparable factors that had to be overcome, the first of which was the total means at the disposal of the adversarial state to pursue their interests and the second the strength of their will to resist. The rub in this knowledge is that as a combination while the former is measurable, the latter is much less easy to determine and can only be gauged by the strength of motivation[16]. This form of calculations will invariably lead to an upward spiral of power application against increased resistance till one or the other breaks, at which point an extreme would have been reached. In a nuclear context this may mean the end of purpose.

China perceives CNP as the single most critical indicator and measure of the aggregate economic, political, military, and technological prowess of a nation. In its calculus the nature of power is made up of two ingredients; the first and the primary is that set of dominance that manipulates and forces desired outcomes, termed as Command Power; while the second are ideational virtues (soft power) that serve to influence and mould finales with no great certainty. Professors Hu Augang and Men Honghua, in their paper on CNP and grand strategy[17] identify three core factors that establish

---

[15] Clausewitz, Carl Von. 'On War' Princeton University Press, 1976, pg75.

[16] Ibid, pg.77.

[17] Prof Hu Augang and Associate Prof Men Honghua. 'The Rising of Modern China CNP and Grand Strategy'. A paper presented

the CNP of states: Strategic Resources, Strategic Capability and Strategic Outcomes. They go onto add that while the latter two are a function of the former, CNP, is in fact a summation of the total Strategic Resources of a nation.

Strategic resources in their scheme of things come in eight categories which are a summation of the attributes listed by political economists of the past with a difference that in their impact on power, the weightage given to knowledge and technology and the state of economy is double that of the remaining six. This was in recognition of the arrival of the information era. The strategic resources identified are: capacity of the economy; human capital as a function of those in the working age and their educational qualifications along with total numbers; natural resources with an emphasis on energy consumption and those that have a direct impact on building infrastructure; capital resources in terms of FDIs and institutional investments; knowledge and technological resources; government resources in terms of government expenditure; military resources including nuclear capabilities and lastly international resources as a function of the influence of soft power. The key strategic resource is military power and capability since it is seen as an all pervasive enabler for internal security and also to provide the external power for maximizing interests overseas. In addition military power is not only an explicit function of CNP but is also a tangible expression of the will to power. The Chinese approach is a natural progression of the various formulations that we have seen thus far from ancient times through the cold war and to the present day global scenario. What is of particular significance is the all pervasive nature of military power from the precision it provides to the National Power of a nation, to the abstract as a manifestation of the will to power.

The Study

The study undertaken to evaluate the role of the military's contribution to CNP began with the use of the Carver Delphi method to elicit the views of 150 middle and senior grade Indian and foreign military officers along with other scholars on what they considered to be the determinants of military capability. In order to arrive at an objective analysis each determinant was rated on a scale of 1 to10 as a relative integer for eight countries besides India. Fifteen determinants were initially identified as shown in Table1.

Table 1: Military Capability Average result of the Poll

Determinants	US	Germany	Japan	Russia	China	India	Indonesia	Brasil	South Africa
Institutions to Regenerate Military Thinkig	8.60	6.38	5.60	6.80	7.24	5.73	3.59	4.40	4.27
Defence Expenditure/ GDP	8.44	5.55	5.05	6.44	7.83	5.18	3.59	4.43	4.21
Ordinance Delivery	8.56	5.84	4.68	7.03	7.09	5.45	3.43	4.37	4.41
Defence R&D as % of Total R&D	8.52	6.16	5.15	6.78	7.16	4.43	2.91	4.25	4.39
% of Regular Forces employed in Internal Security Forces	5.29	4.85	4.75	5.35	5.44	5.53	4.56	4.63	4.52
State of Indigenisation of conventional	8.53	6.62	5.56	7.58	6.96	4.56	2.97	4.35	4.51
Expeditionary/ Transnational Capability as % of Defence Expenditure	8.55	5.94	4.74	6.76	6.46	5.05	3.09	3.90	4.07
Omniscience as % of Defence Expenditure	8.43	6.00	5.16	6.76	6.84	5.00	3.06	4.02	4.16
Networking as % of Defence Expenditure	8.44	6.43	5.71	6.25	6.57	4.77	3.00	4.01	4.18
Command Structure for Speed of Battle	8.56	6.63	5.52	6.94	6.82	5.50	3.52	4.33	4.35
Independent Defence of Space Assets or in Alliance	8.57	5.85	5.47	7.20	6.70	5.10	2.69	3.59	3.58
Civil Military Relations	8.02	0.86	6.25	6.48	6.66	5.32	4.03	5.14	5.04
Tactical Capability	8.24	6.34	5.38	7.02	7.30	6.63	3.96	4.61	4.71
Nuclear Capability	8.81	3.95	2.64	7.59	7.26	5.88	1.55	2.20	2.68
Arsend	8.81	3.76	2.24	7.75	7.19	5.28	1.61	2.27	260

Source: Based on the Carver Delphi Method. A USI Study, 2010.

The following paragraphs are devoted to providing an insight into each of the determinants for clarity of the subsequent arguments and to give them weightage on a relative scale for an aggregate of 1. Product of weightage with the poll results will give an indication of country standing in terms of 'perceived' military power:

(a) **Institutions to Regenerate Military Thinking**: In warfare as with most matters that affect human affairs, change is the only certainty. And change is driven by need, technology, the times, human vision and creativity. Planners' device strategies, lay down doctrines, evolve tactics and commandeer technologies in order to contend with and harness change so that the operational 'high ground' is not surrendered. In years gone by it was the humble stirrup that caused a revolution in the manner in which horsemen could free their arms and provide rapid mobility to the archer; much in the same way as information technology has today laid bare the battle space enabling precision assault of targets that yesterday were discrete and near invulnerable. The continuous regeneration of military thought is the only tool to anticipate, challenge and confront change. To institutionalize it provides the wherewithal to transform and come out with war winning strategies. In its absence the war is lost before the first salvo is fired. Barring the US military, this has been an area of conspicuous weakness with most military establishments. This is attributable to three factors; firstly most militaries are slow and uneasy with change, secondly the immediate economics of change can be forbidding and lastly training in the military is incestuous in form; unfortunately it thrives on yesterday's battles. (**Weightage awarded is 0.15**).

(b) **Defence Expenditure as a Percentage of GDP**: Defence expenditure and human resource development will remain key indices of a qualitative and quantitative measure of military capability as long as they are a part of integrated force planning. In our specific context the blindness to the indivisibility force, if not remedied, can only result in the frittering away of resources and fragmenting of force. In this circumstance integrated force planning attains critical proportions. Defence expenditure as a percentage of GDP in a democratic system such as ours is representative of national will to power; having said that this percentage in the vein of other major democratic powers maybe pegged in the region of 3-3.5% of GDP. Countries such as Indonesia which have turned their sights inwards have done so at the cost of there ability to have their will in global affairs. (**Weightage awarded is 0.033**, this is on the assumption that defence spending will be pegged at 3 to 3.5% of GDP).

(c) **Ordnance Delivery**: Delivery systems must at all times be cognizant of the impact technology has on the effectiveness of munitions over time. This is a truism that is plain to all defence planners. The problem arises with the pace at which technological interventions are available and the time compression that this feature enjoys. On the other side of the argument is the danger of chasing technology for its own sake which can result in economically wasteful expenditure. The key lies in determining what technologies will serve the interests of effectiveness over the life of the delivery system; for this precision technology forecast along with its adaptation should be an intrinsic part of the acquisition/developmental process keeping scope for upgradation through technology injections. The technologic aging of hardware in most countries including Japan, Brazil, Indonesia and South Africa is symptomatic of the growing economic burden of unplanned upgradation and an unwillingness to transform. (**Weightage awarded is 0.1**).

(d) **Defence R&D as a percentage of total R&D**: By nature R&D is a stand alone investment. It is the application of its fruits that may take various forms. The need is to continuously sponsor and promote basic research. This is a national endeavour and must not find itself curbed by viewing defence R&D as something different. Therefore investments in this field will remain a part of national planning. The essence lies in being able to build structures that extract, innovate and apply. To this end R&D forecasts and tasking should find expression in the defence planner's agenda. The problem is that fundamental research is not an area that works like other enterprises where you plough in money and you get returns. The US are leaders because they are willing and have the financial clout to invest without expecting returns for each investment. Paradoxically it is failures that often indicate resolve. To give some idea of the relative differences, the US budget for R&D is $148 billion of which $71B is allocated to pure defence R&D [18]. The second big investor is China at $36B (reported) while India is at about $9B. At $4.1B Brazil's approach is particularly significant for the success of its collaborative ventures (**Weightage awarded is 0.033**).

(e) **Percentage of Regular Forces Employed in Internal Security**: The Chinese in their formulation of the role of the military in CNP, as mentioned earlier, do not make any bones about its significant and abiding role in assuring internal security. While it maybe argued that this is natural to authoritarian states, it must also be said that it is equally relevant to emerging powers. The external dimension will remain hollow unless the internal is secured. Our calculus must at all times allow for this without it being made to seem as an 'add-on' extraneous and avoidable function. Resource planning in this field must factor the Internal Security facet. (**Weightage awarded is 0.05**).

(f) **State of Indigenisation of Conventional Forces**: In a globalised economy indigenization as a mantra would need to be retooled. While past experience has made us sensitive to sanctions, one would not fail to note that as the means of production move out of the boundaries of origin, the bite of sanctions have diminishing effect. There are, indeed, key areas of technology that must be identified and indigenization investments enhanced in those fields. After all, the object not being to reinvent the wheel but to boost our design, adaptation and innovation capability. The ubiquitous personal computer has components from practically all over the world put together by a second agency for wide spectrum application. The same would apply to components that would go into making ships, aircrafts and other vehicles. The US model is much too finance intensive; what perhaps presents an optimal compromise is the collaborative strategy adopted by China and Brazil. (**Weightage**

[18] Limpinen, Edward.AAS.org, 18 Mar 2010 and Info USA, US dept of state, 05 sep 2010.

awarded is 0.1).

(g) **Expeditionary/Transnational Capability as a Percentage of Defence Expenditure**: To have a military establishment out of sync with the larger strategic objectives of the nation is the surest recipe for a fall. Our interests today range from our oil commissions in Kamchatka through the Middle East to South America, our interests in Antarctica and the burgeoning trade with China would all demand a military capability to secure these interests either through cooperative ventures or individually. In this perspective we must witness a growing transnational force structuring. Many of these capabilities will have multi tasking competence. The growth of China's Navy is a case in point. (**Weightage awarded is 0.05**).

(h) **Omniscience as a Percentage of Defence Expenditure**: The contemporary global scenario is marked by the omnipresence of knowledge and it is the availability of this knowledge that makes for potency in every endeavour including the battlefield. To not just be aware of this but also to grasp and invest in omniscient (all knowing) structures is an imperative of the future. As our interests expand our transnational forces will find themselves handicapped unless this capability is intrinsic to their make up. (**Weightage awarded is 0.05**).

(i) **Networking as a Percentage of Defence Expenditure**: In an era where mass of the industrial age has been transformed through knowledge to precision in all activities; the enabler that has made it possible has been rapid networks that moved information from the gatherer to the warrior. Exceedingly the dependence on precision and shielded networks will be the nervous system of future battlefields. (**Weightage awarded is 0.05**).

(j) **Command Structure for Speed of Battle**: Flatter structures will be the order of the day. This would imply not just empowering our future leaders at every level with authorizations to act but also equipping them intellectually with the necessary material and knowledge base to come out winners. To this end our investments in training and preparing our officers and men would have to be enhanced. Also command structures would have to be sensitive and flexible enough to permit action at every level. (**Weightage awarded is 0.1**).

(k) **Independent Defence of Space Assets or In Alliance**: Space assets would be central to all networks, surveillance, targeting and knowledge denying activities. Their defence would therefore have to be through providing physical, electronic and force shields; a field which is new and would have to take the form of integrated space defence structures. (**Weightage awarded is 0.033**).

(l) **Civil Military Relations**: Traditionally in our context civil military relations has been an area of considerable weakness. This frailty is more on account of a refusal to accept that the larger aims of harnessing CNP are better served by having the military a part of and deeply involved with the decision making process that goes into providing security in all its dimensions to the nation. Till such time that institutionally and structurally it is accepted that the military is not only an explicit instrument of CNP but also an implicit statement of the nation's will to power, this frailty will remain a critical flaw. (**Weightage awarded is 0.1**).

(m) **Tactical Capability**: Hitherto prowess in the tactical field was an area of considerable strength of the Indian military establishment. However the future demands far more integration in planning, equipping and force structuring than is currently apparent. In India the absence of the CDS, squarely on account of the reluctance of individual service headquarters is a damning case in point. The future holds no place for tribal approaches and turf centric decision making. Transformation of individual tactical capability into a larger joint operational competence is the key. The strength of yesterday may well be the fatal failing of today if not remedied forthwith. (**Weightage awarded is 0.15** on the premise that transformational goals in India are addressed forthwith).

The last determinant is nuclear capability and the nuclear arsenal that the nation has stockpiled. The quandary that arises when dealing with nuclear weapons is that on the one hand is the absolute nature of destruction that they represent while on the other is that its efficacy lies in its non use; that is in the deterrent effect that it thrusts upon belligerents. This brings us to an interesting understanding of how nuclear weapons have in fact changed the nature of warfare and the dynamics that condition military confrontation between nations. In the nuclear age armed conflicts are largely predicated on the two faces of warfare, the primary face as defined by conventional forces and the shadow face as circumscribed by the nuclear forces. **Application of the former is an active art while the latter scripts the perimeter and imposes cut offs. It is this distinctive ability of nuclear forces to lay down limits to the conventional war that gives it weight when computing national power.** It is also for the same reason that in our study we give this feature special attention.

Table 2 gives the relative standing of the nine countries listed in Table 1. Product of the poll average and weightage awarded for each determinant decides standing. In as much as the nuclear dimension is concerned it is, due to its special nature, dealt with separately and finds expression as a 'power limiter'.

Table 2:   Relative Standings

Determinants	US	Germany	Japan	Russia	China	India	Indonesia	Brasil	South Africa
Institutions to Regenerate Military Thinkig	1.29	0.96	0.84	1.02	1.09	0.86	0.54	0.66	0.64
Defence Expenditure/ GDP	6.29	0.19	0.17	0.22	0.27	0.18	0.12	0.15	0.14
Ordinance Delivery	0.86	0.58	0.47	0.70	0.71	0.55	0.34	0.44	0.44
Defence R&D as % of Total R&D	0.28	0.20	0.17	0.22	0.24	0.15	0.10	0.14	0.14
% of Regular Forces employed in Internal Security Forces	0.26	0.24	0.24	0.27	0.27	0.28	0.23	0.23	0.23
State of Indigenisation of conventional	0.85	0.66	0.56	0.76	0.70	0.46	0.30	0.44	0.45
Expeditionary/ Transnational Capability as % of Defence Expenditure	0.43	0.30	0.24	0.34	0.32	0.25	0.15	0.20	0.20
Omniscience as % of Defence Expenditure	0.42	0.30	0.26	0.34	0.34	0.25	0.15	0.20	0.21
Networking as % of Defence Expenditure	0.42	0.32	0.29	0.31	0.33	0.24	0.15	0.20	0.21
Command Structure for Speed of Battle	0.86	0.66	0.55	0.69	0.68	0.55	0.35	0.43	0.44
Independent Defence of Space Assets or in Alliance	0.28	0.19	0.18	0.24	0.22	0.17	0.09	0.12	0.12
Civil Military Relations	0.80	0.69	0.63	0.65	0.67	0.53	0.40	6.51	0.50
Tactical Capability	1.24	0.95	0.81	1.05	1.10	0.99	0.59	0.69	0.71
Standing	**8.28**	**0.25**	**5.39**	**6.81**	**6.92**	**5.45**	**3.52**	**4.41**	**4.43**
Ranking	**1**	**4**	**6**	**3**	**2**	**5**	**9**	**8**	**7**

Source: Author Sept 2010, Based on the Carver Delphi Method and standings based on empirical weighted mean . A USI Study, 2010.

Nuclear Capability and Arsenal

At first appraisal, nothing can appear more ludicrous than to approach the total power of a nation through the sights of an aimer armed with nuclear weapons. For if war is a continuation of politics by other means then, a weapon of total annihilation obliterates the very purpose of that polity and therefore must be an absurdity. Yet, nuclear weapons exist and nations have over time, evolved a theology that not only recognizes its influence on international relations but have granted it a certain grudging legitimacy as an ultimate currency of power and, as we have noted earlier, an agent that scripts the perimeters of conflict. Therefore, in the overall context of the role of "hard" power in CNP, not to factor nuclear forces would be to suspend ourselves in denial of its existence, influence and of technology.

Strategists have long developed a doctrine of rationality (which some may call the doctrine of the absurd) which breathes life to the implementation of a deterrent relationship between nations. This doctrine has only one purpose and that is to establish solidarity between all the elements of CNP. It is in the absence of such a theory that India, in its short independent history, has suffered an awkward fragmentation in strategic posture whether it was to contend with the Chinese in the past and in the present or in the immediate wake of 26/11. The theory of strategic deterrence begins with an understanding that sovereign leaders are rational and will always be willing to engage in "interest-benefit" calculations while making policy decisions. The assumption of rationality is considered universal in terms of context, challenges and responses. It is, indeed a labour in mirror imaging. It is this factor that removes strategic forces from the realm of abstraction and places it on the pedestal of reality.

Strategic nuclear forces, as mentioned earlier change the very nature of the application of power by scripting perimeters and drawing limits. There are five considerations related to strategic forces and their operationalising that have an impact on CNP. These are:

(a) Doctrine

(b) Credibility

(c) Vulnerability

(d) Command and Control

(e) Will and Resolve

Doctrine for strategic forces is its soul for it drives development, structure and nature of arsenal; it serves to develop deterrent relationships based on rationality. Its absence contributes negatively to CNP for one very good reason that is nations do not readily take to unpredictability or clandestine programmes. A declared doctrine provides the necessary strategic cohesion within and, more importantly, without. For having evolved and operationalised nuclear forces the absence of visible guiding principles for their command and control leaves the larger global community in a state of deep suspicion of both capability and intent. This brings with it a host of responses triggered by the uncertainty of not knowing ranging from economic sanctions to frosty relations to downright hostility; all of which in a globalised situation hurts acutely the development of national power.

Credibility is the key to operationalise doctrine, its value is largely determined by resolve, alternatives, readiness, reliability, technology and nature and survivability of the Arsenal. Credibility lies in the eyes of the beholder and its absence is a source of instability which casts a negative shadow on CNP. Credibility is to doctrine what the 'Emperors new clothes' were to that naïve child! The empty nakedness of words must be clad by all the elements listed above.

Vulnerability is the chief anxiety that invites technologies. It is minimized by providing options of vectors, locations, security of enabling codes and stealth. Vulnerability of an arsenal is again a source of instability with its negative impact on CNP.

Command and Control is central to nuclear deterrence. Its survivability and redundancy not only enhances credibility but will also avert the temptation of a decapitating strike. It provides a positive inflexion to CNP.

Will and resolve are essential features that reinforce the stability of a deterrent relationship. They must be backed by selective transparency with the aim of periodically exposing our will and assured security. Both factors add positively to CNP.

As long as our nuclear doctrine and its operationalising is sufficiently transparent; credibility of the arsenal assured and periodically emphasized; and the vulnerability of the arsenal minimized, nuclear forces will remain a factor that changes and limits the military application of power.

Effects of Determinants on Perceived Power – The Matrix

The matrix at Fig 2 is indicative of the effects of the determinants on perceived military power and provides cues as to how best it could be enhanced. The Ray Cline expression for perceived power has been adapted in order to develop the matrix. The grey wash is suggestive of the impact of credible nuclear forces to circumscribe the limits to which conventional power can be applied, the spread of the wash into the -X region would imply that under certain circumstances conventional military power may be totally inhibited, also when credibility of the deterrent breaks down or when doctrine abandons nuclear capability to a potential that does not translate to an operationalised arsenal then the limits imposed on conventional warfare are nonexistent.

In Clines equation, perceived power $(Pp) = (C + E + M) * (S + W)$, C and E are taken as positive constants; for in India's case, demography in terms of work age, technological grounding and geography (C) is positive till at least 2050; economic growth (E) is positive in the 8% - 9% range and is likely to remain in that region for the next decade or more. Strategic purpose (S) and the will of the people (W) are taken as 0.5 each, as may be appreciated, this is game changing factor which through soft means can alter the slope of the line a-b enhancing perceived power. The equation in this instance is linear and is represented by the line a-b. The point (a) is taken as the origin since even if military power due to obsolescence or technological anachronism is near zero, there remain the other elements of CNP that contribute to (Pp). At the same time a situation defined by point (d) is also possible when the internals of the country are in turmoil and obsolete hardware makes up military power (Indonesia in the 1970s). By increasing weightage of the determinants through investments the slope of a-b can be altered to enhance perceived power.

Fig. 2   Effects of Determinants on Military Power

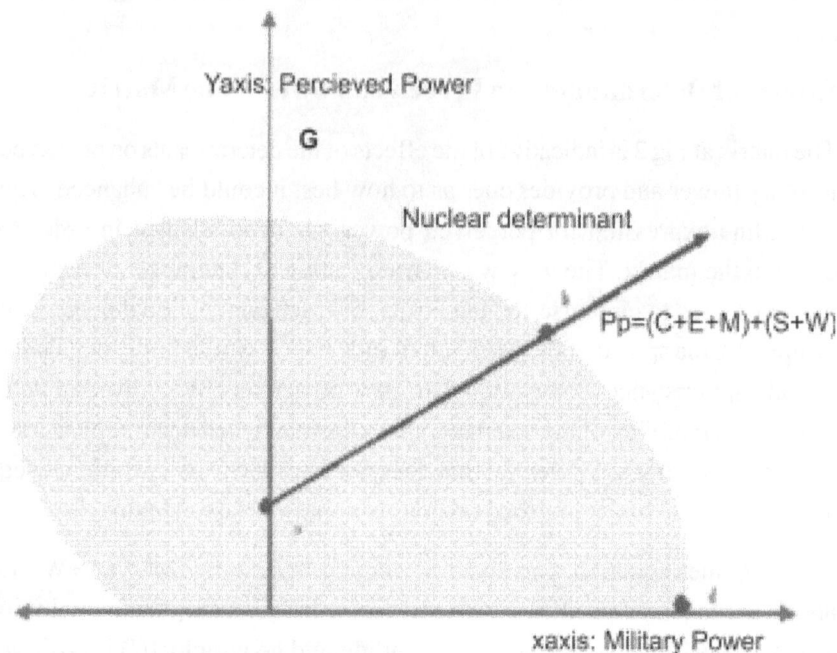

(Source: Author Sep 2010)

Note: We have adapted Ray Cline's equation of Perceived Power using weightages as applied in the previous section of this paper. These determinants are subject to the limits set by the nuclear determinant.

C & E are taken as constant positives, demography (C) in terms of work age and technical qualification is positive till at least 2050. Economic Growth (E) is positive in the 8% to 9% range.

M is the summation of the weightages while S and W are the intangibles represented by strategic purpose will of the people and resolve of leadership.

Conclusion

In the past, as peoples of the Indic civilization, we as a society were marginally troubled by the role that the military played in National Power. If our fate was ruled by our 'karma' or by providential laws then, that was as satisfactory as if there had been no such divine intervention; for we assumed that the future of mankind would be secured by the activities of free and intelligent people. If even this was not quite satisfactory, nature's law of inexorability took over. Unfortunately by the middle of the 20th century such convenient illusions were well and truly dispelled. Civilizations and empires had collapsed with increasingly rapid frequency and at times in violent storms, leaving in its wake broken ideologies, battered leadership and impoverished societies.

At the heart of the matter lay power. Its quest, accretion and relevance have been the only constant through all of history. It has provided a rationale for stability and, in its own right, been a regulatory agent. We have noted that given the international system that we are a part of and the realism that pervades it; of all the determinants of power, military muscle is explicit in its application and at the same time implicit as an expression of a country's will to power. An attempt has been made to place this abstraction within the larger framework of the nation's standing, or in Fukuyama's words the 'Stateness' of the country. While the task of the international system has been to tame the exercise of power, it is a paradox that the same power provides the facility to regulate and control its exercise. Nuclear power takes the debate to its logical extreme of absolute destruction and in arriving at this macabre conclusion it provides the basis of drawing boundaries and limiting conflicts.

We have in the course of our debate examined the views of several scholars on the subject and noted in some details the Chinese approach to the formulation of CNP and the manner in which they have transformed their centralized approach, which to some schools appear as a weakness, into strength. Decision making that is command and control and integration of our resources including civil military relations, technology adaptation and our propensity to operate in stove pipes are areas of weakness that we must remedy. Failing which our ability to rise beyond the tactical will remain an enduring impediment. The sage voice of Kautilya reminds us that the military power of a state is not just the mere counting of armed physicals, but also of 'mantra yuddha' the power of good policies, sound judgement, precision command, analysis and good counsel.

FOR A BETTER GOVERNED INDIA

Introduction

With the rapid pace of urbanisation, the percentage of India's population living in cities and urban areas has almost doubled to 27.8% in 2001 from 14% at the time of Independence. This is expected to accelerate even further, and by 2021 over 40% of Indians is expected to be living in urban areas. By 2012, Urban India will contribute over 68% to Indian GDP. Indian Cities provide settings as engines of economic growth, and at the same time face enormous challenges.

The quality of governance is an issue of increasing concern in countries around the world, both developed and developing. The UN Secretary-General has stated, "Good governance is perhaps the single most important factor in eradicating poverty and promoting development." However, a lack of systematic data, both over time within countries as well as between countries around the world, ensures that fundamental questions remain to be answered adequately. How can we best measure governance? How does governance performance differ across time and space? Which are the most critical issues of governance?

While there has been a growing realisation among some chief ministers on the need to improve governance, a few have already been able to translate this into concrete action. Some of the ways of improving governance are enumerated in the succeeding paragraphs.

Focus on Outcomes

At present, officials at all levels spend a great deal of time in collecting and submitting information, but this is not used for taking corrective and remedial action or for analysis, but only for forwarding it to a higher level, or for answering Parliament/assembly questions. Equally, state governments do not discourage reporting of inflated figures from the districts, which again renders monitoring ineffective. As data is often not verified or collected through independent sources, no action is taken against officers indulging in errant reporting. The practice is so widely prevalent in all the states that the overall percentage of malnourished children of 0-3 years, according to the data reaching the government from the field, is 8% (with only 1% children severely malnourished), against 46% (with 17% children severely malnourished) reported by an independent National Family Health Survey (NFHS-3) sponsored by the government. The field officials are thus able to escape from any sense of accountability for reducing malnutrition.

The situation can easily be corrected by asking the state governments to show greater transparency in district and central records by putting them on a website, and by frequent field inspections by an independent team of experts, nutritionists and grass roots workers. The Centre should also pull up the states for not recognizing almost 90% of the severely malnourished children.

Fiscal Transfers

Very little of the government transfers of roughly Rs 4 trillion (this amount does not include subsidies such as on food, kerosene and fertilizers) annually to the states is linked with performance and good delivery. The concept of good governance needs to be translated into a quantifiable annual index on the basis of certain agreed indicators, and Central transfers should be linked to such an index (it is informally learnt that the 13th Finance Commission has recommended giving additional funds to states that do well on certain indicators such as infant mortality rate, forest cover and so on).

Accountability

Departments such as the police and rural development, which have closer dealings with the people, should be assessed annually by an independent team consisting of professionals such as journalists, retired judges, academicians, activists, non-governmental organisations and even retired government servants. They should look at the departments' policies and performance, and suggest constructive steps for their improvement. At present, the system of inspections is elaborate, but often precludes the possibility of a "fresh look" as they are totally governmental and rigid. The system should be made more open so that the civil service can gain from the expertise of outsiders in the mode of donor agency evaluations of projects. It is heartening to note that the government has already started doing so for some of its flagship programmes such as in education and health. Petitions under the Right to Information Act have also empowered citizens, but its use is still dominated by civil servants on personnel issues of appointments and promotions.

Personnel Issues

Appointments and transfers are two well-known areas where the evolution of firm criteria can be easily circumvented in the name of administrative efficacy. Even if the fiscal climate does not allow a large number of new appointments, a game of musical chairs through transfers can always bring in huge rentals to corrupt officials and politicians. As tenures shrink, both efficiency and accountability suffer.

Several reforms are needed here. The powers of transferring all class II officers should be with the head of the department and not with the government. At least for higher ranks of the civil services, for example Chief Secretary and Director General of Police, postings may be made contractual for a fixed period of at least two years (as is being done in the government for secretaries in the ministries of home, defence and finance), and officers should be monetarily compensated if removed before the period of the contract expires without their consent or explanation.

A stability index should be calculated for important posts such as secretaries, deputy commissioners and district superintendents of police. An average of at least two years for each group should be fixed, so that even though the government would be free to transfer an officer before two years without calling for an explanation, the average must be maintained at above two years. (The government has accepted this suggestion, and has made changes in the IAS rules. However, the choice of posts for which this would be applicable has been left to the states. Predictably, no state has declared any post under the new rules.) This would mean that for every officer with a short tenure, someone else must have a sufficiently long tenure to maintain the average.

Conclusion

A good civil service is necessary, but not sufficient for good governance; a bad civil service is sufficient, but not necessary for bad governance. Thus, a dilapidated civil service has been a key factor in Africa's economic decline. Conversely, a strong civil service is one of several reasons why in several East Asian economies, especially Japan, Singapore and South Korea, authoritarianism has coexisted with excellent economic performance. It can be argued that the link between authoritarianism and economic decline, so evident in Africa, has been inoperative in these Asian countries largely because of their strong civil service. Greater responsiveness and openness can legitimately be demanded of public administrations in many East Asian countries. Clearly, civil service systems in most East Asian countries cannot be considered a problem; they are, rather, an important part of the solution to these countries' other problems.

Governance reforms are intractable under a "kleptocracy" that exploits national wealth for its own benefit and is, by definition, uninterested in transparency and accountability. A pliable and unskilled civil service is actually desirable from its point of view—public employees dependent on the regime's discretionary largesse are forced to become corrupt, cannot quit their jobs, and reluctantly become the regime's accomplices. Providing financial assistance from the government to such states without linking it with performance and reforms would be a waste of resources. In all other cases, reform is manageable, albeit difficult complex and slow. Therefore, considering that the states would need external pressure on them to improve outcomes, certain control by the government of India over IAS and policy domain in the social sector is necessary, till such time that the states show signs of improvement in governance.

Governance in India

Service Delivery in India

India is today one of the fastest growing economies of the World. However high growth achieved through private enterprise has not been translated into satisfactory progress on the public front, suggesting limited impact of government programmes. Delivery of public services requires financial resources, but more importantly the quality of expenditure and government-public interface in these areas must improve. It is not the size of allocations on pro-poor services alone that matters. Government of India transfers more than four lakh crore Rupees every year to the states. If even half of it was to be sent to the six crore poor families directly through a money order, they would receive more than 90 Rupees a day! Thus public expenditure needs to be effectively translated into public goods and services for it to have an impact on public satisfaction. Unfortunately different kinds of distortions can come in the way of resource allocations reaching the intended beneficiaries.

In most states, about 70% of all government employees are support staff unrelated to public service – drivers, peons and clerks. A highly feudal culture of hierarchies detrimental to clear lines of accountability or effective decision-making prevails. Key public services – education, healthcare, police and judiciary are starved of people, whereas many wings are overstaffed. Even when employees are deployed in productive sectors, their productivity is low and accountability is weak. The prevalent rent-seeking behaviour makes most basic services inaccessible to the poor and marginalized sections.

More often than not, weak governance, manifesting itself in poor service delivery, high cost, and uncoordinated and wasteful public expenditure, is one of the key factors impinging on development and social indicators. For instance, teachers need to be present and effective at their jobs, just as doctors and nurses need to provide the care that patients need. But they are often mired in a system where the incentives for effective service delivery are weak, and political patronage is a way of life. Highly trained doctors seldom wish to serve in remote rural areas. Since those who do serve are rarely monitored, the penalties for not being at work are low. Even when present, they treat poor people badly.

Democratic Politics and Bureaucracy

In a well-functioning democracy, the political process would ideally find answers to governance problems. To be fair to the modern brand of politicians, and balance our analysis on the issue of politicians' vs civil servants, it must be admitted that except for high integrity, neutrality towards party politics, and provision of minimal administrative services in times of emergency, the senior civil service even in the past had on occasions little to commend for itself.

A discussion on political and electoral reforms (restriction on the number of ministers and ban on criminals fighting elections through law could be a good beginning), though absolutely vital, is outside the scope of this paper. Good governance is undermined by lack of transparency, weak accountability, poor organizational and technical capacity, lack of responsiveness, inefficiency and poor motivation. These are the areas where civil servants have to take initiative. Some of the ways it can be done is described below.

Improving Transparency and Accountability

Transparency builds external demand for reform and makes administration more responsive and performance oriented. As an experiment, all muster rolls in employment schemes should be put on the internet in at least one block of a district where internet facilities exist. The Official Secrets Act should be repealed and replaced with a less restrictive law. Property and tax returns of all senior officers and politicians should be available for scrutiny by the public. Land records should be made available on-line through a web-site.

'Outward accountability' is essential for greater responsiveness to the needs of the public and thus to improve service quality, and prevent bogus and inflated reporting. Departments such as the Police and Revenue, which have more dealings with the people, should be assessed once in three years by an independent Commission, consisting of professionals such as journalists, retired judges, academicians, activists, NGOs, and even retired government servants. These should look at their policies and performance, and suggest constructive steps for their improvement. At present the systems of inspection are elaborate but often preclude the possibility of a 'fresh look' as they are totally governmental and rigid. The system should be made more open so that the civil service can gain from the expertise of outsiders in the mode of donor agency evaluations of projects.

Making the Civil Service E-governance Friendly

There are several reasons why e-governance should figure prominently in any programme of administrative reform and modernisation. First and foremost, technologies have advanced rapidly and cost effectively in recent years to bring e-governance applications within the reach of governments. Second, these applications are easier to implement today than many other types of administrative reforms. A lot of experience has now been gained with respect to their introduction. Technology can inject greater transparency, discipline in terms of deadlines, systematic monitoring, and security of data that standard administrative systems are unable to enforce. Third, they can make the citizen- state interface much easier, reducing transaction costs and public dissatisfaction. Finally, e-governance is less threatening to those in authority in contrast to some of the complex administrative reforms that have remained dormant in official reports. An e-governance application may look simple and limited in scope, yet it may have far reaching implications for the operating culture and performance of governments.

Conventional administrative reforms in India have had a mixed record for several reasons. A major problem is in mobilizing the kind of political and administrative will necessary to implement them. It could also be that people are not certain about the final outcome of some of these reforms. As a result, many ambitious reforms are proposed in official reports that are seldom acted on. Much time and money are wasted on exercises that produce no impact on the ground. Today, technology can be used to bypass these barriers, using a low key approach that need not be so threatening to many interest groups. We need not therefore wait till complex administrative reforms are accomplished to tap the potential that technology has to offer. E-governance applications are a good example of how the discipline of information and communication technologies could be used to compensate for the inherent difficulties in implementing organization intensive administrative reforms. They could in fact be used as short cuts to demonstrate "quick wins" while the ground is being prepared for the more difficult administrative reforms.

What are the expectations from e-governance? What has this approach achieved elsewhere? Developed countries are at the forefront in e-governance applications. They have used new technologies to streamline and speed up their interactions with and services to the public in almost all sectors of activity. They have also used IT in a big way in improving the internal management of their systems with respect to funds, personnel and assets (internal housekeeping). Based on this experience, the benefits of e-governance can be summarized as follows:

(a) It improves government's overall productivity.

(b) It promotes greater transparency and public accountability.

(c) It simplifies and speeds up the delivery of a wide range of public services.

(d) It improves service quality and thus increases citizen satisfaction

(e) It aids dissemination of information and thus empowers people.

Shift from Input Controls to Monitoring of Outcomes

Officials at all levels spend a great deal of time in collecting and submitting information, but these are not used for taking corrective and remedial action or for analysis, but only for forwarding it to a higher level, or for answering Parliament/ Assembly Questions. Often data on performance reaches late, or is not available district-wise, with the result that accountability cannot be fixed. On the other hand, state governments do not discourage reporting of inflated figures from the districts, which again renders monitoring ineffective. As data is often not verified or collected through independent sources, no action is taken against officers indulging in bogus reporting. For instance, in UP the number of fully immunized children that was being reported by the state government a few years back was almost cent percent, though the evaluated figure is less than 30 per cent. It is not enough that the central government departments and the state governments use professional and academic organisations to undertake impact studies from time to time. Their findings must be publicised and discussed with key stakeholders so that improvements in design and delivery can be effected at the earliest. Governments should also put on its website findings of the impact studies, and distribute these in the workshops it organizes. Dissemination of results is critical for use.

Assess Quality

There are unfortunately no indicators for assessing the quality of programme outcomes. GOI and civil society may like to fill this void and produce reports that assess the quality of outcomes. For instance, one would like to know how many newly constructed toilets are being used, and what impact has it had on peoples' health and hygiene. The district administration is not held responsible for poor utilisation, because information is collected on construction, but not on usage.

Measure Satisfaction

If the objective is to increase public satisfaction, one must begin by measuring it over a period of time. Even when people have physical access to a service (school, PHC), they are largely dissatisfied with its quality. In Bangalore the satisfaction from public hospitals improved from 25 to 34 percent between 1994-99, but jumped to 78 per cent in 2003 due to frequent measurement of public satisfaction. This highlights the importance of regular information flows.

The system of information flows in government does not report on satisfaction. For instance, data on drinking water reports the number of taps and villages covered, but not the quantity, quality and availability of water distributed. An all-India survey by Public Affairs Committee, a professional organisation based at Bangalore, revealed a big gap between access and satisfaction in rural India with government services, as shown below.

Access and Satisfaction in rural India

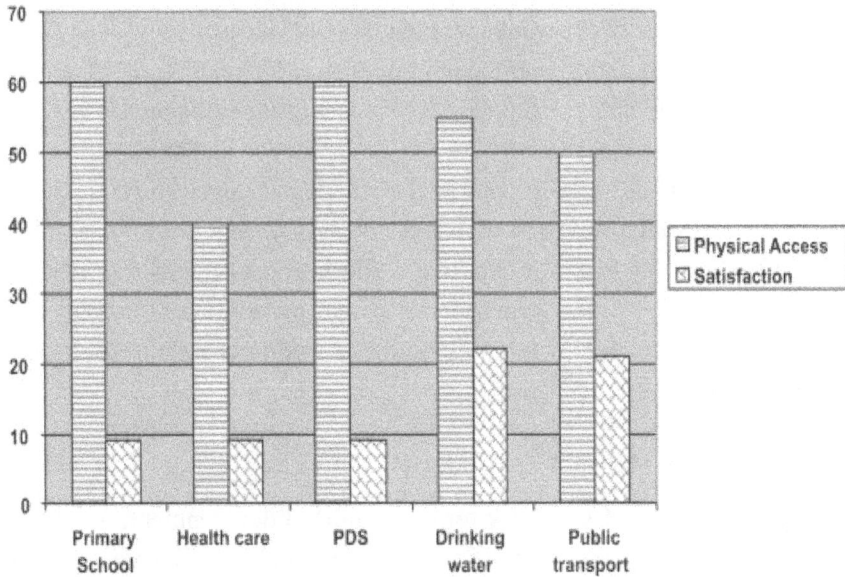

Measure Absenteeism

While satisfaction may be subjective, and with economic progress people's aspirations for high quality services may have increased, quantitative data on absenteeism of both service providers and service receivers (students in classrooms, or women turning up for institutional deliveries) throws a great deal of light on the quality of service. Pratham, a voluntary organisation, has evolved a simple test in education which judges the extent of learning in primary schools. Such results should be widely disseminated.

Promoting Public Private Partnership

The role of private sector in social sector is not sufficiently recognised in India. For instance, most health care is now given in the private sector and, for the poor, by very poorly or untrained practitioners. Rather than trying to replace private services, the Government should try to improve the private market, with the carrot of training and the stick of public information. Public funds should be reallocated to combating communicable diseases.

The PHCs account for less than 5 percent of deliveries in many states and provide full ante-natal care to less than a quarter of pregnant women. It may be worthwhile to experiment contracting out PHCs to civil society and private sector. Although government is responsible for health care outcomes, it does not need to deliver all public health care through the public system. Governments must distinguish between public funded and public provided health care. In many cases it is more efficient to have government purchase health care from the private sector. India has several successful examples of contracting out PHCs in Andhra Pradesh and to a lesser extent in Karnataka. Both models illustrate what can be achieved through the contracting model while both pilots have great room for improvement and potential scale-up.

Accountability Through Panchayats

Though providing a framework for decentralized development, trends so far suggest that the panchayati raj and the municipal system have not been able to enhance participation and empowerment. Despite the fact that some village level panchayat leaders have done commendable work, on the whole the PRIs have not benefited the people to the extent of funds provided by government.

The control which is exercised by the Block level officials over the village panchayats and gram sabhas (which rarely meet) has not only buttressed corruption and diluted accountability, but it has also led to pessimism that villagers at their own level cannot change and improve performance. Today PRIs are not yet 3rd tier of the government, but an extension of the 2nd tier. They are not functioning as institutions of self-governance, but only as agencies for executing a few programs of the state government/GoI.

PRIs at the intermediate and district level and their processes appear opaque and distant to the common person. Many important decisions related to identification of beneficiaries under various schemes, handling of funds, accounting and documentation are finalised out of sight of the ordinary person. Details of several important provisions and schemes remain unknown and unpublicised. The role and powers of government officials in PRI related processes is very complex, and known to only a few persons in each community.

The elected members of the PRIs at the block and district level behave more or less as contractors, with no institution of the gram sabhas at that level to put moral pressure on them. ZP and panchayat samiti members look upon devolved funds as equivalent to MP or MLA quota funds, and the Adhyakhsha and the block President have been coerced to distribute these funds equally between all members. They in turn choose the contractor and the nature of schemes. Obviously schemes that offer maximum commission and least risk of verification (such as earth work, which of course is done by machines but shown to be performed by fake labourers) are preferred. It may not be a bad idea to abolish one of the two tiers, district or block, if any state so desires.

Panchayats are mostly busy implementing construction oriented schemes, which promote contractor - wage labour relationship. These do not require participation of the poor as equals, on the other hand these foster dependency of the poor on Sarpanch and block staff. In such a situation panchayat activities get reduced to collusion between Sarpanch and block engineers. Panchayats are not active in education, health, SHGs, watershed, nutrition, pastures and forestry programs, which require people to come together as equals and work through consensus.

However, it does not mean that panchayats or other peoples' organisations have no potential. In fact their capability for achieving transparency, participation, inclusion and ownership can be enhanced by introducing some important reforms discussed below.

Suggested Reforms

Local collection of taxes - Rather than receiving a share in taxes and Central grants the panchayats should have the right to levy and collect taxes on their own in order to reduce their dependence on state and central governments. Today the PRIs hesitate to levy and collect taxes, as they prefer the soft option of receiving grants from GOI. This must be discouraged and the local bodies be encouraged to raise local resources for development and then receive matching grants from the Centre/States. The more dependent a PRI is on the mass of its citizens for financial resources, the more likely it is to use scarce material resources to promote human development and reduce poverty. External funds with no commitment to raise internal funds make PRIs irresponsible and corrupt.

There is an urgent need to transfer the task/function of levying of taxes to local bodies. One should collection of taxes collectable from within the geographical spread of the local bodies like the land revenue, irrigation cess etc unlike those from outside the area such as Octroi. Panchayats should not only collect taxes on land, irrigation drinking water, power, and houses, but also be given the authority to levy taxes on politically unpopular subjects such as agricultural income tax on large holdings.

Untied grants – In addition, panchayats would need a share in state and central revenues. States need to increase the share of transfers to PRIs from state governments as untied grants The formula of transfer should no doubt give weightage to population and poverty, but also to efficiency, so that there is incentive to them for increasing the sources of own revenues of PRIs through own and assigned taxes and increasing their capacity to collect. State grants should be given to them only when the PRIs are able to collect a minimum percentage of the taxes assigned to them.

Rank panchayats - Through a carefully designed methodology, it is quite possible to measure the performance of panchayats, and to what extent they are inclusive and participative.

Connecting the three tiers - There ought to be a system of representation of Gram Panchayat Presidents in the Taluka Panchayat with direct election of Taluka Panchayat President. A similar system ought to be in place for the Zilla Panchayats too.

Do we really require three tiers? In most states one of these two tiers is weak, district unit is weak in Tamil Nadu and Rajasthan, whereas the block unit is weak in Maharashtra and Gujarat. Some people have suggested that the states should be given the option of doing away with one of the levels, in case they so desire. Its implication for efficiency, equity and participation should be studied.

Linking MLAs with block panchayats - There is a nebulous domain of executive powers into which MPs, MLAs, and the PRIs all foray, each one working in this space by legitimate or illegitimate means. Back seat driving promotes irresponsible decision making and encourages corruption. Therefore why not legitimize the power for the MLAs and make them block (taluk panchayat) president by making their constituency co-terminus with the Panchayat Samiti/Taluka Panchayat? By giving a role to MLAs in the panchayat system, one would make them strong supporters of delegation of functions and funds to the panchayats. To hold that the directly elected MLA is wily, corrupt, and irresponsible, while the indirectly elected Adhyaksha or Taluk President can be trusted with crores, is honest, and committed to public welfare is neither good theory, nor is empirical valid.

CBOs and PRIs - The institutional links between political decentralisation, in the form of Panchayati Raj (PRIs), and administrative decentralisation, in the form of user committees promoted by the central Ministries needs to be strengthened. Linkages between these two institutions will also reinforce the voice of the weaker sections of the society.

Lastly, effective panchayats/user groups would also require effective district and block level administration. Hence efforts towards better accountability and performance from local bureaucracy should go simultaneously along with building local PRI capabilities, otherwise the elected PRI leaders would not change their perception of the state being an 'open treasury'.

Respecting Civil Society's Autonomy

Despite the enormous burden posed by mal-governance, civil society action has been weak. This could be a reflection on the general state of civil society in the country and its priorities, but largely it is because government has unwittingly promoted bogus or pliable organisations, and has either ignored or has hostile relations with those NGOs that wish to speak for the poor and empower them. There are organisations that have sprung up in the last two decades for self-aggrandisement, and for the sake of easy money.

It must be recognized that improvement in governance would take place only when countervailing forces in society develop confidence and autonomy to oppose inefficiency and corruption in government. Therefore in addition to promoting genuine organizations, the Home Ministry should relax FCRA provisions so that NGOs have access to independent funding.

A vibrant civil society movement towards participatory governance would itself create a demand for better services from the people, thus putting pressure on politics to move away from non-issues or sectarian gains to take more interest in the real livelihood issues of the people. Therefore governments must involve professional organizations in monitoring of programmes and dissemination of information to the stakeholders, so as to increase their sense of ownership and strengthen participatory democracy. Civil society should also take up sustained work among the poor and marginalised people, especially in the rural areas for increasing their awareness and for putting pressure on the panchayats/municipalities and making them accountable.

Role of GoI

In the Indian situation (where foreign donors provide very little aid to the states as compared with what is provided by the Centre) self-correction in administration can come only from the Centre, backed by strong civil society action. The GoI must, at the very least, do the following:-

(a) Improve incentive mechanism by linking fund transfer with performance

(b) Improve monitoring mechanisms so that authentic information is available to planners about the quality of implementation for all important schemes

(c) Amend the All India Services Rules to control the flourishing transfer industry in the states

The concept of good governance needs to be translated into a quantifiable annual index on the basis of certain agreed indicators such as infant mortality rate, extent of immunisation, literacy rate for women, child sex ratio, feeding programmes for children, availability of safe drinking water supply, electrification of rural households, rural and urban unemployment, percentage of girls married below 18 years, percentage of villages not connected by all weather roads, number of class I government officials prosecuted and convicted for corruption, and so on. Some universally accepted criteria for good budgetary practices may also be included in the index. Once these figures are publicized states may get into a competitive mode towards improving their score. Central transfers should be linked to such an index.

Conclusion

Development is an outcome of efficient institutions rather than the other way around. Focus therefore must be shifted from maximising the quantity of development funding to maximising of development outcomes and effectiveness of public service delivery. Despite good achievement on the growth front, India faces significant challenges and needs to take some difficult political decisions. Concerted policy action is needed to lift the 250 million poor, and increasingly concentrated in the poorer states, out of poverty. This requires not so much additional resources, as better participation of stakeholders and sound delivery mechanisms. This requires improving the environment in which the three agencies of delivery - civil service, panchayats and NGOs – function, as described in this paper.

Reforming the IAS

According to a survey[1] on 12 Asian economies done by the Hong Kong based Political and Economic Risk Consultancy, India's bureaucracy was ranked[2] the least-efficient, and working with the country's civil servants was described as a slow process. India's own Second Administrative Reforms Commission is no less scathing in its criticism: The state apparatus is generally perceived to be inefficient. Corruption is all-pervasive, eating into the vitals of our system, undermining economic growth, distorting competition and disproportionately hurting the poor and marginalized citizens. Criminalization of politics continues to exist, with money and muscle power playing a large role in elections. In general there is a high degree of volatility in society on account of unfulfilled expectations and poor delivery. Abuse of authority has become the bane of the democratic system.'

The poor shape of India's bureaucracy has also resulted in indifferent progress on the Millennium Development Goals. High growth notwithstanding, India seems to have failed on two fronts. First, social indicators on health, nutrition, hygiene, and quality of education are either stagnant or moving very slowly. And secondly, a large number of marginalised and disadvantaged people have either not gained from development, or in many cases have actually been harmed from the process. Weak governance, manifesting itself in poor service delivery, uncaring leadership, and uncoordinated and wasteful public expenditure, are the key factors impinging on development and social indicators.

---

[1] Times of India, 3rd June 2009

[2] Ranking by most efficient to least efficient economies: Singapore, Hong Kong, Thailand, South Korea, Japan, Malaysia, Taiwan, Vietnam, China, Philippines, Indonesia and India.

Political Compulsions and Bureaucracy

In a well-functioning democracy, the political process would ideally find answers to governance problems. Political pressure can be healthy if it results in greater demand on administration for efficiency and better services to the people. Pressures properly regulated and wisely tempered, improve the spirit of administration and help to keep it on an even keel, but this is not happening in India.

The state resources are the most valued prize for both politicians and their constituencies, which leads to a client patron relationship between the holders of state power and those seeking favours. Patronage is controlled by individuals, not established institutions bound to follow set procedures. Where power is highly personalised and weakly institutionalised, the decision making process is replaced by arbitrary and behind-the-scene transactions.

Impact on the IAS

A young IAS officer from Bihar described[3] the predicament of honest officers in the following terms:- 'As Project Director (PD) I was handling rural development funds and it was often a problem to release money to the sub-district Blocks and Panchayats (elected village councils). This was so because the Block Development Officer (BDO) or the Mukhia (elected panchayat president) would immediately take up 'n' number of schemes and distribute the total money as advance to either his own relatives who act as agents or Abhikartas (Junior Engineers) in employment schemes or the muscle men or petty contractors of the local MLA. If any action is proposed against the BDO or the Mukhia a report has to be sent to the Minister who often does not take any action. This further emboldens the BDO while the Collector/ PD gets demoralised.

Involvement in partisan politics is understandable, though unfortunate, because between expression of the will of the State (represented by politicians) and the execution of that will (through the administrators) there cannot be any long term dichotomy. In other words, a model in which politicians would be casteist, corrupt and will harbour criminals, whereas

---

[3] Planning Commission, 2000, Mid Term appraisal of the 9th Plan, Govt of India

civil servants will continue to be efficient, responsive to public needs and change-agents cannot be sustained indefinitely. In the long run administrative and political values have to coincide.

While defending the continuation of the all India Services, Sardar Patel had said, "they are as good as we are". At that time it was taken as a compliment that the civil service was being compared with statesmen who had won freedom for the country. One does not know how many civil servants will like to be told today that they are like politicians.

Internal Problems within the IAS

Lack of Professionalism

A high degree of professionalism ought to be the dominant characteristic of a modern bureaucracy.

Creation of Redundant Posts

Often a senior post has required to be split, thus diluting and diminishing the scale of responsibilities attached with the post. For instance, in some states against the post of one Chief Secretary, there are many officers now in equivalent but far less important posts drawing the same salary. In one state, previously where one officer used to be the Secretary of Medical and Health, now there are five officers doing the job of one, four are in-charge of health, family planning, medical, and medical education respectively, whereas the fifth one as Principal Secretary oversees the work of these four Secretaries.

This has apparently been done to avoid demoralisation due to stagnation, but the net result has been just the opposite.

Structure of Reward and Punishment

It may be recalled that even in the 1970's the officers exerted pressure on the system to move to what they thought were more glamorous positions. Some decades back, when "useless" posts were almost non-existent, an informal hierarchy of jobs had existed. The Secretary Industries, as also every one else, thought that he was holding a more important job than the Secretary Social Welfare although they drew the same salary. A collector of a large district felt humiliated if he was transferred as Director of Tribal Development.

The difference between then and now is that previously civil servants had clear ideas about the type of behaviour that would be rewarded or punished; furthermore, control over that, and judgment about it, was in the hands of the civil service itself.

Poor Service Delivery

To be fair to the modern brand of politicians, it must be admitted that except for high integrity, neutrality towards party politics, and provision of minimal administrative services in times of emergency, the civil service even in the past had little to commend for itself. No chief minister seems to be saying to his constituents: 'within three months all canals would run on time, you would get 10 hours of electricity, rations would be available for the poor, you apply for a license today and within a month it would reach your doors, your grievances will be promptly attended to, etc.' One reason why he does not say so is the total lack of faith on the part of voters in such promises which need delivery through the administrative apparatus. Ministers too are conscious of the limitations of the system, and realize that such promises cannot be delivered.

Although many civil servants hold the view that it is the nature of politics which largely determines the nature of the civil service and the ends to which it would be put, and therefore civil service reforms cannot succeed in isolation, causation is also in the other direction. A few competent and ambitious civil servants would be able to rise above all this, by joining the UN and other such organisations. Their material success will further fuel the desire of the ordinary members of the service to enrich themselves by hook or by crook. In the process they would become totally indistinguishable from other rent seeking parasites - politicians, Inspectors and middlemen. Perhaps they had not imagined that they would end up like this at the time of joining the service. Stagnation in their intellectual capabilities and a decline in self-esteem will further demoralise them.

How to Stem the Rot

Government of India transferred almost four trillion Rupees in 2008-09 to the states. If even half of it was to be sent to the sixty million poor families (at 28% as the cutoff line for poverty, 300 million poor would be equivalent to roughly 60 million households) directly by money order, they would receive more than 90 Rupees a day! It proves that public expenditure needs to be effectively translated into public goods and services that reach the poor for it to have an impact on poverty and social outcomes. Unfortunately different kinds of distortions can come in the way of resource allocations reaching the intended beneficiaries.

Although there has been a growing realisation among some chief ministers on the need to improve governance, only a few have been able to translate this into concrete action. This would necessarily involve keeping the MLAs and Ministers under check, which is difficult when the state is under a coalition regime, or the ruling party is constrained by a thin margin in the Assembly, or is divided into factions. In many other states even Chief Ministers seem to be averse to professionalizing administration.

When neither politics nor state administration has the capacity for self-correction, only external pressure can coerce states to take hard decisions that will hit at their money making tactics. In the Indian situation (where foreign donors provide very little aid to the states as compared with what is provided by the Centre) this can come only from the Centre, backed by strong civil society and media action.

Conditions under which the civil servants operate in the social sector Ministries in Government of India (GOI) are somewhat different from the work environment prevailing in the states. First, the central government Joint Secretary does not control field staff and is therefore free from the pressures of transfers and postings. Second, his/her tenure in GOI is for five years, which facilitates growth of professionalism. In the states, when officers fear that they would be transferred within six months there is hardly any incentive to perform. Third, central government officials are more in touch with experts, donors and specialists, and therefore are under peer group pressure to learn their subject and be able to converse with the specialists on equal terms. In some cases, where GOI Ministries (such as in

Education and lately in Health) have started behaving like donors and make states be answerable for results, results in the field are more satisfactory than in the Ministries, such as Tribal Affairs, Food & Civil Supplies, and Women & Child Development, where they are content with just release of funds or foodgrain with little monitoring of outcomes.

Therefore the enhanced control by the Centre on social sector expenditure should provide a window of opportunity to put some pressure on the states to improve their administration and service delivery. Some of the ways it can be achieved are discussed below.

Focus on Outcomes

At present officials at all levels spend a great deal of time in collecting and submitting information, but these are not used for taking corrective and remedial action or for analysis, but only for forwarding it to a higher level, or for answering Parliament/ Assembly Questions. Equally, state governments do not discourage reporting of inflated figures from the districts, which again renders monitoring ineffective. As data is often not verified or collected through independent sources, no action is taken against officers indulging in bogus reporting.

Fiscal Transfers

Very little of the GOI transfer of roughly Rs 4 trillion Rupees (this amount does not include subsidies, such as on food, kerosene, and fertilizers) annually to the states is linked with performance and good delivery. The concept of good governance needs to be translated into a quantifiable annual index on the basis of certain agreed indicators, and central transfers should be linked to such an index[4].

Accountability

As a consequence of its colonial heritage as well as the hierarchical social system administrative accountability in India was always internal and upwards, and the civil service's accountability to the public had been very

---

[4] It is informally learnt that the 13th Finance Commission has recommended giving additional funds to states who do well on certain indicators, such as IMR, forest cover, etc. This would be a good beginning, if the suggestion is accepted by GOI.

limited. With politicisation and declining discipline, internal accountability stands seriously eroded, while accountability via legislative review and the legal system has not been sufficiently effective.

'Outward accountability', therefore, is essential for greater responsiveness to the needs of the public and thus to improve service quality. Departments such as the Police and Rural Development, which have more dealings with the people, should be assessed annually by an independent team consisting of professionals such as journalists, retired judges, academicians, activists, NGOs, and even retired government servants. These should look at their policies and performance, and suggest constructive steps for their improvement. At present the system of inspections is elaborate but often precludes the possibility of a 'fresh look' as they are totally governmental and rigid. The system should be made more open so that the civil service can gain from the expertise of outsiders in the mode of donor agency evaluations of projects. It is heartening to note that GOI has already started doing so for some of its flagship programmes, such as in education and health. Petitions under the Right to Information Act (RTI) have also empowered citizens, but its use is still dominated by civil servants on personnel issues of appointments and promotions.

Priorities for enhancing both internal and external civil service accountability should include: improved information systems and accountability for inputs; better audit; face-to-face meetings with consumers and user groups; publishing budget summaries in a form accessible to the public; a stronger performance evaluation system; scrutiny and active use of quarterly and annual reports; and selective use of contractual appointments.

One way to bring in accountability is to start the system of holding public hearings in matters pertaining to the works handled by each office. Prominent social workers and NGOs should be associated with this exercise for more productive results. The teams would undertake surveys of quality of service delivery in key areas; scrutinize policies, programmes and delivery mechanisms. Civil servant's views on work constraints and reporting fraud and corruption should be elicited. The reviews conducted should also form the basis of time bound changes and improvements which should be monitored.

Needless to say that such comprehensive reforms need for their sustenance strong political and administrative will from the top. In its absence, reforms remain only on paper. Accountability has to be induced; it cannot be decreed by fiat. Accountability is a result of a complex set of incentives, transparency in processes and decision making, and checks and balances at various levels of government. Thus, the Prime Minister and his senior colleagues IAS in GOI have to put their weight behind new accountability systems and review it from time to time.

Personnel Issues

Appointments and transfers are two well-known areas where the evolution of firm criteria can be easily circumvented in the name of administrative efficacy. Even if the fiscal climate does not allow large numbers of new appointments, a game of musical chairs through transfers can always bring in huge rentals to corrupt officials and politicians. As tenures shorten both efficiency and accountability suffer. In U.P., the average tenure of an IAS officer in the last five years is said to be as low as four months!

The topic of reducing political interference is a sensitive one, for the right to transfer government servants is clearly vested within the political leadership of the States under Article 310 of the Indian Constitution, which maintains that civil servants serve at the "pleasure" of the ruling authorities. Yet few would disagree that this power is often abused by both government servants and politicians — the former in seeking prime postings, and the latter for making civil service pliable. The prime concern of the political executive now is not to make policies but to manage jobs and favourable postings for their constituents. This means a high degree of centralisation at the level of the state government and little accountability.

Several reforms are needed here. Powers of transfers of all class II officers should be with Head of the Department, and not with government. At least for higher ranks of the civil services e.g. Chief Secretary and the Police Chief, postings may be made contractual for a fixed period of at least two years (as is being done in GOI for Secretaries in the Ministries of Home, Defence, and Finance), and officers be monetarily compensated if removed before the period of the contract without their consent or explanation.

Stability index should be calculated for important posts, such as Secretaries, Deputy Commissioners, and District Superintendent of Police. An average of at least two years for each group be fixed, so that although government would be free to transfer an officer before two years without calling for his explanation, the average must be maintained above two years[5]. This would mean that for every short tenure some one else must have a sufficiently long tenure to maintain the average.

At the same time it must be recognized that some posts would have more attraction for the employees than others. These may be due to better location where good schools or cheap government housing is available, more challenges, the pull of private practice for doctors, or simply more opportunities to make money. Except for the Indian Foreign Service, no other service categorises posts according to its demand so as to ensure that everyone gets a fair chance to serve on both important and difficult (such as in remote and tribal areas) assignments. One should categorise posts in each department according to the nature of duties and geographical location into A, B and C posts, and chart out the kind of mix that should dictate the average officer's span of career. At least for IAS officers, one should be able to know through websites that total transparency is being observed and whether some 'well connected' officials have not been able to get 'plum' postings and avoid difficult areas.

Conclusion

A strong civil service is one of several reasons why in several East Asian economies, authoritarianism has co-existed with excellent economic performance. It can be argued that the link between authoritarianism and economic decline, so evident in Africa, has been inoperative in many Asian countries largely because of their strong civil service. Greater responsiveness and openness can legitimately be demanded of public administrations in

---

[5] GOI has accepted this suggestion, and has made changes in the IAS Rules, however the choice of posts for which this would be applicable has been left to the states. Predictably, no state has declared any post under the new Rules.

many East Asian countries. Clearly, civil service systems in most East Asian countries cannot be considered a problem; they are, rather, an important part of the solution to these countries' other problems.

The situation in many Indian states that are responsible for achieving the Millennium Development Goals is different. A vast gap exists between the stated and unstated objectives. On paper the avowed objective of government is to give clean administration and work for the poor, but lucrative posts are auctioned to the highest bidder. Corruption is rampant. People have unfortunately accepted the position as *fait accompli* and resigned themselves to their fate. They too tend to seek short cuts and exploit the system by breaking rules or approaching mafia gangs and politicians for favours.

A pliable and unskilled civil service is actually desirable from its point of view—public employees dependent on the regime's discretionary largesse are forced to become corrupt, cannot quit their jobs, and reluctantly become the regime's accomplices. Providing financial assistance from GOI to such states without linking it with performance and reforms would be a waste of resources. In all other cases, reform is manageable, albeit difficult, complex, and slow. Therefore, considering that the states would need external pressure on them to improve outcomes, certain control by GOI over the IAS and policy domain in social sector is necessary, till such time that the states show signs of improvement in governance.

Police Reforms in India – A Historical Perspective

The police organisation in India in its present form is based essentially on the Police Act of 1861, which was legislated "to re-organise the police and to make it a more efficient instrument for the prevention and detection of crime". It constituted a single homogenous force of civil constabulary for the performance of all duties which could not be assigned to the military arm. The management of the force in each province was entrusted to an Inspector General who was assisted by Superintendents of Police in each district. The superintendence of the police was vested in the state government.

The Indian Police Commission of 1902-03, which reviewed the working of the police, found that the system had failed because the importance of the police work had been under-estimated and responsible duties entrusted to un-trained and ill-educated officers recruited in the lowest ranks from the lower strata of society, that supervision had been defective, that the superior officers of the department were insufficiently trained, and that their sense of responsibility had been weakened by "a degree of interference never contemplated by the authors of the system". It concluded that "the police force throughout the country is in a most unsatisfactory condition, that abuses are common everywhere, that this involves great injury to the people and discredit to the government, and that radical reforms are urgently necessary". This was the first time that a responsible body talked of police reforms. Ironically, the battle for reforms continues even after more than a hundred years.

Independence – Status Quo Continues

At the dawn of independence, it was expected that a new role, a new philosophy would be defined for the police, that its accountability to the law of the land and the people of the country would be underscored in unmistakable terms. But that was not to be and "the relationship that existed between the police and the foreign power before independence was allowed to continue with the only change that the foreign power was substituted by the political party in power".

For some years, however, there was no problem, thanks to the quality of political as well as administrative leadership. The politicians were men of great stature, endowed with vision and committed to pursuing the national interests. The administrators were also thorough professionals, keen on playing their role in the independent India. The politicians drew from the professional experience and expertise of the civil servant who, in turn, benefited from the politicians' commitment to democracy and secularism. There was mutual respect for each other, give and take in the pursuit of common objective of taking the nation forward on the road to progress and modernity.

As the years rolled by, however, there was unfortunately a qualitative change in the style of politics. The fire of idealism which had inspired the first generation of post-independent politicians and civil servants started getting dim. Power became an end in itself, and gradually a symbiotic relationship developed between the politicians on the one hand and the civil servants on the other. Vested interests grew on both sides and, as commented by the National Police Commission, "what started as a normal interaction between the politicians and the services for the avowed objective of better administration with better awareness of public feelings and expectations, soon degenerated into different forms of intercession, intervention and interference with *mala fide* objectives unconnected with public interest".

It was around mid-sixties that the political leadership injected the concept of 'commitment' in administration. It caused havoc. Officers were selected and given key placements in consideration of their affinity and loyalty to the ruling party and its political philosophy. Their intrinsic merit and administrative qualifications were given secondary importance. The disastrous consequences of this were seen during the Emergency (1975-77) when, as observed by the Shah Commission in its interim report, "...the police was used and allowed themselves to be used for purposes some of which were, to say the least, questionable. Some police officers behaved as though they are not accountable at all to any public authority. The decision to arrest and release certain persons were entirely on political considerations which were intended to be favorable to the ruling party. Employing the police to the advantage of any political party is a sure source of subverting the rule of law. The Government must seriously consider the feasibility and the desirability of insulating the police from the politics of the country and employing it scrupulously on duties for which alone it is by law intended."

In its third and final report (1978), the Shah Commission warned that "If a recurrence of this type of subversion is to be prevented the system must be overhauled with a view to strengthen it in a manner that the functionaries working in the system do so in an atmosphere free from the fear of consequences of their lawful action and in a spirit calculated to promote the integrity and welfare of the Nation and the rule of law."

The suggested overhaul was, unfortunately, never taken up. The Bureau of Police Research and Development, in a paper *Political and Administrative Manipulation of the Police*, published in 1979, warned that "excessive control of the political executive and its principal adviser over the police has the inherent danger of making the police a tool for subverting the process of law, promoting the growth of authoritarianism, and shaking the very foundations of democracy." The warning went unheeded.

State Police Commissions

Several State Police Commissions, at different period of time, suggested structural reforms in the police and emphasized the need to insulate it form extraneous pressures, but their core recommendations were never implemented by the executive. The Kerala Police Reorganization Committee (1959) said that "the greatest obstacle to efficient police administration flows from the domination of party politics under the state administration... the result of partisan interference is often reflected in lawless enforcement of laws, inferior service and in general decline of police prestige followed by irresponsible criticism and consequent widening of the cleavage between the police and the public." The West Bengal Police Commission (1960-61) found that there were frequent allegations that investigation of offences was sought to be interfered with by influential persons highly placed in society or office. The Punjab Police Commission (1961-62) deplored that "members of political parties, particularly of the ruling party, whether in the legislature or outside, interfere considerably in the working of the police for unlawful ends". The Delhi Police Commission (1968) observed that political interference was a rich source of corruption. The Tamilnadu Police Commission (1971) stated that the problem of political interference had grown over the years in spite of the most explicit public declarations made by the successive Chief Ministers. Observations on similar lines were made by the Police Commissions of Bihar, Maharashtra, Madhya Pradesh, Uttar Pradesh, Assam and Andhra Pradesh also.

National Police Commission

The Government of India appointed a National Police Commission in 1977, as it felt that "far reaching changes have taken place in the country" since independence but "there has been no comprehensive review at the national level of the police system after independence despite radical changes in the political, social and economic situation in the country". It was felt that "a fresh examination is necessary of the role and performance of the police both as a law enforcement agency and as an institution to protect rights of the citizens enshrined in the Constitution". The NPC submitted eight detailed reports between 1979 and 1981 which contained comprehensive recommendations covering the entire gamut of police working.

In the first report, the National Police Commission recommended that the existing system of working of the constables, who constitute more than 85% of the force, be radically changed. They should be so recruited and trained that they could be deployed on duties involving the exercise of discretion and judgement. The Commission also suggested machinery for redressal of grievances within the police organization.

The second report of the Commission stressed that the basic role of the police is to function as a law enforcement agency and render impartial service to the people. It expressed grave concern on the misuse of police, interference by illegal or improper orders or pressure from political executives or other extraneous sources. The Commission recommended that the power of superintendence of the state government over the police should be limited to ensuring that the police perform their duties in accordance with the law. To ensure this, it recommended the setting up of a statutory body called the 'State Security Commission' in each state and also that the chief of police should be assured of a minimum prescribed tenure.

The third report dealt with the procedural laws and the evils of suppression of crime by non-registration of cases. It also examined the role of police in dealing with the weaker sections of society. The Commission emphasised that the posting of officers in-charge of police stations should be the exclusive responsibility of the district Superintendent of Police and similarly the selection and posting of Superintendents of Police should be the exclusive responsibility of the Chief of Police.

The fourth report emphasised the imperative need of co-ordinating the functioning of the investigating staff with the prosecuting agency and suggested reforms in procedural laws with a view to facilitating judicious conduct of investigations. On the subject of enforcement of social legislation, the Commission laid down the parameters of police involvement.

The fifth report dealt with the recruitment of constables and sub-inspectors and laid emphasis on their proper training.

The sixth report recommended police commissionerates in large cities with a population of five hundred thousand and above and also in places which had witnessed rapid industrialization or urbanisation. It also recommended certain measures to improve the police handling and investigation of cases of communal riots.

The seventh report dealt with the internal management of the police force and emphasised that this should be entirely under the purview of the Chief of Police.

The eighth report recommended that the State Security Commission should be provided with an independent cell to evaluate police performance in both qualitative and quantitative terms.

The Commission even drafted a model Police Bill which could be enacted. Its recommendations, however, received no more than a cosmetic treatment at the hands of the Government of India. The political leadership was just not prepared to give functional autonomy to the police because it had found this wing of the administration a convenient tool to further its partisan objectives. As for the bureaucracy, control over the police was - and continues to be - an intoxicant they have become addicted to and are just not willing to give that up. And so, the Act of 1861 continues to be on the statute book even after nearly 150 years – a millstone around the police neck.

Other Committees

Apart from the National Police Commission, several other bodies were constituted from time to time to go into the question of police reforms. These were:

(a) Gore Committee on Police Training (1971-73)

(b) Ribeiro Committee on Police Reforms (1998)

(c) Padmanabhaiah Committee on Police Reforms (2000)

(d) Group of Ministers on National Security (2000-01)

(e) Malimath Committee on Reforms of Criminal Justice System (2001-3)

The Gore Committee was constituted to review the state of police training in the country and suggest improvements. The Ribeiro Committee was set up by the Supreme Court while it was deliberating over the Public Interest Litigation filed for police reforms; the Court wanted the Committee to examine if the National Police Commission's recommendations, which formed the core of the PIL, were still relevant or that any modifications were called for. The Padmanabhaiah Committee examined the requirements of policing in the new millennium. The Group of Ministers examined the reports of various Committees which were set up in the wake of Pakistan's aggression in Kargil, including the one dealing with internal security, and suggested comprehensive measures to strengthen the internal and external security apparatus. The Malimath Committee made far-reaching recommendations to reform the criminal justice system. It was of the view that the present Adversarial System could be improved by adapting some features of the Inquisitorial System, and recommended that 'Quest for Truth' should be the guiding principle of the entire criminal justice system. The Committee suggested significant changes in the Criminal Procedure Code to expedite the disposal of cases and in the Evidence Act to facilitate securing of convictions. Unfortunately, the recommendations of the Malimath Committee were trashed because of the chorus of protest from the human rights lobbies.

Judicial Intervention

The core recommendations of the National Police Commission were resurrected through a public interest litigation filed in the Supreme Court in 1996. The petition argued that "the present distortions and aberrations in the functioning of the police have their roots in the colonial past, the structure and organization of the police which have remained basically unchanged during the last nearly 135 years, and the complete subordination of the police to the executive – an arrangement which was designed originally to protect the interests of the British Raj but which unfortunately continues to this day". It drew attention of the Court to the misuse and abuse of the police in the following forms:

(a) Frequent postings and transfers,

(b) Recruitment procedures vitiated through political recommendations

(c) Promotions influenced

(d) Investigations tampered with

(e) Unlawful directions to police

(f) Intelligence apparatus utilized for political purpose

The petition requested the Court to re-define the role and functions of the police, frame a new Police Act on the lines of the Model Bill drafted by the National Police Commission, and direct the states to constitute State Security Commissions to insulate the police from extraneous pressures, lay down a transparent procedure for the selection of Police Chiefs, and separate the investigation work from the law and order responsibilities of the police.

It was forcefully argued during the pendency of the petition that the continuance of the colonial pattern of policing had contributed to disasters at the national level. In 1984, there were anti –Sikh riots in Delhi in which about 3,000 persons were killed. The Delhi Police, barring some honourable exceptions, remained a mute spectator to the carnage because the rioters were instigated by politicians of the ruling party. In 1992, the disputed shrine in Ayodhya was demolished notwithstanding the presence of state police forces and the formidable presence of central paramilitary forces. These forces were immobilized because the political masters were not keen on preventing the *karsevaks* (volunteers) from vandalising the structure. In 2002, during the riots in Gujarat, the politicians played a dubious role and are alleged to have instigated the rioters at certain places. Police officers who tried to uphold the rule of law were punished by the executive. The National Human Rights Commission, which enquired into the incidents, recorded that "there was a comprehensive failure of the State to protect the constitutional rights of the people of Gujarat" and urged that "the matter of police reforms receive attention at the highest political level, at the centre and in the states, and that this issue be pursued in good faith, and on a sustained basis with the greater interest of the country alone in mind, an interest that must overrule every extraneous consideration". It emphasized that "the rot that has set in must be cured if the rule of law is to prevail".

The writ petition was heard by the Supreme Court over a period of ten years. The dilemma before the Supreme Court was whether it should wait further for the governments to take suitable steps for police reforms. However, as recorded in the judgment, "having regard to (i) the gravity of the problem; (ii) the urgent need for preservation and strengthening of Rule of Law; (iii) pendency of even this petition for last over ten years; (iv) the fact that various Commissions and Committees have made recommendations on similar lines for introducing reforms in the police set up in the country; and (v) total uncertainty as to when police reforms would be introduced, we think that there cannot be any further wait, and the stage has come for issue of appropriate directions for immediate compliance so as to be operative till such time a new model Police Act is prepared by the Central Government and/or the State Governments pass the requisite legislations".

In a landmark judgment on September 22, 2006, the Supreme Court ordered the setting up of three institutions at the state level with a view to insulating the police from extraneous influences, giving it functional autonomy and ensuring its accountability. These institutions are:

(a) State Security Commission which would lay down the broad policies and give directions for the performance of the preventive tasks and service oriented functions of the police;

(b) Police Establishment Board comprising the Director General of Police and four other senior officers of the department which shall decide all transfers, postings, promotions and other service related matters of officers of and below the rank of Deputy Superintendent of Police and make appropriate recommendations regarding the postings and transfers of officers of the rank of Superintendent of Police and above to the State Government; and

(c) Police Complaints Authority at the district and state levels with a view to inquiring into allegations of serious misconduct by the police personnel.

Besides, the Apex Court ordered that the Director General of Police shall be selected by the state government from amongst the three senior-most officers of the Department who have been empanelled for promotion to that rank by the Union Public Service Commission, and that he shall have a prescribed minimum tenure of two years. Police officers on operational duties in the field like the Inspector General of Police of a Zone, Deputy Inspector General of a Range, Superintendent of Police in-charge of a district and Station House Officer in-charge of a police station would also have a minimum tenure of two years.

The Court also ordered the separation of investigating police from the law and order police to ensure speedier investigation, better expertise and improved rapport with the people.

The Union Government was also asked to set up a National Security Commission for the selection and placement of heads of Central Police Organizations, upgrading the effectiveness of these forces and improving the service conditions of its personnel.

Tardy Compliance

The judicial directions were to be implemented by December 31, 2006. Subsequently, the time limit was extended till March 31, 2007. There has been considerable resistance to implementing the directions. The political leadership and the bureaucracy are not prepared to loosen their stranglehold over the police. Eight states, namely, Andhra Pradesh, Gujarat, Punjab, Jammu & Kashmir, Karnataka, Maharashtra, Tamilnadu and Uttar Pradesh filed review petitions. However, all these petitions were dismissed by the Supreme Court on August 23, 2007. The majority of states nevertheless continued to drag their feet in implementation whereupon the petitioner moved for contempt against the defaulting states. The Court was however not inclined to issue any contempt notices to the states. On May 17, 2008 the Supreme Court constituted a Monitoring Committee headed by Justice KT Thomas to oversee the implementation of its directions in the States and Union Territories and apprise the Court about unnecessary objections or delays on the part of any respondent so that appropriate follow up action could be taken, and also examine the legislations enacted by different states to see whether those were in compliance to the letter and spirit of the Court's directions. The Monitoring Committee is expected to submit its report in the near future.

The Union Government, at its level, has not shown the expected commitment to police reforms. It had constituted a committee under the chairmanship of Sri Soli Sorabjee, a former Attorney General, to draft a Model Police Act. The Committee submitted its recommendations on October 30, 2006 "to empower the police to enable it to function as an efficient, effective, people-friendly and responsive agency". The Committee broadly followed the pattern already recommended by the Supreme Court. The Government of India gave assurances on the floor of the parliament that a Model Police Act on the lines of Sorabjee Committee's recommendations would be tabled in the near future, but the promise has not been kept so far.

Some states have almost complied with the directions of the Supreme Court. These include the states of Arunachal Pradesh, Assam Manipur, Meghalaya, Mizoram, Nagaland, Sikkim, Tripura, Uttrakhand and Goa. Some other states like Andhra Pradesh, Jammu & Kashmir, Jharkhand, Madhya Pradesh, Maharashtra, Orissa and West Bengal have partially complied with the directions. It must be clarified however that even in states which have almost complied; the directions have yet to be implemented on the ground. Twelve states (Assam, Bihar, Chhattisgarh, Gujarat, Haryana, Himachal Pradesh, Karnataka, Kerala, Punjab, Rajasthan, Tripura and Uttrakhand) have drafted laws with a view to circumventing the implementation of Supreme Court's directions. The Bihar Police Bill is particularly perverse. Uttar Pradesh and Tamilnadu are among the most non-compliant states.

The Road Ahead

The reforms, it must be emphasized, are not for the glory of the police - they are to give better security and protection to the people of the country, uphold their human rights and generally improve governance. In the context of the growing threat of terrorism and the expanding influence of Maoists, it is all the more imperative that our first line of defense is restructured and reorganized so that it is able to deal with these challenges effectively. Public opinion must be mobilized to put pressure on the executive to accelerate the process of police reforms. Media should also be involved in the process. A number of NGOs have evinced interest in pushing police reforms. They must join hands and pool their efforts. Police reforms are absolutely essential to uphold the country's democratic structure and sustain its economic progress.

The Importance of Internal Security

Apart from defence preparedness against foreign invasion, external security is largely determined by exigencies that are domestic and internal in nature. Even in the case of direct armed warfare, intelligence gathering and identifying quislings and fifth colouminst must take into account domestic issues that make such activities either widespread, or ideologically acceptable to many, and sometimes both.

Besides these security pressures largely determined from outside, it is also necessary for the state to take care of problems, dissensions and fissures within so that external enemies cannot take advantage of them for their enemy designs. This aspect is not adequately emphasized for which reason, all too often, matters which are internal in nature are projected as outcomes of international manipulation. This postpones a correct reckoning of the situation, and, more dangerously, may make matters worse.

This can be exemplified with the help of two illustrations.

First, the question of fundamentalist terrorism. If truth be told, the major fear behind violence generated by religious bigots is because of the belief that there are partisans within who make the job of *jehadis* easy. The more conscientious among this set of thinkers go on to advocate greater understanding of the religion and rituals of the other, involve diverse communities in religious meetings, holding peace marches, and so on.

All this is very well, but there is much more that demands attention. If we take the case of Muslim victims in Ahmedabad, post 2002, one finds that they are not keen on the fundamentalist option at all. If anything, there is a perceptible distance between them and the religious clerics. Muslims in Ahmedabad do not want religious education, there is little evidence of burqa amongst them, and they all want their children to learn Gujarati in school.

None of these demands are even faintly religious in character. They have ambitions for themselves, and more so for their children. They also want safety; and as they are constantly terrorized on this score, they naturally seek neighbourhoods where Muslims are in a majority. As long as there is the feeling among Muslims that they are easy and soft targets, the urge to ghettoize will dominate their thinking.

How can these issues be addressed? By holding hands and organizing marches, by singing devotional songs (whether Sufi or Bhakti), by hosting iftaar parties, or by paying attention to what Muslims really want.

The Muslims demand justice. Even after all these years those who killed, brutalized, looted and maimed them are walking free and without remorse. Muslims of Ahmedabad, indeed, in Mumbai and elsewhere too, want to be recognized as full citizens. They want to forget the trauma they went through, but cannot do so without the law of the land taking its course.

Second, Muslims in Ahmedabad want good secular schools where the medium of instruction is either Gujarati or English. It must be noted in this connection that even Jamaat-i-Islam and Jamait-i-Ulema in Gujarat support this policy. In many Anjuman schools in Ahmedabad, learning Urdu is not even an option for the boys.

Under these conditions, if Muslims are to be satisfied and kept outside the sway of fundamentalism, what should the state do? Very simply, give them justice and give them secular schools. Once this is done the threat of Muslims turning fundamentalist will diminish significantly. If this is not done, then fundamentalism may become a self-fulfilling prophecy.

The second example is Maoism. The ruling belief in media and policy circles is that there is a red corridor extending from Nepal to Chattisgarh. Perhaps, some would even like to remind us that the corridor has spikes into China. So the fear of Maoism is aggravated because there is an external dimension to it.

A close look at this issue will tell us that the tribals of India are not Maoists, do not want to fight landlords (because they are next to non-existent in those regions), and do not bear arms that can match the might of the state. What tribals want is a way out of poverty, but who doesn't? In which case, why is Maoism such a threat only in certain areas? The politics of left wing violence should have enveloped all of India. If it has not, can we argue that it is because of topographical and geographic reasons? Or even if it is not there, our policy advisors would caution us that the external enemies of India are conspiring with dissenters within to break our state to its knees.

In this context again, what are the facts? One needs to ask oneself why there was no tribal unrest, let alone Maoism, when Bokaro and Bhilai were created. They too were bang in the middle of what is today Jharkhand and Chattisgarh. When answering this question one must recall that from the 1960s to the mid 1980s Maoist ideology springing from the Naxalite movement was very powerful in India, particularly in Bengal, Bihar and Andhra Pradesh.

Does this mean that the way land is being acquired now is different and needs to be examined?

If this is partly true can we avoid asking the follow up questions? How tainted are the officials in Jharkhand and Chattisgarh? Is it possible that they are involved with rapacious miners, timber merchants and smugglers? Is Maoism a cloak to cover and make opaque to the outside world, corrupt commercial and bureaucratic practices? Is the violence in the so-called Maoist areas really Maoist and tribal led, or are there wheels within wheels which implicate business and bureaucracy?

Answers to questions like this will give us a clearer idea of the nature of internal threat in our country. It is the failure to answer these questions that make matters internal take on an external bearing and in the fullness of time become self fulfilling prophecies, as mentioned earlier.

As Rabindranath Tagore said: Satan comes in only when he finds a flaw. Let us not let the external Satan in. Let us attend to our internal flaws.

India's Urban Awakening and Consequences for National Power

Over the next 20 years, India will see one of the most significant transformations in its history. The country will see urbanization of its population and economy on a scale and scope that is, outside of China, unprecedented in history. This transformation will throw up enormous opportunities and challenges for the country. How India responds to this economic and social shift will have lasting consequences on its ability to sustain its economic growth and social stability, and its capacity to generate new levers of power and influence internationally.

India's Urban Awakening

Historically, urbanization and growth have been inseparable companions in a country's evolution. As a country develops, more and more of its economic activities shift from agriculture in rural areas to manufacturing and services in urban areas. The vast improvement in productivity that this shift entails is one of the fundamental drivers of economic growth. Every major country in the world has exhibited this transformation as an inherent element of its development. According to the United Nations[1], the share of the global population living in cities surpassed 50 percent for the first time in 2008, and is continuing to trend upwards, with the global urban population expected to increase by another 1.6 billion people between 2005 and 2025.

---

[1] World Urbanization Prospects, United Nations, 2007

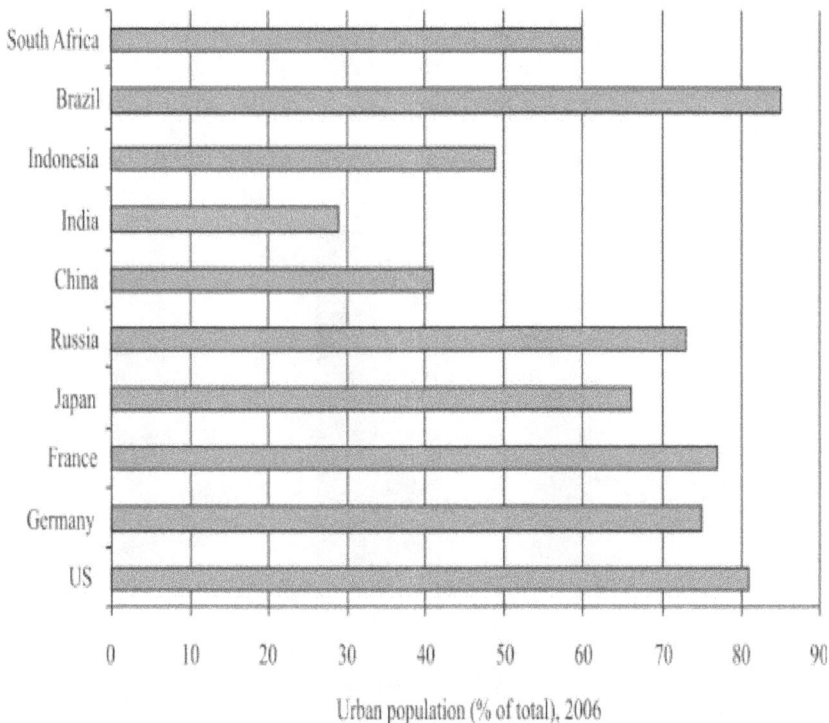

Urban population (% of total), 2006

Source: World Development Indicators, 2008

This same shift has been happening in India, and will continue to be a central tenet of India's economic development. New research from the McKinsey Global Institute (MGI)[2] projects that India's GDP can grow from 49 trillion rupees in 2008 to 238 trillion rupees by 2030. Accompanying this economic growth, India's urban population will grow from 340 million in 2001 to 590 million by 2030. For the next 20 years, around 11 million people will be added to India's urban population each year.

---

[2] India's Urban Awakening: Building inclusive cities, sustaining economic growth, McKinsey Global Institute, April 2010

India: Urban-Rural Divide

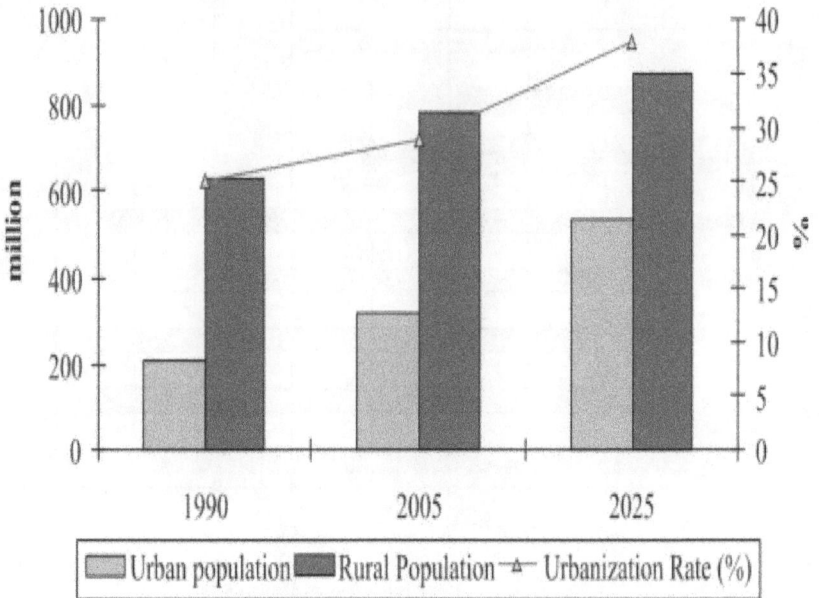

Source: McKinsey Global Institute, India's Urban Awakening, April 2010

Economic output produced in urban India will grow from 54 percent of the total in 2001 to nearly 70 percent in 2030. 70 percent of net new employment will be generated in cities. By 2030, 68 Indian cities will carry more than a million in population and the largest mega cities in the country, including Delhi, Mumbai and Kolkata, will be larger in population and economic output than even medium sized countries today like Malaysia, Colombia and Israel.

The rise of the minority: Cities will account for 70% of GDP by 2030

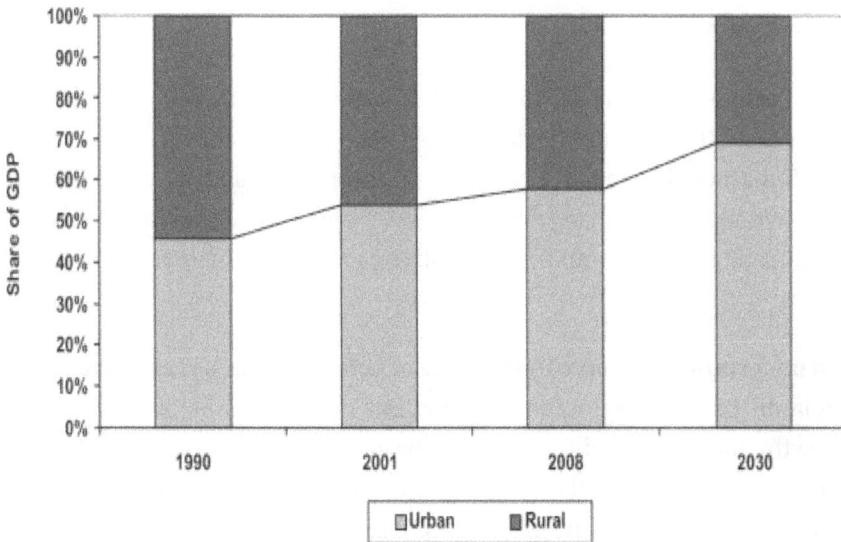

Source: McKinsey Global Institute, India's Urban Awakening, April 2010

However, the research also points out that India's current policy approach is woefully inadequate to addressing the challenges of this urban transformation. Building the backbone of basic infrastructure in cities alone will need $1.2 trillion in new capital investments over the next 20 years. Bringing cities to acceptable living conditions by expanding access to water supply, sanitation, waste management, affordable housing, and public transportation for citizens will require India to build infrastructure at a pace that is more than 20 times what the country has managed to achieve in recent years. Building world-class urban centers that can compete with cities around the world in attracting talent and investments will be an even greater challenge.

The evidence of the failure of India's current approach is readily apparent in each one of its cities today. Across states and across cities of every size, the economic growth unleashed by reforms has translated to rising incomes and consumption levels but steep declines in living conditions. In fact, worse is to come. Every independent forecast estimates that the shortage of basic services in Indian cities will go up dramatically (by some estimates, by as high as 4 times the gap today), were the country to continue its current approach.

A Broken Approach

So what explains India's inability to translate its dramatic economic growth in the last 20 years into the desperately needed renewal of its cities? Why has India not developed a coherent philosophy around its cities and an effective approach to managing them? The roots of India's uninspiring record in managing its accelerating urbanization can be found in three, intertwined issues.

An uncertain philosophy on the role of cities in India's transformation. India still has not recognized the importance of cities in sustaining economic growth, and in expanding access to basic services for the poorest of its population, including those who currently live in rural areas. This has translated to a political and governance approach that just does not recognize cities as discrete units that deserve policy and administrative attention at the same level as states and economic sectors.

In India today, political and social attitudes towards cities vary dramatically. At one end, there is still a constituency that looks at the failure of the country to create livable cities and then argues for exploring ways to limit the expansion of the urban population. This school of thought calls for migration to be curbed through greater focus on rural employment and living conditions, thus (presumably) reducing the incentive to leave villages for cities. At the other end is a constituency of urban thinkers and scholars deeply aware of the economic and social rationale for greater and more effective urbanization, but who are left to preach to each other's convictions. In the vast middle lie two important constituencies. The political leadership, who by and large remain unconvinced about the intellectual arguments and are forced to make tradeoffs between the benefits of allocating resources to rural poverty programs that are compellingly simple and have a clear and perceptible impact (even despite enormous leakage) on the ground in the short term (and, therefore on the preferences of voters, the vast majority of who are still in rural India), and investing in cities that may be economically vital in the long term but have comparatively better living conditions and a complex and arduous path to renewal. Community organizers and activists, the other important constituency, have been hesitant to embrace advocacy for cities, especially on the back of the evidence of the last few decades where wealthy, entrenched interests have always won the competition for resources and investments within cities, at the cost of the poorest communities. To make matters worse, to both these constituencies, advocacy for cities still carries with it the stigma of elitism and the presumption of the urban agenda being the agenda of wealthy city dwellers.

In the introduction to his latest book[3], historian Ramachandra Guha argues that there are five revolutions simultaneously occurring in India: the urban revolution, the industrial revolution, the democratic revolution, the national revolution, and the social revolution. Clearly, India is in the midst of navigating an enormously complex transformation, and one that, as Guha explains, requires India to address these five forces simultaneously, in contrast to most developed nations, which had the advantage of facing these same big changes in a sequential manner over a period of decades. The recognition of these simultaneous revolutions, each with its own set of characteristics, constituencies and champions, places into context why the urban transition has not received the focus and attention due to it.

The deeper truth, though, is that while there are indeed five revolutions, cities are at the forefront of each of the other four revolutions.

Driven by persistent advantages in productivity, cities will continue to be at the center of the industrial transformation, and will likely account for at least 70 percent of economic output by 2030. Out of the 150 million new jobs that are likely to be created between now and 2030, 120 million are going to be in cities. Some of the most competitive service sectors that will be at the heart of job and income growth can only be nurtured in cities. While improving rural incomes and livelihoods in the short term is an important agenda on its own merit, no amount of directed public investments in rural areas will address the fundamental economic advantages of cities. The size and momentum of India's continued economic growth is inextricably linked to the fate of its cities. India's industrial revolution is its urban revolution too.

---

[3] Makers of Modern India, Edited and Introduced by Ramachandra Guha, 2010

India is one of the few democracies in the world where cities are still run as extensions of state governments. Even in states with a strong record of devolution, real power continues to rest with state governments. And in a country proud of its democratic ethos and institutions, there is a democracy vacuum at the city level. In sharp contrast to the common threads of effective governance and administration around the world, the third layer (and especially cities more than villages) continues to be unformed and under evolved. Creating local representation and accountability will have to be a defining feature of India's democratic revolution.

On the social front, there have always existed two opposing points of view on the impact of cities on social and community fabrics. One argues that with migration representing a break from a life influenced by deep rooted under currents of caste in India's villages, cities offer the possibility of new beginnings shod of old habits and legacies. The other argues that the absence of deep community and social linkages at a time of mobility and disruption makes migrants especially prone to the influence of divisive ideologies. Either way, cities will clearly be a central theatre of India's social revolution too.

And above all, cities have a vital role to play in nation building, primarily as the most effective instrument to expand access to basic services to an increasing number of Indians at the fastest pace possible. As the MGI research points out, cities account for a disproportionate share of taxes (around 80 percent), key to financing development expenditure. The same research highlights that the cost of building and delivering basic service networks can be 30 to 50 percent cheaper in concentrated population centers, making cities an effective platform to attract and serve the poorest segments of the population, many of whom will be first generation migrants. This is especially relevant at the current stage of India's growth, where scarce development revenues need to be deployed where returns can be the most effective.

The politics of real estate and the governance of political parties. The internal functioning of political parties in India has received much attention from political scientists. Pratap Banu Mehta has often argued that greater internal democratization of parties should be an essential agenda of reforms in the country[4] His argument is that with internal democracy, where the criteria for advancement is clear and non whimsical, newly mobilized social groups are likely to work within existing party structures and therefore be less tempted to set up on their own, thus preventing the fragmentation of the party system. Further, political leaders used to the sanctity of democratic procedures are less likely to circumvent democracy in government, and in the process, the politics of patronage stands a chance of being circumvented by the politics of ideas in the long term.

The agenda of reform in the funding and functioning of political parties has very significant relevance to the agenda of urban renewal on two fronts. Arbitrating the competing interests for physical space is a key function of city governments around the world. In well functioning cities, this negotiation is usually conducted through formal urban planning processes where choices are transparent and, for the most part, defendable. The robust economic growth of the last two decades has translated to a thriving real estate sector characterized by rising land values in most of India's cities, especially the large metropolitan centers. Generating revenues through outright sale of public land as well as through making choices that have a significant impact on the value of private land (including usage and floor area ratio) have always been a key income source for cities around the world, especially at an equivalent stage of development. Even in India, land sales have often funded regional development authorities; sale of Bandra-Kurla land in the early 1970s has allowed the Mumbai Metropolitan Regional Development Authority to fund multi billion dollar infrastructure projects in the city. The MGI research estimates that the city of Mumbai can generate as much as 4,000 to 5,000 rupees per square foot through leveraging development control rules that guide the permissible floor area ratio. The same report also highlights that Indian cities can raise more than $25 billion a year through effective monetization of urban land. Clearly, significant value is at stake in the decision processes that guide the use of real estate inside cities.

It is no surprise then that, in a political system built around patronage, and where the rapid rise in the cost of elections forces political parties to look for substantial sources of funding from private interest groups, chief

---

[4] "Reform Political Parties First", Pratap Banu Mehta, India Seminar, January 2001

ministers and state leaders would be reluctant to devolve power over such decisions to city governments and systematic urban planning processes. In the arbitrariness of urban land allocation lie power, wealth, and the possibility of political patronage. Thus, one of the most important and effective instruments of public policy at the city level – the optimal allocation of space that should be a negotiation of competing demands amongst legitimate stakeholders as well as longitudinally – remain blunted by patronage politics.

At the same time, the absence of democratic processes inside political parties also undermines what has been a proven pathway for career progression inside parties in democracies around the world: a record of executive leadership and success at the city level providing a platform for national leadership. In fact, cities have been the training grounds of national politics even in autocratic states like China, where the mayors of Shanghai and Beijing have often used success in local administration to pivot into leadership positions in the central leadership of the communist party. The absence of a clearly defined tier of government at the city level, accentuated by lack of democratic processes inside political parties, has therefore taken away a compelling lever of change in other societies: the ability to attract enterprising political leaders who seek higher national offices through reputations built on track records of success at the city level.

The absence of functioning, well-formed governments that can attract credible political talent, therefore, continues to hurt the ability of cities to devise and implement an agenda of renewal for the long term.

Failure of imagination. The agenda of transformative urban renewal has still not caught the imagination of India; not just its political leaders but also its planners, architects, designers, engineers and, to a large extent, its private sector. At a time when there are substantial city initiatives under way in China, Southeast Asia and the Middle East, the other major theatres of urbanization in the world, including the renewal of commercial centers, renovation of neighborhoods and the massive build-out of new transportation systems and housing projects, India's canvas, by and large, still remains empty.

To an extent, this is because the forces of enterprise and creativity have been stifled by the absence of a public framework where the rules of the game are clearly outlined. Such a framework has to include an approach to the usage of city space and resources, raising funds for investment in basic infrastructure, ensuring environmental sustainability and building alignment on the separation of roles between the public, private and social sectors. City management remains one of the most difficult and complex administrative challenges globally that will require the application of the best technical and professional talent available. And unlike in other sectors of reform focus in the country, for example telecommunications and financial services, success in urban is extraordinarily reliant on the quality of public governance; change cannot be led and driven by the private sector, it will only be a locally accountable city government that can build and refine such a framework of change.

To some extent, this has also been about the absence of compelling signposts and benchmarks that then inspire the best engineers, designers and architects into the field of urban renewal. Aside from interest in some select sectors such as housing and transportation, the private sector too has not recognized the enormous opportunities inherent to the process of transforming India's cities. For a country lined with thousands of cities and towns that are all very visibly straining at the edges, there has been no significant post-Independence story of success that can provide the inspiration for emulation.

Exacerbating these is an attitude of misplaced faith in India's ability to catch up, to correct mistakes and to get things right, even if at the very last minute. However, more than any other sector, urban is one area where building proactive solutions does matter, and reactive solutions can often be extremely expensive and generate sub optimal outcomes. For example, in the absence of a process that actively facilitates the creation of affordable housing units, it is almost guaranteed that urban slums will come up, which then require enormous policy attention and investments to turn around over an extended period of time. Cities exhibit enormous path dependencies, where choices on the allocation of space and investments have lasting effects for decades. The laissez faire attitude that characterizes India's governance approach will reveal its worst outcomes in urban renewal.

Why is urbanization important to national power? The outcome of India's urbanization is of enormous consequence to the well being of its citizens and the sustainability of India's economic growth and social development. And ultimately, it will also shape the nature and tenor of the influence that India will wield in the global order of the 21st century.

Urbanization and economic heft. At the most fundamental level of the power determinant, India's economic heft is very reliant on its urbanization approach. Whether India can continue to grow at a near double digit rate will determine whether India can evolve into a global economic power and the extent to which it can shrink the economic gap with its most meaningful competitor, China.

In 1950, China's urbanization rate was 13 percent and India's urbanization rate was 17 percent. By 2005, Chinas urbanization rate reached 41 percent and India's 29 percent. During the same period, China's economic output grew 25 times its 1950 level while India's only grew about ten fold.

This is not to give the credit for China's economic growth to more rapid urbanization. Nor is the argument here that India should grow its military expenditure at the same rate as China's or spend the same proportion of public resources on the military. But, with its presence in a troubling neighborhood and proximity to a great power that could evolve into an economic and military hegemony, India's ability to protect its interests and further its domestic agenda will be greatly influenced by its ability to shore up its security, which in turn will be dependent on the scale and depth of its economic growth.

And India's ability to manage its urban transition will drive the pace and nature of its economic growth and social development. Given the reliance of economic growth and jobs on cities, it is inconceivable that India will be able to maintain or accelerate its current growth level without a substantial renewal in its urbanization approach. There is no conceivable development path in which growth will continue even as its main geographical theatres crumble. There is no possible approach that allows India to continue to accelerate private incomes even as the government fails to deliver basic public goods in at least the places where it is easiest to deliver.

The necessity of developing an effective approach to renewing cities becomes even clearer when observing two fundamental characteristics of India's economic growth.

In their paper comparing China and India's economic development approaches[5], Huang and Khanna highlighted one substantial difference between the growth drivers of the two countries. China's economic growth (at least till date) has been export led and largely driven by foreign direct investment while India's growth has come on the back of thriving domestic entrepreneurship. The authors attributed this to the presence of a comparatively stronger supporting infrastructure in India to facilitate private enterprise, including transparent capital markets and a functioning (although flawed) legal system. In comparison, China continues to be constrained by the legacy of a top-down approach that imposes legal and regulatory constraints on private firms, largely designed to prevent domestic businesses from challenging China's state-owned enterprises.

Private entrepreneurship as the driver of growth in India means cities become even more relevant to India's ability to sustain its economic transformation. Cities are the proven engines of entrepreneurship and innovation around the world. In Richard Florida's book [6] analyzing the relevance of cities in the 21st century, he traces recent economic research and thinking that have explored the increasing significance of location to economic growth. From Joseph Schumpeter's theories on innovation to Robert Solow's research on the role of technology through to the more recent work of Paul Romer, Robert Lucas and Jane Jacobs, it is now firmly established that talent clustering is a primary determinant of economic growth. Their work shows that it is the underlying power of the clustering force (of people and productivity, creative skills and talents) that powers growth. And cities are the geographical manifestation of the desire of talent to cluster, and the evidence of how this clustering produces a virtuous cycle of innovation, entrepreneurship and growth. Therefore, cities become extraordinarily important in a country whose primary engine of growth is

---

[5] Can India Overtake China?, Yasheng Huang and Tarun Khanna, Foreign Policy, July-August 2003

[6] Chapter 4: The Clustering Force, Who's Your City?, Richard Florida, 2008

bottom up innovation and entrepreneurship.

The second characteristic of India's economic growth is closely linked to the first but is worth attention on it own merits: that India's growth has been largely driven by services and not manufacturing. This is a fairly distinctive development trajectory in India that is in sharp contrast to that seen in China and almost every other large economy in the world at an equivalent stage of development, where manufacturing was the lead sector. According to MGI, the share of the services sector in India's GDP has grown from 42 percent in 1990 to 51 percent in 2000 and 59 percent in 2009. Based on sectoral growth projections, share of services is likely to reach around 70 percent by 2030. The same report also highlighted that the services sector is more productive in cities than in rural settings and that higher value added services inevitably gravitate towards cities (partly due to the value of the clustering force mentioned earlier). In fact, global evidence shows that some services (for example, high end financial services) almost always can only be sited in cities of a certain scale.

The message on economic growth and leverage is clear. Developing an effective urbanization approach is critical to India's ability to continue on an economic trajectory that, from the perspective of hard power, will give it the heft and leverage to protect its national interests and allow it to focus on its agenda of inclusion and equity.

Potency of disruptive changes. As discussed earlier, both China and India are going through a scale and pace of urbanization that is unprecedented in human history. And in many ways, the two emerging global powers face a common challenge when it comes to their urbanization trajectories: the possibility of disruptive changes that could undermine their power and global standing.

As the MGI report pointed out, to a large extent, China has succeeded in developing an effective approach to its urbanization by developing an internally consistent set of practices that address key elements such as funding, governance and planning. It has made public investments in its cities ahead of demand, created city governance structures that are accountable even in the absence of democratic institutions, and adopted urban planning and renewal approaches that have learnt from global practices. These methodical approaches have enabled Chinese cities to grow at annual rates that have sometimes reached 30 percent, a remarkable achievement by any standard.

At the same time, China will face four substantial challenges, any of which could turn out to be disruptive and derail its momentum. First, there is a substantial gap between its largest, coastal cities and the smaller cities and towns in the hinterlands. While many of the coastal cities have grown at 15-30 percent annually, the hinterland has grown at a far less scorching pace, registering growth between 5 and 9 percent[7]. This disparity also shows up in per capita incomes – the per capita income of Shanghai is above $6,000 today while that of a hinterland city like Taiyuan is below $2,000. The national government has recognized this disparity and has started to move its resources more aggressively to the hinterlands, most recently with a fiscal stimulus that disproportionately invested in public transportation and housing in the hinterland. However, it remains a challenge of consequence. Secondly, China largely succeeded in navigating the challenges of rapid urbanization and migration from the villages to the cities by imposing a *hukou* system, directing internal population flows by issuing visas for legally residing in cities. While draconian by modern democratic standards, it allowed the country to systematically plan for the provision of basic services for even the lowest income groups. More recently, the government has moved to create a social welfare system that is also open to the 'illegal' non-*hukou* residents of cities.

As cities expand in size, it is unclear if the domestic population will continue to abide by such a system and whether the opening up of internal migration flows through reforms in the social security system will create disruptions. Thirdly, city governments in China have often succeeded in pushing through renewal of neighborhoods through autocratic measures that have disregarded property rights. While these have enabled China's cities to make transformative changes in its urban form and structure at a rapid pace, it again raises the possibility of social disruptions if newly mobilized groups start to resist renewal by fiat. And, above all, urban China has a severe environmental crisis on the cards. A recent report from the Urban

---

[7] China's Urban Billion, McKinsey Global Institute, 2009

China Institute pointed to the cleanliness of China's cities as being woefully behind the West. Air pollution and sulphur dioxide emissions lag World Health Organization norms. Smog filled mega cities are as much a health disaster in the making as they are potential sparks in the powder kegs of urban dissatisfaction in China.

India's challenge is very different but equally daunting. In the competition for resources inside cities, very often, the interests of the lowest income groups and first generation migrants have often been sacrificed to serve the rising aspirations of the wealthiest residents. The alliance between business interests, entrenched incumbents and the political establishment has resulted in appalling living conditions in its largest cities, despite rising incomes and the possibility of substantial public investment resources. The fissures that are now evident in India's rural hinterlands (often triggered by the losers of the very same competition for resources) may well be a precursor to what awaits urban India if it is not able to meet at least the most basic requirements of its poorest citizens.

Both China and India, therefore, face the possibility of disruptive changes in its urban trajectories. And given their size and aspirations, the possibility is troubling of two emerging powers that face disruptive domestic pressures simultaneously.

New Frontiers and the Battle of Ideas

China and India are major competitors for foreign investment, capital, trade, resources, and markets[8]. Much has been written about the emerging competition between China and India for strategic space and leverage, including in their quests to lock up raw materials and resources in Africa, Middle East and Central Asia to power their surging economies. The competition has already pitted governments, government linked companies and private sector interests from the two countries against each other in markets around the world. This competition for resources will of course be a key arena of international relations in the 21st century.

An equally interesting and consequential theatre of competition between

---

[8] India-China Relations, J. Mohan Malik, Berkshire Encyclopedia of China, 2009

the two countries will be driven by ideas and contrasting economic and social approaches. With the acknowledgment of the increasing importance of soft power in international relations, India faces a question of what its key levers are in the battle for disseminating compelling ideas around the world.

In a rapidly urbanizing world, where around 450 million people will be added to the cities of Africa and Latin America alone in the next 20 years, ideas based on China and India's urban experiences will be an important driver of their growth and influence. This competition will revolve around the structures, products and services that allow a country to effectively manage its urbanization. From building affordable houses at low cost and at a large scale to green technologies that reduce emissions in dense cities, from innovations in mass transit systems to technologies and approaches to manage urban waste, rapidly urbanizing countries in Africa and Latin America will look to the rest of the world for ideas and solutions. And as they do, they are more likely to find parallels in their challenges in India and China than in the cities of the West. And the innovations and products and services that emanate from the two countries' urban experiences are, therefore, likely to find eager markets and recipients in these two continents, creating another theatre of competition between the two.

Even here, crafting an effective urbanization approach creates the possibility for India to develop an asymmetric advantage in its competition with China. As pointed our recently by an observer of Africa[9], China has already created a significant conventional advantage over India in Africa through preferential tariff lines, size and speed of aid delivered, intensity of defense relations and regularity of bilateral conversations. The opportunity for India, points out the same paper, lies in contributing to the quality of Africa's economic growth, not just its quantity. And here India has two advantages over China: the aspiration of many of the stakeholders in Africa to create solutions that are based on a democratic framework (and one that can deepen democratic institutions), and the emphasis on business models that ride on private entrepreneurship and local productivity.

---

[9] Strategic Competition between China and India in Africa, Stratsis Incite, August 2010

However, before India can evangelize its ideas, it needs to craft a compelling new approach to its urbanization, including creating a framework that allows new ideas, products and services to thrive in its own backyards.

Imperative for Change

The quest for equity as well as the search for global power and leverage both point to the same compelling need for India to renew its approach to its rapid urbanization.

And crafting a new approach requires India to fundamentally renew its political and governance structure even as it creates a framework for bringing together the public, private and social sectors in a generational mission to build the 80 percent of the country that still remains to be built.

The starting point of this approach has to be a genuine recognition that cities need to be a third tier of government at par with the central and state governments, deserving of autonomy and structures that allow them to function as discrete administrative units. India needs to unleash the immense potential of its cities and doing so requires accepting that, in the short term, in the competition for talent, political leadership and resources, there will be winners and losers. Yet, that is the only way forward for cities in India to chart their own paths and pursue development approaches that are responsive and accountable to the needs of city voters. Accountability for outcomes in cities has to be driven by local elections and the promise of career progression for political leaders who show results on the ground.

And the freeing of cities through devolution will have to be accompanied by the development of a new framework that, while exhibiting variation across the country as cities implement their own priorities and choices, provides a guide on the focus of public delivery, the involvement of the private sector, and the use of public policy instruments to drive urban development and investments.

On both the above, many compelling proposals remain on the table. What has been missing to date has been a sense of urgency in addressing the challenge head on, and a sense of commitment from the country's leadership to unleash cities from the clutches of entrenched political and private interests. Crafting a new approach to India's rapid urbanization and renewing its cities and towns remains one of the defining missions of this generation, the outcome of which will determine the extent to which India will play a meaningful role in the international order of the 21st century.

Caste in India: From System to Identity

With the breakdown of the closed natural economy of the village, status and economic relations between different castes have radically altered. No longer can the once "dominant castes" exercise their sway over the rest. The reason is simple: they are no longer economically powerful. Landlordism is a thing of the past and though land reforms were not properly implemented, demography and sub-division of holdings have played their role. Consequently, the "big land holders" in India today rarely operate more than 20 acres of land. This is why most farms are family operated and there is little scope for hired labour other than during the peak harvesting season.

This has changed the way in which the caste system operated. The caste of the rural landed oligarchs was the one on top of the heap and other castes were arranged in status order depending upon their relationship with such families. So a goldsmith of the biggest landlord had a higher position than the goldsmith of a lesser one. The same logic held for the Brahmans too. The priest who performed rituals for the land lords held a higher position than those who did the same for the less powerful landed families. Yet together they were superior to the temple priests who had to serve all those who came to worship.

Patron client relationships were neatly ordered and each caste knew its boundaries of social interaction. Most castes resented their lowly position, but they could not openly express them for fear of inviting the wrath of the oligarchs and the lesser oligarchs of traditional rural India. Even the Brahman was a service caste, albeit of a higher order. In practice, the caste of the dominants was on top and the others arranged according to the vision of the superior community, which nearly always, except perhaps in Gujarat, called itself a warrior caste of one kind or another.

With the breakdown of the closed, natural economy of the village, the caste system does not quite operate in the same way. Interestingly though, it is because the old hierarchy has been dismantled that caste identities have come up quite ferociously. The once subjugated people, including the Scheduled Castes, are not willing to accept their earlier status and role and are freeing themselves from traditional duties, wherever they can manage to. Urbanization may not have entered the village, but non-farm occupations constitute roughly 50% of the rural economy today. When this feature is coupled with smaller land holdings, it becomes quite clear why the old caste pyramid is finding it hard to survive in contemporary India

Is Caste Dangerous if Untackled?

Caste beliefs cannot be tolerated in a democratic society where the accidents of birth have no place in determining an individual's life chances. Hence, caste background should have no place in a modern polity. It does not really matter what caste values a person may hold indoors or in one's personal space, but it cannot be allowed to spill over into the public domain. Even at the level of the family, a person has the right to choose who to marry or where to work and what kind of occupation to pursue. If the family as a whole believes in endogamous intra-caste marriage, then that is a different matter, but it cannot be forced on sons and daughters.

At any rate, there is just no room to exercise caste prejudices in the public domain. If a person wants to eat with members of the same caste, then it is that person's individual choice, but it cannot be enforced as a public policy in the work place outside the home. Likewise, caste views should not stop people from aspiring to jobs at any level demanding any kind of specialization. In other words, some people can be as bigoted as they want to be, but cannot let those prejudices step out of their skin. If they do, the law should come down heavily and unequivocally on them for fundamental rights are here in threat.

Caste therefore needs to be tackled at the public plane. No quarter can be yielded on this ground without damaging the basis of our democracy.

Nor should one allow different castes competing against each other as castes for educational positions and offices in the public or private sector.

To slice such openings on the basis of caste would strengthen caste prejudices though the caste system itself would not be enlivened. In the caste system, there is no scope for competition. Yet, because the system is not operative, that does not mean that the free play of competitive caste identities, which overvalues one's own background while stigmatizing others, is to be tolerated.

Is Caste Disappearing in India?

One should be careful in wording such a question. If we mean the caste system then that is disappearing for reasons mentioned earlier, most importantly, the breakdown of the old village economy and with it the oligarchy of dominant castes.

Caste, however, continues as identity and this needs to be confronted four square. Just because the system is not operative, it does not mean the matter is over. Caste identities feature in caste politics and too much of that is already in evidence in our everyday experience.

However, we should be cautious before we announce that caste passions rule us at all times. Caste politics weighs in heavily at the level of village politics. This is why it is important to keep track of how *panchayat* level decisions are taken. Local self government in India has to constantly be on guard, for the vote can often be misused if the marginals and the weak are not protected.

This danger is considerably lessened at the level of legislative or parliamentary constituencies. Constituencies in such cases are so large that they often comprise as many as 12 to 13 castes of roughly equal size. This makes it difficult for pure caste politics to rule as there are only two, or three, viable contenders. Therefore, while voting, regardless of how caste prejudiced a person may be, it is imperative to rise above caste considerations when facing the ballot box. Thus, from a distance it might appear that castes are playing a decisive role, but that is not strictly true. Yadavs, under the best of circumstances, constitute only about 18%-20% of the population in any legislative constituency. Jats are at best about 8% of the population in west UP, often considered to be a Jat lair.

Why do we then think that caste politics is so dominant? The main reason for this is that the elite in politics think along caste lines in nominating people to positions, and most importantly, in handing out tickets. Not every caste is equally well organized or connected. In west UP, for a long time, the Jats were for a long time the most forward agrarian castes and hence their networks were strongest, so they determined who should contest from where. The same can be said of Yadavs in Bihar and east UP. In Maharashtra the picture is a little different. About 33% of Maharashtrians are Marathas and that is why this community is politically fractured- from Maoist to Shiv Sainiks and everything in between.

As the political elite are caste conscious in the way they operate they like to encourage the view that people vote on caste grounds. This makes their position strong in both the popular mind as well as within their own parties. What really helps them in this quest are members of the media. As most journalists spend time with politicians they legitimize their views for public consumption. At the empirical level, caste alone cannot play a decisive role because the numbers just do not add up. This also explains why Mayawati lost every seat in Mirzapur in 2002 and won practically every seat in 2007. This also explain the rise and fall of Maulayam and Laloo.

Can Urbanization Kill It?

Urbanization is the only measure that will eventually kill caste. This is not because urbanization by itself makes one more liberal and less prejudiced. Human beings are incapable of being bigotry free.

However, in an urban setting it is very difficult for parents to monitor who their children meet and where. Boy can meet girl at bus stops, in schools and colleges, in the work place, anywhere. Parents are, therefore, no longer sanguine about who their son-in-law is going to be. Once people from different castes begin to marry then that will break the back of identity based caste prejudices.

In caste theory proper, when X caste marries Y caste the children are not half X and half Y (as would be the case with inter racial unions), but of Z caste. Let us be more frank. The children of such inter caste unions are actually outcastes.

For such unions to happen on an increasing scale a family needs to be roughly two to three generations urban. When a villager is initially introduced to the city it is very likely that there is a strengthening of caste prejudices because such people are looking and longing for roots and social connections. As time goes on, this tendency diminishes, till eventually, with inter caste marriages, it makes no sense to hold on to it at all.

If we then look at the full cycle, it begins with the caste system, which then gives way to caste identities, and these in turn are gradually dissolved in in the anonymity of urbanization.

In this connection it should also be borne in mind that poor, subaltern rural castes and peoples are the most keen to migrate from the countryside. As long as they remain rural they cannot exit from the dense interactive network that defined them in their village and made their pasts an ever present reality. Once they come to cities what matters most is not their past, or their ancestry, but what they themselves have managed to become. With urbanization then there is a shift from the interactive nexus to the appreciation of attributes. Now it is relevant to be able to speak English, own a colour TV and live in South Delhi. So long one has these attributes the fact that one's great grandfather was a day labourer is of little consequence and can be properly concealed. However, the trajectory is not a smooth one for most people. After the village they move into a urban slum and only a lucky few eventually make it to white collar jobs within two to three generations. Most never do, yet the slum is the beginning of hope in a way their rural homes were not.

Will Education Finish It?

The short answer is: No. Remember, the rural elite and Brahmans were educated. Education by itself is not the answer, the social cauldron is. This is why urbanization is so important. Why should **we ever** believe that education can eradicate castes? Education has not eradicated racism or religious intolerance. Education has to do with literacy, with getting degrees and holding jobs. Education has to do with learning skills that will make life better, easier and more prosperous. Education cannot remove prejudices in a lasting fashion.

Will Reservation Perpetuate Caste?

Please note that the caste system is dead. What reservation was supposed to do was to end its systematic nature where the hierarchy was upheld in theory and practice. When Ambedkar presided over the making of the Constitution, the Reservation policy envisaged at that time was supposed to root out caste completely from public life.

How does Reservation of the Ambedkar kind help in this matter? When democracy is inaugurated it must take on board the fact that there are certain communities that have suffered for generations because of prejudices against them that could be based on caste, religion, race or language. Democracy requires that everybody compete equally without the drag of the past. But not everybody is equal at the starting point, thanks to our inglorious traditions. Reservations were targeted at those who had no socially valuable assets because they were victimized in the past and held back from acquiring them. The provisions of Reservations were, therefore, designed to help such communities acquire such assets as early as possible so that they can then participate as equals in the near future. In due course of time, a critical number of people from previously persecuted backgrounds would occupy positions of power and status and would take the fight forward to make sure that caste prejudices have no place in public life.

Reservations were then envisaged to be (i) for those who had no social assets and were actively persecuted whenever they sought to acquire them, and (ii) they were time bound. The time element and the constant monitoring of Reservations were insisted upon most of all by Ambedkar, so that this provision would not become a political resource to be exploited in perpetuity by certain castes.

The second round of Reservations came with Mandal in 1999. This system differed from the earlier Ambedkar inspired policy in significant ways. First, it was not meant to eradicate caste, but to represent it. Second, most dangerously, it was not aimed at those who had no socially valuable assets whatsoever but rather at those who could convert their rural assets (land and power) to urban ones (jobs in the public or private sector.

We need to make this distinction very categorically. Mandal advocates do not want Reservations to be time bound or denied to those who already possess socially valuable assets. This is why there is an unholy combine today of elite Scheduled Castes and the OBCs. Interestingly, OBC in the Constitution refers to Backward Classes but not to Backward Castes. Mandal cunningly made Backward Class synonymous with Backward Castes in the popular mind. But there is no such term in the Constitution.

Look closely at the formula set out by Mandal for determining backwardness. The least points are given to economic backwardness and the most for social backwardness. Further, the criteria for social backwardness are so vague that any community with political power, numbers and gumption can easily lay claim to it.

In conclusion, the Mandal system of Reservation perpetuates caste identities and caste politics, whereas the Ambedkar version was aimed to extirpate caste in all its forms, including the one that harps on identity. It may also be noted that Mandal Reservation exploits the view that the caste system is still in operation as its underlying rationale. However, ask any rural Scheduled Caste and he or she will tell you that the worst perpetrators of caste prejudices in rural India are the Yadavs, Thevars, Marawars, Okkaligas, Gujars, and so on. It is the leaders of these castes, or, more correctly, the elite of these castes, who have benefited most from OBC reservations, and yet they are the most vicious in their relationships with the poor in their respective village settings.

The Communal Divide and the Perennial Anthropological Failing

Human beings, the world over, believe their own community to be the most evolved and look at other people disparagingly. This negative attitude may be one of benign and amused tolerance to one of active persecution. For the latter to happen, social prejudices must correlate with economic and political power.

Nationalism came up in the 19th century on the basis of blood, soil and tradition, real or imagined. During that period it was usually the exploited who used these stirring passions to establish a less elitist regime. The ancient regime was ousted by such strivings at the popular level.

In India the divide between religious communities takes on a militant and violent form not only because these ancient prejudices are difficult to eradicate but also because in the making of our nation-state religion played a very important role in dividing territories between India and Pakistan. That this happened with bloodshed and wanton violence resulting in personal tragedies has allowed religious sectarianism to flourish in India. This is particularly the case if it can be made out that the minority religious groups are out to create another Pakistan, or to further break up the territorial possessions of the Indian nation-state. When Sikh extremists were drawing public attention (from the mid 1980s to the early 1990s) the majoritiarian view at that time was that another partition was being planned and that it had to be halted. When Muslims were killed in Gujarat in 2002, the cry went up that they were Pakistani agents.

In communal conflicts of this kind it is important to note that there are no economic motives behind it. Unlike caste competition, linguistic rivalry, territorial disputes, river water tensions, in Hindu-Sikh or Hindu-Muslim killings it is not as if the majority community wants the jobs of the minority community. The bloodshed draws its charge from a nationalist passion and not an economic one. As the killers on the rampage are not motivated by economic drives, it is incorrect to analyze such social tragedies with the methods of social science for that only gives legitimacy to the killers. What we need to do is to suspend social science but to introduce instead social forensics: who killed whom for how much and for what. The format and techniques of social science take away attention from these questions. Instead, social science sets one to seek causes behind ethnic massacres in asymmetric economic distribution or tradition value constructs. Such efforts give the ideological structure of ethnicits a boost as well as to those efforts that are aimed at hand holding, prayer meetings, or "education". What is needed instead is the strict implementation of the law.

If the law is *not* used strictly in such conditions then the perennial tendency in human kind to spontaneously divide will constantly find political patrons.

Why not Roll Back an Inefficient State?

The state should be rolled back if it unnecessarily interferes with normal trade and economic initiatives. However, we should remember that the market came after society. If market rules are to trump social arrangements then we shall constantly be prone to economic philippics.

Having taken note of this foundational fact, a kind of social ontology, if you will, we must remember that countries that are advising India to roll back the state in fact did just the reverse in their climb to economic pre-eminence. In the USA the state has always played an important role in education and social welfare on a scale that India is nowhere near matching. Even the subsidies they give to their farmers are much higher than what our rural cultivator can avail of. In Europe, the involvement of the state is much greater. Unless the state provides quality public goods at quality levels, a strong economy based on private initiative cannot develop. Instead, you will have a continent of indigent and ill trained migrants who will work for anything. This makes labour intensive industry more attractive and there is therefore much lesser insistence on increasing productivity through innovation and mechanization. If the poor have little or no access to quality health and education not only will their bargaining power be low, but the need for entrepreneurs to be properly innovative will also be absent. The pressure to do so will just not be there.

There are some good reasons why the Indian state should not be rolled back, but should be made more responsible. Consider this: over 80% of all health expenditure in India is out of pocket: one of the highest in the world, second only to war ravaged Iraq. In USA the state pays about 45% of all health costs in the country; in Europe it can go up as high as 85% to 90%. While on this subject of public goods, the government in the USA pays about 83% of all educational expenditure. The Indian state only picks up 15% of educational cost.

The Indian state has already rolled back when it comes to delivery. The point is not to let it roll back further but to pressure it to deliver as it should to citizens. This is the lesson India should learn from USA and Europe. Unfortunately, the Indian state has been so closely identified with corruption that the idea that the state should be around to deliver to citizens for that is their right, does not easily surface.

It must be borne in mind that no private initiative can deliver quality health or education to the population as a whole. Private initiative on these issues can only attract the well to do, and when NGOs sponsor health and educational measures they are not just limited in their scope, but they also serve beneficiaries and not citizens.

To make citizenship substantial the state must deliver public goods to the public at quality levels and not appropriate the state machinery for the aggrandizement of a few.

Why do Intellectuals think India is Falling Apart?

To a large extent the feeling among intellectuals that India might quite easily fall apart is because we believe that there is just one route to being a proper nation state and that is the one Europe and America took. What they overlook is that even in western settings language rarely united people; and in some cases, like Germany or UK, not even religion. When Italy became Italy only 2% spoke Italian and when the French Revolution happened only about 17% spoke French.

By the time India became Independent in 1947 the world had moved on. No longer was it politically possible to stamp out other languages or to privilege any one religion. Democracy had taken great strides in the intervening decades and centuries for India to turn its back to them.

Ultimately, we need to recognize that there is not just one privileged path to nation-statehood. Language and religion do not always coalesce to give a nation-state its durability. It is however more important to judge a nation-state not by how it came into being but what it does successfully once it has arrived on the world stage. All viable nation-states are able to successfully sacralize their territorial holdings and to delineate their borders in the public psyche. In India this happened with the Partition and hence it remains for many a live source of political symbolism. This is the negative side. On the positive side, there has not been any major political movement to partition the country, other than the disturbances in the North East and Kashmir. To understand these specific issues, one needs to pay attention on how the borders were drawn in these regions. Even here, one must be careful in one's analysis as there are great differences in the centrifugal forces in J&K and in the North East.

In the majority of the Indian land mass there is no discernible move towards secession. Even the Khalistani movement was supported by a few. The overwhelming numbers of Sikhs who were deeply hurt by what happened in the wake of Mrs. Indira Gandhi's assassination were, however, not in favour of Khalistan. To go back in time, once the State Reorganization Committee had done its work, it was noticed that regional passions also subsided. It was initially believed that the call for Maharashtra would end in wanting to unfurl the flag of a sovereign Maharashtra, but that did not happen. When India became Independent in 1947, the leaders of the DMK had to realign their positions with what they saw was a popular sentiment around them. A few years later, in the early 1950s, Annadurai had no option but to announce that the freedom of India was the freedom of all India and not just of North India.

The Age of City: Challenges of Urbanisation

Urbanisation will be a defining feature of India's growth in the next decades. Opportunities provided by a urbanisation will provide impetus to economic growth and innovation and enable vast segments of population to be lifted out of poverty.

In the last three-four decades, nations like China, Korea, Singapore have recorded unprecedented economic growth by becoming the manufacturing destinations of the entire world. These countries have managed to wean away global industrial entrepreneurs and giant multinational corporations from the developed countries to set up manufacturing bases in Asia, not just because of cheaper labour, but equally importantly, by creating manufacturing cities which on account of their infrastructure are great places to live, work and play.

In contrast, during the last couple of decades, India has made huge strides in the IT and Services Sector, but not so successfully in manufacturing. So far, the major attempts towards infrastructure for industrial development in the country have been largely confined to the establishment of industrial parks and industrial estates. These do not stand any comparison with the scale and high quality of developed infrastructure and lack integration and convergence with social development to enhance quality of life.

To maintain sustained national GDP growth of 9-10% per annum it is essential that the manufacturing sector in India also grows steadily at 14-15% per annum over the next three decades. To achieve this India needs to rapidly enhance its competitiveness in manufacturing by attracting global investors through the creation of world class infrastructure and reduced logistics costs. A major initiative of developing the Delhi Mumbai Industrial

Corridor (DMIC) on the backbone of the western leg of the Dedicated Freight Corridor (DFC) has been initiated. The DMIC is essentially aimed at the **development of 24 futuristic, new, industrial cities** in India which can compete with the best manufacturing and investment destinations in the world.

The development of new cities has been initiated at a time when the scorching pace of urbanisation is a major challenge facing the country. According to McKinsey's recent studies by 2030, 40% of India's population will be living in urban areas, 68 cities will have a population of more than 1 million, and 70% of net new employment will be generated in cities. It is estimated that, on average about 75% of global economic production takes place in cities. Indian urban areas will also follow the trend and account for nearly 70% of the country's GDP by 2030. While such unprecedented growth is welcome from an economic perspective, it would also bring about severe attendant challenges. A report on Intelligent urbanisation by Booz & Co. has alluded that by 2020, housing shortage will reach about 30 million dwelling units, 200 million new water connections will be required, 250 million people will have to be given access to sewage, 160 GW of power generating capacity to be added and the number of vehicles on our urban roads will increase by 5 times.

India needs to also create several new-generation, greenfield cities that are planned, financed, developed, operated and managed more efficiently, in harmony with future urbanisation trends and requirements. The late Prof. C.K. Prahalad, author of "The Fortune at the Bottom of the Pyramid" had stated that "India needs to build 500 new cities urgently to provide better quality life to its migrating people; otherwise every existing city will become a slum when Independent India becomes 75 in 2022

Most of the cities built in Europe and America were established in the 19th century when there was easy availability to public goods like gas and water. This led to sprawling cities with residence being far away from the place of work and utilities operating in vertical silos. Today's world is far more crowded and complex and requires much more efficient, long term solutions for servicing urban areas. Today's cities have to be compact, based on scientific master planning, must evolve and grow on a public transport axis with integration of publics services.

The DNA of a new cities is formed based on its public transport system. As has often been said, we should move people and not cars, through an efficient public transport system. Cycling and walking are an integral component of the planning for new cities. Bogota for instance built 400 kilometers of bicycle paths used today by 3,50,000 cyclists. Land use and transportation plans have to be integrated alongwith land requirement for housings. Curitiba has the highest rate of public transport ridership in Brazil (45%). It has the lowest rate of urban air pollution. Fuel loss due to traffic congestion in 2002 was US$ 930,000 as compared to US$ 13.4 million in Rio-de-Janeiro. The cities must also recycle waste and sewage water. Yokohama city in Japan generates US$ 23.5 million from selling recyclables and another US$ 24.6 million from electricity generated from incineration.

India is in the process of developing world class industrial regions in the corridor between Delhi and Mumbai. This development, in part is being facilitated by a new Dedicated Freight Corridor in the form of a railway between Delhi and Mumbai. The objective is to create a strong economic base in this band with a globally competitive environment (dedicated power & water supply), reduced logistic costs and state of the art infrastructure. The project provides a unique opportunity for the country to plan, develop, build and manage cities that are both ecologically and economically sustainable.

The Delhi-Mumbai Industrial Corridor has completed the master planning of a new city of almost 900 sq. Kms. at Dholera in Gujarat, the Manesar-Bawal Industrial region in Haryana, the Indore-Pithampur-Mhow industrial region in Madhya Pradesh and is at an advanced stage with the master planning of the Dighi Port Investment region and the Nasik-Sinnar-Igatpuri region in Maharashtra. The master plans being prepared, the strategic urban approaches being adopted and the infrastructure decisions being made with respect to these regions will have consequences for future generations.

There are several challenges we face – our preliminary estimates reveal that a greenfield global competitive city with all its external and internal infrastructure will require an outlay of around Rs. 60,000-70,000 crores. It is possible to commercialise and structure private public partnership (PPP) models on approximately 65-70% of this outlay. Almost 30-35% of the outlay is required in phases for trunk infrastructure which are key to the city and are not capable of commercialisation. This is critical as we should not create new "Gurgaon's" without drainage and sewerage. Taking a city's life span of thirty years the city as an economic model is highly viable and would generate substantial resources. This is in addition to its high multiplier impact on other aspect of the economy. However, there is a revenue-expenditure mismatch in the first eleven-twelve years of the project cycle. This necessitates, infrastructure financing of long tenor at reasonable rates. Governance of the cities is a key issue to ensure better and more efficient management of the assets being created. Thus the organisational structure holds the key for long-term sustainability of the new cities.

Proposed Model For India and Interpreting the results of the CNP quantitative model

The concept of comprehensive national power (CNP) is, in the final analysis, a relative concept. Only when relating a state's national capabilities across a range of metrics among a selected peer group of countries can we assess and rank nations. As eluded to in the *Introduction* and *Conceptualizing Comprehensive National Power* chapters, the authors selected 8 countries that constitute India's peer group. The reason for this narrow selection was the following: In the hierarchical order that has defined international politics over the past millenia, a handful of nations have wielded disproportionate strength in international relations. In the contemporary era, US, Russia and China are the obvious great powers. Germany and Japan follow as technologically advanced and prosporous states that posess many of the ingredients that define a great power. In the third tier, come the emerging and middle powers such as India, Brazil, South Africa and Indonesia. These four states that have the potential – in terms of economy, demography, human capital, geography, natural resources and military capacity – to emerge as regional or great powers in the coming decades.

When developing the model the authors felt that a multi-variable approach would be the most suitable method to assess a state's CNP. The reason for this is that the traditional approach of a single variable analysis that focuses either on war making capacity or combat capabilities of nations or their economic potential provides an incomplete assessment of national power.

One of the reasons for pursuing single variable analyses conducted mainly by western political scienctists has been their interest in evaluating and ranking great powers that had already arrived on the international system. Hence, focusing on a single economic or military metric was sufficient as this became a proxy for capabilities within the domestic system of the studied countries. This study, since it is being conducted from the perspective of an emerging power, which has yet to cross the threshold in multiple underlying ingredients that make a great power, is therefore primarily interested in understanding what are the building blocks of national power. To put it more plainly, the process of first generating wealth for sustained periods and simultaneously converting acquired wealth to power is neither linear nor inevitable. In sum, a multiple-variable analysis was necessary given the objective of this study.

In addition, the complexity of contemporary interstate interactions suggests that power does not always "flow from the barrel of a gun". The two defining characteristics of international relations in the modern era – economic interdependence or globalisation and the nuclear revolution – have combined to make the conduct of foreign policy and inter-state interactions a more complex endeavor. Globalisation aided by the advancement of transport and connectivity technologies has made economic interactions more extensive and deeper than in earlier eras. The nuclear and misile revolution has made unrestrained state action that was witnessed in the first half of the twentieth century impossible. Today, while military force matters its political use is often restricted to preventing war or conflict from escalating to high levels of violence (i.e. deterrence) or conducting limited expeditions or wars or to extend security assistance to other weaker states. In short, military power matters, but its use is more complex, limited and circumscribed by the overall logic of maintaining strategic stability.

States can no longer pursue their interests in a Clauzwitsian sense where use of force or threat of force is the sole driver of their foreign policies. Other factors such as economic do matter and in many cases have become significant aspects of inter-state interactions.

Our model will not only provide a snapshot of the contemporary international hierarchy (based on our 9 country peer group) but also flag areas or aspects of power where India lags behind other states. A graphical representation of the model is appended at the end of this chapter. *(Please refer the CD enclosed with the book for graphical representation)*

The determinants of CNP

The idea of CNP is premised on the primacy of the state as the principal actor in the international system. Yet, to gauge the relative power of different states, one needs to disaggregate national power whereby each constituent or *determinant* of national power has a relative capability to be gauged. The notion of CNP, however, implies that the sub-components of power are greater than the sum of its individual parts. Thus, the *interdependencies* within the state's various internal components are implicitly recognised and these determinants dynamically interact to produce what is known as CNP.

What influences a state's 'extractive capacity' or in other words its ability to convert wealth to power?

(a) **Economic structure** – material and natural resources. This determinant has a dual feature in the sense that aside from providing the surpluses to transform physical and human resources into tangible capabilities it also serves as a non-coercive instrument of power by itself. Economic power is the source or foundation of nearly all other aspects of material power. **In our model, the economy received a weightage of 25 percent.**

(b) **Science & Technology** – S&T is what enables states to not only sustain growth but enhance the productivity of their economies. By itself, it also is a source of leverage in international politics since countries that possess cutting edge technologies can extract higher surpluses and influence by allowing weaker states from plugging into high-technology industries. **In our model, S&T received a weightage of 12.5 percent.**

(c) **Governance** – Governance has five underlying facets – accountability, political stability (absence of violence), government effectiveness, rule of law and control of corruption. **In our model, Governance received a weightage of 15 percent.**

(d) **Human Capital** – Measures the institutional and knowledge capability of the system to leverage its human resource endowment (demography). Education and health are the main sub-determinants of guaging the quality of human capital across nations. **In our model, Human Capital received a weightage of 12.5 percent.**

The above may be considered as the "building blocks" or "inputs" of CNP. These building blocks embody latent power and only the state's political performance can convert these building blocks into useable power instruments.

And since in an anarchical or "self help" international system, the ultimate currency of useable power is military force the principal objective of a security seeking state is to convert its "building blocks" into military capabilities. Thus, for CNP to be complete the chain, the extractive process *must* produce a tangible output - combat capabilities. This is captured by the determinant of Military Capability. **In our model, Military capability received a weightage of 20 percent.**

The final component of CNP is one that provides it a strategic character or grand strategy.

In our study the 'Foreign Policy' Determinant attempts to measure the capacity of the state in terms of its autonomy, grand strategy (or the institutional and ideational ability to generate and adapt one), and the quality of the strategic bureaucracy (those assigned to implement national security goals) as they combine to maneuver the state in international life by leveraging all the material and ideological strengths that a state can mobilise. Finally, **in our model, Foreign Policy received a weightage of 15 percent.**

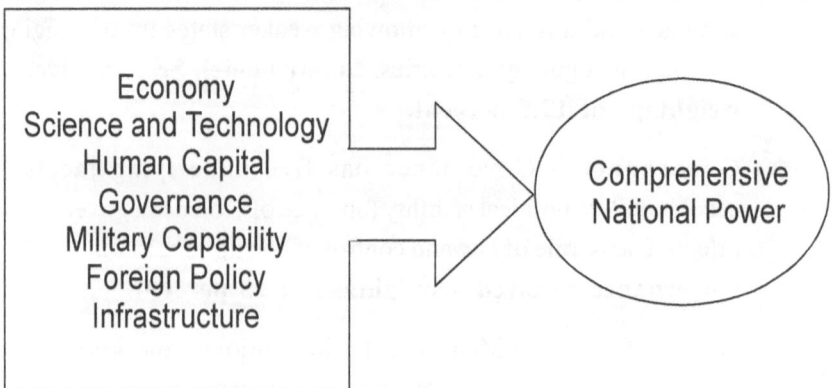

Economy
Science and Technology
Human Capital
Governance
Military Capability
Foreign Policy
Infrastructure

Comprehensive
National Power

Mathematically, this study's CNP function would be defined as,

CNP= F (D1, D2....D6)

Where,

D = Determinant (consisting of sub-determinants)

(Note: The entire quantitative data set and it computation has been placed in the Annexure and is available in electronic format for the reviewer to scrutinise the data and methodology.)

Explaination of methodology and interpretation of the final results:

1. Economy

In order to assess the quality and structure of a state's economy, the economic determinant was disaggregated into seven sub-determinants:

(a) **Leveraging GDP**: This seeks to measure the ability of the state (central government) to draw resources from society. Ratios such as public debt to GDP, tax revenue to GDP, and government expenditure to GDP are deemed to be the most important proxies. Given the importance of this measure, leveraging GDP was assigned a weight of 20 percent.

(b) **Exposure and Interdependence of Economy:** This seeks to measure a state's dependence on the global economy. For example, a state that relies on international trade to a large extent would find its foreign policy was constrained than a state that can generate economic value or complex divisions of labour from its domestic system. Similarly, a state with a high share of foreign debt to GDP would be exposed to international capital and creditors, and thus potential foreign pressure. Nations that run trade surpluses are considered economically and politically stronger than nations that consumed more than they produce indigenously. Finally, states that have a high stock of net FDI possess leverage over another state's political economy. Given the importance of this sub-determinant in shaping a state's overall economic power, it was assigned a weightage of 20 percent.

(c) **Modernity of Economic System:** This seeks to measure the structure of a state's economy in terms of sectoral contributions by agriculture, industry and services. It also evaluates a country's level of urbanisation, level of investment rate as a percentage of GDP. A weightage of 10 percent was assigned.

(d) **Human Development Index:** Based on the United Nations HDI, this metric seeks to evaluate states on life expectancy and state spending on healthcare and education. It received a weightage of 17.5 percent.

(e) **Demography:** This sub-determinant seeks to measure a nation's potential workforce available for economic activities. It received a weightage of 12.5 percent.

(f) **Non-energy resources:** This sub-determinant seeks to evalute a nation on three important measures indicative of resource pressures and food security facing a state: Arable land as a percentage of total land area, which would reveal the potential for domestic food production; renewable freshwater available per capita is again important in flagging which states are likely to face resource deficits; the population density is a good proxy for the overall pressure on the ecological system and natural resource base that a nation possesses. A weightage of 10 percent was assigned.

(g) **Energy Security:** It evaluates a state's import dependence on energy resources and percentage of clean consumption in a state's overall energy mix. A weightage of 10 percent was assigned.

Data for all the above metrics was mined from diverse by internationally credible sources such as the World Bank, IMF, UN and Economist Intelligence Unit.

Leading powers in economic strength

Rank	Country	Score
1	China	0.0444
2	Japan	0.0391
3	Germany	0.0358
4	Russia	0.0283
5	Indonesia	0.0250
6	India	0.0234
7	South Africa	0.0213
8	Brazil	0.0197
9	US	0.0130

2.   Science and technology

In order to assess the science and technology capabilities of a state, the peer group was assessed on eleven different metrics related to S&T. For a detailed description of the eleven metrics vis-à-vis the rationale for selection, weightages and data sources please refer to chapter on Science and Technology.

Leading powers in S&T

Rank	Country	Score
1	Japan	0.0294
2	US	0.0272
3	Germany	0.0229
4	China	0.0126
5	Russia	0.0097
6	Brazil	0.0083
7	South Africa	0.0079
8	India	0.0063
9	Indonesia	0.0008

3.   Human Capital

This determinant seeks to evaluate the fundamental of a state's system for human capital development. It includes an extensive look at several educational indicators including traditional mesasures such as adult and youth literacy, state spending on education to more detailed measures such as school life expectancy at various levels of education. It also seeks to assess a state's health care system both in terms of manpower adequacy, state spending and household affordability. Data was primarily sourced from the World Bank's Annual World Development Indicators.

Leading powers in Human Capital

Rank	Country	Score
1	US	0.0190
2	Germany	0.0177
3	Russia	0.0160
4	Japan	0.0157
5	Brazil	0.0144
6	SA	0.0128
7	China	0.0107
8	Indonesia	0.0100
9	India	0.0087

4.   Governance

Governance has five underlying facets – accountability, political stability (absence of violence), government effectiveness, rule of law and control of corruption. These five fundamentals of governance indicate the sustainability and control of a state's leadership or elite or single party regime to maintain societal order. Data was primarily sourced from the World Bank's Annual World Governance Indicators.

Leading powers in Governance

Rank	Country	Score
1	Germany	0.0290
2	USA	0.0257
3	Japan	0.0253
4	South Africa	0.0175
5	Brazil	0.0165
6	China	0.0120
7	India	0.0117
8	Russia	0.0072
9	Indonesia	0.0052

5.   Military Capability

Given the importance of this determinant the authors undertook a comprehensive assessment of relative military potential of the peer group. Furthermore, since the study seeks scrutinise military capability beyond the most common metric – state military spending as a percentage of GDP – it was necessary to rely on expert opinion as a substitute for data for many of the variables that might not exist in open source formats or would be costly to assemble for the purposes of an analytical study or was of a qualitative nature where subjective judgments are the only means of gauging a relative score. In fact, the Delphi method is a well established way of surveying the opinion of experts on a range of metrics. The sub-determinants were presented to a closed group of 150 officers at the National Defence College. The participants were then asked to assign scores ranging from a minimum of 1 to a maximum of 9 for the entire peer group of 9 countries. Below is the result of that poll. The average score for each country was used to determine its relative rank in the country set.

Military Sub-Determinants	US	Germany	Japan	Russia	China	India	Indonesia	Brazil	South Africa
Institutions to Regenerate Military Thinking	8.6	6.38	5.6	6.8	7.24	5.73	3.59	4.4	4.27
Defence Expenditure/G-DP	8.44	5.55	5.05	6.44	7.83	5.18	3.59	4.43	4.21
Ordnance Delivery	8.56	5.84	4.68	7.03	7.09	5.45	3.43	4.37	4.41
Defence R&D as % of Total R%D	8.52	6.16	5.15	6.78	7.16	4.43	2.91	4.25	4.39
% of Regular Forces Employed in Internal Security Forces	5.29	4.85	4.75	5.35	5.44	5.53	4.56	4.63	4.52
State of Indigenisation of Conventional	8.53	6.62	5.56	7.58	6.96	4.56	2.97	4.35	4.51

Military Sub-Determinants	US	Germany	Japan	Russia	China	India	Indonesia	Brazil	South Africa
Expeditionary/Transnational Capability as % of Defence Expenditure	8.55	5.94	4.74	6.76	6.46	5.05	3.09	3.9	4.07
Omniscience as % of Defence Expenditure	8.43	6	5.16	6.76	6.84	5	3.06	4.02	4.16
Networking as % of Defence Expenditure	8.44	6.43	5.71	6.25	6.57	4.77	3	4.01	4.18
Command Structure for Speed of Battle	8.56	6.63	5.52	6.94	6.82	5.5	3.52	4.33	4.35
Independent defence of Space Assets or in Alliance	8.57	5.85	5.47	7.2	6.7	5.1	2.69	3.59	3.58
Civil Military Relations	8.02	6.86	6.25	6.48	6.66	5.32	4.03	5.14	5.04
Tactical Capability	8.24	6.34	5.38	7.02	7.3	6.63	3.96	4.61	4.71
Nuclear Capability	8.81	3.95	2.64	7.59	7.26	5.88	1.55	2.2	2.68
Arsenal	8.81	3.76	2.24	7.75	7.19	5.28	1.61	2.27	2.6

Leading powers in Military Capability

Rank	Country	Score
1	US	0.0368
2	Russia	0.0311
3	China	0.0304
4	India	0.0234
5	Germany	0.0215
6	Japan	0.0167
7	South Africa	0.0151
8	Brazil	0.0141
9	Indonesia	0.0108

6.   Foreign Policy

Foreign Policy in our model attempts to capture not only the infrastructural capacity of the Ministry of Foreign Affairs but also the strategic flexibility, ideational capabilities and geopolitical relevance of a state. In sum, foreign policy is deemed to be a proxy for assessing the quality of a grand strategy and all the institutional pre-requisites such as inter-agency coordination, jointness of the armed services etc.

Foreign policy can be disaggregated into four variables:

(a) **Strategic Autonomy:** Strategic flexibility of a Great/Regional Power versus alliance commitments, level of conformity and strategic dependence on an alliance leader for other states. For instance, Germany, France, Japan, Turkey, Australia, South Korea have partial autonomy having forfeited an independent foreign policy for security under the US security umbrella compared to Russia, China and India who have autonomous foreign policies. To defend an autonomous foreign policy a state must possess autonomous military-industrial capabilities. Thus, absence of alliance commitments is not sufficient for strategic autonomy.

(b) Geopolitical Relevance: This sub-metric has been included to capture the impact of geography on a state's position in the international system. For example, Brazil's geopolitical location would not offer it any significant leverage in international politics to say Japan given the latter's proximity to Asia Pacific's great powers, even though the latter has limited foreign policy autonomy (bilateral alliance with the US).

(c) Ideational Capability: Ideational capability seeks to evaluate a state's capacity to generate a strategic template that can guide its national security managers. Three factors capture a state's ideational capability:

(i) Does the state have a recognizable grand strategy?

(ii) Prestige of policy planning process.

(iii) Quality of national security decision making process, interagency efficiency etc. The above three metrics are interdependent – a grand strategy is of little value without accompanying institutions to aid its implementation, and great institutions require a worldview and strategy to guide them.

(d) Foreign Policy Infrastructure: This is captured by following metrics:

(i) Size of cadre;

(ii) No. of personnel per desk (for major powers and functional areas like arms control, climate change, international trade and finance etc.);

(iii) Training frequency (periodicity of mid-career courses);

(iv) Outsourcing flexibility for non-available expertise/Lateral access options. The above four metrics seek to capture the quality, specialization and scale of human resources involved with foreign policy conception, monitoring and implementation.

Given the qualitative aspects of many of these variables, it was again found that a Delphi approach would be the most efficient and suitable means of arriving a relative scores for the peer group. Each variable was assessed on a scale of 1-9 and expert participants were polled to provide their subjective opinion after being provided a descriptive essence for each variable.

Foreign Policy Sub-Determinants	US	Germany	Japan	Russia	China	India	Indonesia	Brazil	South Africa
Strategic Autonomy	8.34	5.78	5.09	7.21	7.26	5.71	4	5.1	4.92
Relevance in Great Power Calculations	8.76	5.78	5.59	6.98	7.51	5.35	3.1	4.27	4.01
Ideational Capability	8.54	5.93	5.74	6.9	7.58	5.5	3.35	4.52	4.33
Foreign Policy Intellectual Infrastructure	8.64	6.26	5.95	6.71	7.33	5.2	3.63	4.72	4.58
Foreign Policy Infrastructure Institutional Adequacy	8.61	6.03	5.81	6.72	7.49	5	3.57	4.48	4.36

The average score for each state was then used to determine its relative position in the peer group.

Leading powers in Foreign Policy

Rank	Country	Score
1	US	0.0245
2	China	0.0213
3	Russia	0.0197
4	Germany	0.0170
5	Japan	0.0161
6	India	0.0153
7	Brazil	0.0132
8	South Africa	0.0127
9	Indonesia	0.0101

Final CNP ranking

As a multiple-variable study, this model assessed each state on 88 variables spread across 6 master determinants. Based on the weighted results of each determinant, the computation of the final CNP score and rank for each state is straightforward. A state's total CNP score is the summation of its score on each of the 6 sub-determinants discussed earlier. **India's rank is 6th in the peer group of 9 states.**

Country	CNP Number	Rank
US	0.146	1
Germany	0.144	2
Japan	0.142	3
China	0.131	4
Russia	0.112	5
India	**0.089**	6
South Africa	0.087	7
Brazil	0.086	8
Indonesia	0.062	9

Graphical Representation of Relative Ranking:

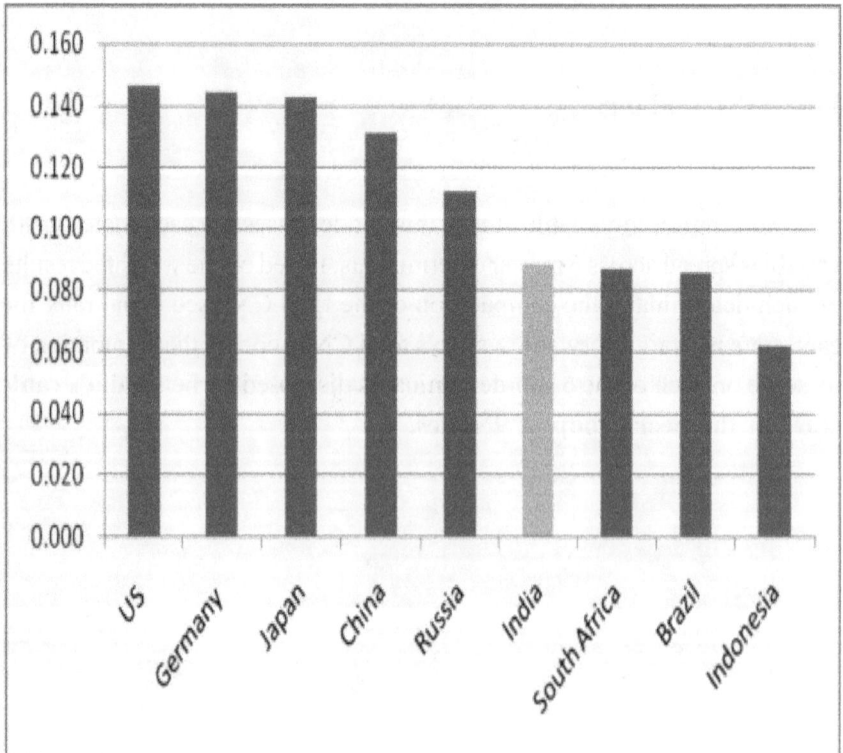

Comprehensive National Power- India's Road Ahead To Great Power Status

India's aspirations to become a great power in the Asia-Pacific region and beyond can be traced to the time of Jawaharlal Nehru, its first post-independence prime minister. At that time, however, India's hopes of assuming great power status were based on an aspirational world view of constructing a new global order based on international law, reliance on multilateral institutions and an end to balance of power politics. This world view was based both on expediency and a moral component.

Six decades after it secured independence, can India emerge as a great power? The question is far from trivial. At an international level, India's rise, if peaceful, would challenge a widely held belief in the study of international politics that holds that the rise of new great powers can lead to major war as their interests clash with those of existing great powers. Yet, so far at least, no state has expressed serious misgivings about India's rise. There's little question that India is on a renewed quest for great power status. However, as it embarks on this path, it still faces a number of pitfalls—its rise is far from certain or inevitable.

There's no arguing with the fact that India has been able to bring about dramatic changes, both at home and abroad. However, it still has a long and tortuous path to travel before it can achieve its grand hopes of becoming a great power. A host of barriers still lie along the road and it's still unclear if it can overcome them.

For a start, and despite significant and sustained economic growth, a sizeable portion of India's population still remains mired in abject, dehumanising poverty. According to survey data, close to 26 percent of the population still lives below the official poverty line. Meanwhile, after 65 years of independence, almost 27 percent of the rural population still lacks access to safe drinking water. Despite varied efforts to promote literacy, only about 65 percent of the population has achieved basic literacy. The list of such statistics goes on. Unless India can find ways to forge policies that address these deeply disturbing shortcomings, rapid economic growth and the consequent emergence of a robust and vibrant middle class will amount to little.

Ironically, the emergence of this new middle class has placed even greater stress on the country's woeful infrastructure. For example, only very belatedly has India transformed the airports of three of its four principal cities–those in New Delhi, Mumbai and Hyderabad. Yet the very roadways and highways that connect the airports to their respective cities have yet to be commensurately improved. Similar limitations continue to dog India's principal ports, many of which operate with antiquated equipment and docking facilities.

Apart from this persistence of endemic poverty and poor infrastructure, India faces other critical challenges in its search for great power status: its acute shortage of critical human capital. At one level, the country can justifiably claim that it has some institutions of higher education which can compete with their peers on a global basis. But these institutions are mostly confined to the realms of science, engineering and management and despite the existence of these centres of excellence; mediocrity is the hallmark of many of India's other educational institutions. For example, with the possible exception of the discipline of economics, India lags woefully behind in the other social sciences such as sociology, anthropology and political science. Few, if any, significant contributions to these fields of intellectual endeavour have emerged from India in recent decades. Most scholarship in these areas is derivative, or worse, still mostly descriptive and hortatory.

A critical component of one of these disciplines, the study of international relations, is essentially in the doldrums. In a nation of well over a billion people, the country has perhaps a dozen or fewer international relations scholars of international repute and stature. Worse still is the state of area studies at Indian universities. Despite adversarial relations with both the PRC and Pakistan, not one Indian university has a world-class South Asia or China studies program. As a consequence it lacks scholars who might be able to provide policy-relevant advice to India's decision-makers. Such a paucity of trained academics will inevitably compromise the quality of India's foreign policy analyses and choices.

Aside from these critical educational shortcomings, the efficacy of India's bureaucratic apparatus is problematic–or worse. The civil service, which is composed mostly of generalists, is increasingly unequal to the complexity of the tasks that they are expected to perform. Yet few reforms have been enacted to impart the requisite training that would enable them to meet the challenges of governance in a modernizing state. The curricular changes that have been made in their training upon entry into the civil service are piecemeal and incremental. Furthermore, a cadre of less than 5,000 officers constitutes the national work force of the civil service. To compound matters, thanks to India's recent economic success the civil service, with its limited pay scale, is no longer attracting the best talent available in the country.

These institutional infirmities, in turn, have prevented the country from tackling various on-going social tensions and associated violence with vigour. For example, for the better part of the last decade, a resurgent Maoist movement, referred to as the Naxalites, has stalked significant parts of the country. Today it afflicts at least 20 states and some 223 districts across the country. Despite sporadic efforts to tackle this movement, the Indian state has yet to fashion a coherent national strategy to contain and suppress it. Meanwhile, the Naxalites have grown bolder, attacking police stations and various large-scale commercial projects with seeming impunity. Admittedly, India has had ample experience in dealing with insurgents and has managed to cope with a host of insurgencies in its 65 year history as an independent state. Yet the intransigence of this movement poses a genuine threat to foreign investment in the country and therefore to its overall economic well-being.

Finally, the Indian state has yet to come to terms with another growing social cleavage which could prove to be even more consequential for its continued political stability and economic growth. There's evidence, for example, that the Pakistan-based terrorists who attacked Mumbai in November 2008 had received assistance from domestic sources. Unless India's political class forthrightly comes to terms with this emergent internal threat, its hopes of extending its influence beyond its shores could well be thwarted.

It's said that Charles de Gaulle once mordantly quipped that Brazil is the country of the future and always will be. The same, unfortunately, could be said about India. It has obviously longed to be a great power but has never marshalled the requisite resources with the necessary sense of purpose to make a breakthrough on multiple fronts. As a consequence it has made significant progress in some areas but has remained a hopeless laggard in others. Unless it can summon its human and material resources to tackle the myriad challenges that it confronts, both at home and abroad, its fond hopes of achieving great power status will continue to remain a fleeting mirage.

The Road Ahead

A recent study of input-output structure identified 10 vital sectors in the Indian economy based on growth impacts on GDP of efficiency improvements in these sectors. These sectors include electricity, water and gas supply, transport services, railway transport services, coal and lignite, etc. The study found that India's growth rate is at least as sensitive to these sectors as it was prior to the 1991 reforms. It is inefficiencies and underinvestment in these infrastructure sectors that has prevented both a take-off in manufacturing industries and deprived the latter from receiving export-oriented foreign direct investment (FDI).

In contrast, the services sector in general and the information technology and software sectors in particular, which are relatively less capital-intensive in their operations and less reliant on core 'public goods', have unsurprisingly flourished, as have certain niche manufacturing sectors that have created their own captive sources of private infrastructure. For instance, 30 percent of industrial electricity consumption is accounted for by captive generation, predominantly diesel generator sets.

More generally, supply-side bottlenecks continue to constrain Indian industry. In the 1980's, India had higher infrastructure stocks in power, roads and telecommunication, and, was only surpassed by China in 1990. After the mid-1980s, the pressure on public expenditure from rising deficits constrained public investment. From 1986, public investment in GDP began a steady decline from 11.2 per cent to 5.6 per cent of GDP in 2003–04. Even today, for every $1 that India spends on infrastructure, China spends $7. Over the past 20 years, India's self-reliance in the production of machine tools has fallen from 80 per cent to the current 20 per cent.

The gap in infrastructure stocks is now so large that for India to catch up with China's present level of stocks per capita by 2015, it would have to invest 12.5 percent of GDP per year on infrastructure. For India to maintain growth rates of 8-10 percent, it is estimated that it would have to invest a $1 trillion over the next decade.

The Indian economic story over the last decade has clearly drawn the attention of the world, evidenced by the flood of heads of state who visited in 2010. Much of this traffic drew attention to India as a customer of foreign goods, a fact which was reflected in the big-ticket deals that India struck during the visits of the leaders of the US, Britain, France, Russia and China. The largest component of India's GDP is services, a statistic which lends itself to the question: how much does or can India innovate or generate intellectual property in Science and Technology (S&T)?

In the measurement of innovative capacity in a global context, India ranks poorly on all of the selected indicators in comparison with the selected countries. India's ranking in these areas predicts some important choices for Indian policymakers, if incentivizing innovation is a major goal.

While practical innovation or *jugaad* in India may be lauded, and even important for domestic markets, India's competitiveness as a global innovator lies in generating export-competitive innovation. As Hussein Kanji describes, Indian companies that are ready to innovate struggle with locating engineering talent. Further, the studied data clearly shows India lacking in the production of resident researchers.

Given the objective factors in India's favour, India is bound to be one of the leading powers of the world. There is no escaping this. We are the second largest demographically and by 2050, we will be largest economy doing very well. Militarily we are doing well, we have manpower empowered well to propel the country move fast. The reasons for not exercising effective power are internal instability, structural weaknesses, and multi religious and multi-ethnic historically. Our democracy has enabled us to deal with these factors in our society. Democracy should be our strength, which is and one can give many examples where democracy has not helped us achieve potentially what we could have achieved. Our priority has to be that of development. Our external challenges are adding to our internal challenges at home. But our challenges remain internal. That is the problem of ethnic spill over, and about our vulnerability to terrorism. We have unsettled borders. We have continuity with powerful neighbours which are our adversaries. These are the reasons which make us appear we are not bold and robust in foreign policy choices because we constantly going wrong in the house, as we have not been able to deal with street issues.

In the past, as peoples of the Indic civilization, we as a society were marginally troubled by the role that the military played in National Power. If our fate was ruled by our 'karma' or by providential laws then, that was as satisfactory as if there had been no such divine intervention; for we assumed that the future of mankind would be secured by the activities of free and intelligent people. If even this was not quite satisfactory, nature's law of inexorability took over. Unfortunately by the middle of the 20th century such convenient illusions were well and truly dispelled. Civilizations and empires had collapsed with increasingly rapid frequency and at times in violent storms, leaving in its wake broken ideologies, battered leadership and impoverished societies.

At the heart of the matter lay power. Its quest, accretion and relevance have been the only constant through all of history. It has provided a rationale for stability and, in its own right, been a regulatory agent. We have noted that given the international system that we are a part of and the realism that pervades it; of all the determinants of power, military muscle is explicit in its application and at the same time implicit as an expression of a country's will to power. An attempt has been made to place this abstraction within the larger framework of the nation's standing, or in Fukuyama's words the 'Stateness' of the country. While the task of the international system has been to tame the exercise of power, it is a paradox that the same power provides the facility to regulate and control its exercise. Nuclear power takes the debate to its logical extreme of absolute destruction and in arriving at this macabre conclusion it provides the basis of drawing boundaries and limiting conflicts.

We have in the course of our debate examined the views of several scholars on the subject and noted in some details the Chinese approach to the formulation of CNP and the manner in which they have transformed their centralized approach, which to some schools appear as a weakness, into strength. Decision making that is command and control and integration of our resources including civil military relations, technology adaptation and our propensity to operate in stove pipes are areas of weakness that we must remedy. Failing which our ability to rise beyond the tactical will remain an enduring impediment. The sage voice of Kautilya reminds us that the military power of a state is not just the mere counting of armed physicals, but also of 'mantra yuddha' the power of good policies, sound judgement, precision command, analysis and good counsel.

Development is an outcome of efficient institutions rather than the other way around. Focus therefore must be shifted from maximising the quantity of development funding to maximising of development outcomes and effectiveness of public service delivery. Despite good achievement on the growth front, India faces significant challenges and needs to take some difficult political decisions. Concerted policy action is needed to lift the 250 million poor, and increasingly concentrated in the poorer states, out of poverty. This requires not so much additional resources, as better participation of stakeholders and sound delivery mechanisms. This requires improving the environment in which the three agencies of delivery - civil service, panchayats and NGOs – function, as described in this paper.

A good civil service is necessary but not sufficient for good governance; a bad civil service is sufficient but not necessary for bad governance. Thus, a dilapidated civil service has been a key factor in Africa's economic decline. Conversely, a strong civil service is one of several reasons why in several east Asian economies, especially Japan, Singapore, and South Korea, authoritarianism has co-existed with excellent economic performance. It can be argued that the link between authoritarianism and economic decline, so evident in Africa, has been inoperative in these Asian countries largely because of their strong civil service. Greater responsiveness and openness can legitimately be demanded of public administrations in many East Asian countries. Clearly, civil service systems in most East Asian countries cannot be considered a problem; they are, rather, an important part of the solution to these countries' other problems.

The situation in many Indian states who are responsible for achieving the Millennium Development Goals is different. A vast gap exists between the stated and unstated objectives. On paper the avowed objective of government is to give clean administration and work for the poor, but lucrative posts are auctioned to the highest bidder. Corruption is rampant. People have unfortunately accepted the position as *fait accompli* and resigned themselves to their fate. They too tend to seek short cuts and exploit the system by breaking rules or approaching mafia gangs and politicians for favours.

Governance reforms are intractable under a 'kleptocracy' that exploits national wealth for its own benefit and is, by definition, uninterested in transparency and accountability. A pliable and unskilled civil service is actually desirable from its point of view—public employees dependent on the regime's discretionary largesse are forced to become corrupt, cannot quit their jobs, and reluctantly become the regime's accomplices. Providing financial assistance from GOI to such states without linking it with performance and reforms would be a waste of resources. In all other cases, reform is manageable, albeit difficult, complex, and slow. Therefore, considering that the states would need external pressure on them to improve outcomes, certain control by GOI over the IAS and policy domain in social sector is necessary, till such time that the states show signs of improvement in governance.

The reforms, it must be emphasized, are not for the glory of the police - they are to give better security and protection to the people of the country, uphold their human rights and generally improve governance. In the context of the growing threat of terrorism and the expanding influence of Maoists, it is all the more imperative that our first line of defense is restructured and reorganized so that it is able to deal with these challenges effectively. Public opinion must be mobilized to put pressure on the executive to accelerate the process of police reforms. Media should also be involved in the process. A number of NGOs have evinced interest in pushing police reforms. They must join hands and pool their efforts. Police reforms are absolutely essential to uphold the country's democratic structure and sustain its economic progress.

The quest for equity as well as the search for global power and leverage both point to the same compelling need for India to renew its approach to its rapid urbanization.

And crafting a new approach requires India to fundamentally renew its political and governance structure even as it creates a framework for bringing together the public, private and social sectors in a generational mission to build the 80 percent of the country that still remains to be built.

The starting point of this approach has to be a genuine recognition that cities need to be a third tier of government at par with the central and state governments, deserving of autonomy and structures that allow them to function as discrete administrative units. India needs to unleash the immense potential of its cities and doing so requires accepting that, in the short term, in the competition for talent, political leadership and resources, there will be winners and losers. Yet, that is the only way forward for cities in India to chart their own paths and pursue development approaches that are responsive and accountable to the needs of city voters. Accountability for outcomes in cities has to be driven by local elections and the promise of career progression for political leaders who show results on the ground.

And the freeing of cities through devolution will have to be accompanied by the development of a new framework that, while exhibiting variation across the country as cities implement their own priorities and choices, provides a guide on the focus of public delivery, the involvement of the private sector, and the use of public policy instruments to drive urban development and investments.

On both the above, many compelling proposals remain on the table. What has been missing to date has been a sense of urgency in addressing the challenge head on, and a sense of commitment from the country's leadership to unleash cities from the clutches of entrenched political and private interests. Crafting a new approach to India's rapid urbanization and renewing its cities and towns remains one of the defining missions of this generation, the outcome of which will determine the extent to which India will play a meaningful role in the international order of the 21st century.

To a large extent the feeling among intellectuals that India might quite easily fall apart is because we believe that there is just one route to being a proper nation state and that is the one Europe and America took. What they overlook is that even in western settings language rarely united people; and in some cases, like Germany or UK, not even religion. When Italy became Italy only 2percent spoke Italian and when the French Revolution happened only about 17percent spoke French.

By the time India became Independent in 1947 the world had moved on. No longer was it politically possible to stamp out other languages or to privilege any one religion. Democracy had taken great strides in the intervening decades and centuries for India to turn its back to them.

Ultimately, we need to recognize that there is not just one privileged path to nation-statehood. Language and religion do not always coalesce to give a nation-state its durability. It is however more important to judge a nation-state not by how it came into being but what it does successfully once it has arrived on the world stage. All viable nation-states are able to successfully sacralize their territorial holdings and to delineate their borders in the public psyche. In India this happened with the Partition and hence it remains for many a live source of political symbolism. This is the negative side. On the positive side, there has not been any major political movement to partition the country, other than the disturbances in the North East and Kashmir. To understand these specific issues, one needs to pay attention on how the borders were drawn in these regions. Even here, one must be careful in one's analysis as there are great differences in the centrifugal forces in J&K and in the North East.

In the majority of the Indian land mass there is no discernible move towards secession. Even the Khalistani movement was supported by a few. The overwhelming numbers of Sikhs who were deeply hurt by what happened in the wake of Mrs. Indira Gandhi's assassination were, however, not in favour of Khalistan. To go back in time, once the State Reorganization

Committee had done its work, it was noticed that regional passions also subsided. It was initially believed that the call for Maharashtra would end in wanting to unfurl the flag of a sovereign Maharashtra, but that did not happen. When India became Independent in 1947, the leaders of the DMK had to realign their positions with what they saw was a popular sentiment around them. A few years later, in the early 1950s, Annadurai had no option but to announce that the freedom of India was the freedom of all India and not just of North India.

Urbanisation will be a defining feature of India's growth in the next decades. Opportunities provided by a urbanisation will provide impetus to economic growth and innovation and enable vast segments of population to be lifted out of poverty.

In the last three-four decades, nations like China, Korea, Singapore have recorded unprecedented economic growth by becoming the manufacturing destinations of the entire world. These countries have managed to wean away global industrial entrepreneurs and giant multinational corporations from the developed countries to set up manufacturing bases in Asia, not just because of cheaper labour, but equally importantly, by creating manufacturing cities which on account of their infrastructure are great places to live, work and play.

In contrast, during the last couple of decades, India has made huge strides in the IT and Services Sector, but not so successfully in manufacturing. So far, the major attempts towards infrastructure for industrial development in the country have been largely confined to the establishment of industrial parks and industrial estates. These do not stand any comparison with the scale and high quality of developed infrastructure and lack integration and convergence with social development to enhance quality of life.

To maintain sustained national GDP growth of 9-10percent per annum it is essential that the manufacturing sector in India also grows steadily at 14-15percent per annum over the next three decades. To achieve this India needs to rapidly enhance its competitiveness in manufacturing by attracting global investors through the creation of world class infrastructure and reduced logistics costs. A major initiative of developing the Delhi Mumbai Industrial Corridor (DMIC) on the backbone of the western leg of the Dedicated

Freight Corridor (DFC) has been initiated. The DMIC is essentially aimed at the development of 24 futuristic, new, industrial cities in India which can compete with the best manufacturing and investment destinations in the world.

The development of new cities has been initiated at a time when the scorching pace of urbanisation is a major challenge facing the country. According to McKinsey's recent studies by 2030, 40percent of India's population will be living in urban areas, 68 cities will have a population of more than 1 million, and 70percent of net new employment will be generated in cities. It is estimated that, on average about 75percent of global economic production takes place in cities. Indian urban areas will also follow the trend and account for nearly 70percent of the country's GDP by 2030. While such unprecedented growth is welcome from an economic perspective, it would also bring about severe attendant challenges. A report on Intelligent urbanisation by Booz & Co has alluded that by 2020, housing shortage will reach about 30 million dwelling units, 200 million new water connections will be required, 250 million people will have to be given access to sewage, 160 GW of power generating capacity to be added and the number of vehicles on our urban roads will increase by 5 times.

India needs to also create several new-generation, greenfield cities that are planned, financed, developed, operated and managed more efficiently, in harmony with future urbanisation trends and requirements. The late Prof CK Prahalad, author of "The Fortune at the Bottom of the Pyramid" had stated that "India needs to build 500 new cities urgently to provide better quality life to its migrating people; otherwise every existing city will become a slum when Independent India becomes 75 in 2022

Most of the cities built in Europe and America were established in the 19th century when there was easy availability to public goods like gas and water. This led to sprawling cities with residence being far away from the place of work and utilities operating in vertical silos. Today's world is far more crowded and complex and requires much more efficient, long term solutions for servicing urban areas. Today's cities have to be compact, based on scientific master planning, must evolve and grow on a public transport axis with integration of publics services.

The DNA of new cities is formed based on its public transport system. As has often been said, we should move people and not cars, through an efficient public transport system. Cycling and walking are an integral component of the planning for new cities. Land use and transportation plans have to be integrated along with land requirement for housings. The cities must also recycle waste and sewage water.

There are several challenges we face – our preliminary estimates reveal that a green field global competitive city with all its external and internal infrastructure will require an outlay of around Rs 60,000-70,000 crores. It is possible to commercialise and structure private public partnership (PPP) models on approximately 65-70 percent of this outlay. Almost 30-35 percent of the outlay is required in phases for trunk infrastructure which are key to the city and are not capable of commercialisation. This is critical as we should not create new "Gurgaon's" without drainage and sewerage. Taking a city's life span of thirty years the city as an economic model is highly viable and would generate substantial resources. This is in addition to its high multiplier impact on other aspect of the economy. However, there is a revenue-expenditure mismatch in the first eleven-twelve years of the project cycle. This necessitates, infrastructure financing of long tenor at reasonable rates. Governance of the cities is a key issue to ensure better and more efficient management of the assets being created. Thus the organisational structure holds the key for long-term sustainability of the new cities.

Ever since independence our "military capability" determinant has remained woefully inadequate in terms of defending and furthering the Country's security and National interests. Immediately after independence Pakistan attacked and captured a significant portion of Kashmir (POK) which is yet to be recovered. Besides since 1990 Pakistan has brazenly and with impunity waged a covert war against us. Our response has never gone beyond threats and talks. In 1962 the Chinese subjected us to a humiliating defeat. Though the Chinese withdrew in the North Eastern sector to the McMahon line, in the Ladakh Sector they remain in possession of almost 40,000 sq kms of our territory. Since then despite continual dialogue and diplomacy the territorial issues between us remain unresolved. The Chinese continue to claim some 90,000 sq kms in Arunachal Pradesh and another small chunk in the middle sector. Crank in the military equation on the border areas only to discover how perilous the situation can be.

Apart from the sacred charge of ensuring territorial integrity the military has an equally important function in securing an environment that facilitates economic growth. This is an aspect often lost sight of. It should be assumed that potential adversaries are likely to try and derail or impede our economic growth. The military and other national instruments are meant to be an insurance against such designs.

Increasing the budgetary allocation for defense is important but not enough. There are other equally important measures to be taken to enhance our defence capability. The study has dwelt on them. To briefly recapitulate; first is the imperative of integration, cohesion and synergy of the three services. The integrated headquarters has been created but for a whole range of entirely extraneous reasons the CDS has not yet been appointed. This must be done without further delay. Otherwise let us disband the integrated headquarters and create another model for higher defense management. The headless integrated defense headquarters cannot be anybody's idea of efficient higher defense management. We must swiftly eject from the comfort zone of drift.

Another extremely important but neglected facet of higher defense management is the relationship and rapport between senior defense officers and the political leadership. Over the last six decades or so the absence of direct and meaningful communication between them is perhaps the single most important reason for the perennial infirmities that have persisted within the Nation's defense machinery. The role of the bureaucracy is an equally important element that determines the efficacy of the higher defense management set up. To address this intricate issue reflection and introspection by the defense services is called for, instead of believing that by apportioning blame they are absolved of their responsibilities. Concurrently for better management of national security the political leadership together with the support of the bureaucracy should begin to initiate measures that encourage better understanding, better synergy and better cooperation amongst all the players at the apex level.

While on the subject of defense capability there are three more sub-determinants that merit emphasis. The first is Institutions to "Regenerate military thinking". The US gets the highest rating and is closely followed by China, Russia and then India. Weapons and equipment are important. But equally or perhaps more important are ideas, concepts, doctrines and innovations. This is an area that deserves much greater attention by the Services.

The second is the state of indigenization of our conventional military weapons platforms, support systems and munitions. Recent reports have labeled India as the world's largest importer of defense equipment. This is lamentable. Some surgical and radical steps must be taken to progressively reduce the outflow of national wealth. Clearly the much touted efforts to reform the defense industry has yet to yield results and maybe there is a case to revisit and engage in a fresh exercise to accelerate the process of modernizing our defense industry. While we do this we must also examine our strategy for acquiring sensitive defense technology that can catapult us into the frontiers of defense R&D.

The third and no less important sub determinant is our nuclear capability. Curiously after the signing of the Indo-US nuclear deal there has been virtually no national level debate on our nuclear weapons capability, the quality of our nuclear deterrence and our nuclear doctrine. This cannot be attributed to a new found trust in the establishment. Within the framework of the deal there would have been a requirement to recast our strategy for acquiring the requisite capability. Is the Nation's assumption that the needful would have been done justified? For national security the vital importance of a credible nuclear deterrent cannot be overemphasized.